Catholic Thought Since The Enlightenment

Catholic Thought Since The Enlightenment

A SURVEY

Aidan Nichols, OP

University of South Africa, Pretoria
Gracewing, Leominster, England

© 1998 University of South Africa
First edition, first impression

ISBN   1 86888 029 X
UK ISBN   0 85244 474 5

Published in South Africa by
Unisa Press
University of South Africa
PO Box 392, 0003 Pretoria

Published outside South Africa by
Gracewing
2 Southern Avenue, Leominster,
Herefordshire HR6 0QF, England

Electronic origination by Iskova Image Setting, Johannesburg
Printed by Sigma Press, Koedoespoort

It is banal to note that the succession of figures moves successively through the history of thought; the part of wisdom is to find a continual conversation taking place, a conversation to which each generation makes its contribution and from which it derives its tradition as it evokes from the other members latent insights and discoveries which emerge only during this continued encounter. Chronology is appropriate in intellectual history, but it is not the final word.

MICHAEL BUCKLEY, SJ
At the Origins of Modern Atheism

CONTENTS

PREFACE

Constraints of length in this survey have obliged me to be selective. The bibliographies offered will enable students to fill gaps — and I have included books and articles in languages other than English for advanced students into whose hands this book may fall. The same need for conciseness has encouraged me to pass some swiftly enunciated judgements, which may assist the student to gain a handle on the topics, whether he or she agrees eventually with my assessment or not.

Apart from its intrinsic interest, the theological history of Catholicism in the last two hundred years is essential reading for anyone who wishes to gain an understanding of the present state of the Catholic Church — most of all for anyone who would care to offer it informed counsel with the benefit of a historical (and not merely contemporary) feeling for its identity and the *juste milieu* of the tendencies of its schools.

I am grateful to Professor Gerald Pillay, formerly of the University of South Africa, for suggesting that I write this work, and to the Liturgical Press, Collegeville, and T and T Clark, of Edinburgh, for permission to include some short extracts from earlier material published through their kindness.

Aidan Nichols, OP
Blackfriars
Cambridge

Memorial of our Lady of Ransom, 1996

I CATHOLIC THEOLOGY AND ENLIGHTENMENT

1 | Intellectual antecedents

The eighteenth-century 'Enlightenment' (the light metaphor is found in
all the principal European languages — *siècle des Lumières, Aufklärung, illuminismo, prosveshchenie, siglo de las Luces*) took various
forms, not all of them intentionally hostile to the Christian faith in its
Catholic expression. Indeed, it could be argued that Catholicism played
a vital, if unwitting, part in the Enlightenment's making. In the previous
hundred years or so, Catholic thinkers had sometimes considered epistemological scepticism to be a necessary therapy. If people recognise
that all knowledge is precarious, they should more easily realise that
only faith founds solid convictions about God. Such would-be defenders
of the faith as Michel de Montaigne (1533–1592) had become unwitting
ancestors of deism in spurning the rational metaphysics of creation
theology by means of which the philosopher-theologians of mediaeval
Christendom explored a God-dependent world. Moreover, the characteristic deistic denial of the necessity of any special, supernatural revelation in history had an unintended forebear in the global missionary
strategy of the Society of Jesus (the Jesuits) in the sixteenth and seventeenth centuries. Faithful to what had been known in the Renaissance
as 'primitive theology' — whereby a devout Catholic such as Giovanni

Pico della Mirandola (1463–1494) had argued that a shadowy sketch of Judaeo-Christianity already existed in the higher civilisations of ancient times — Jesuit missionaries postulated a universal natural religion, laying the ground for the religion of revelation. And in the more imprudent formulations of some Jesuit ethnographers and anthropologists that natural religion bore a distinct resemblance to the religion-without-mysteries which the later deists desired. Voltaire (François Marie Arouet, 1694–1778), a former pupil of the Jesuits, held that evidence for the reality of God certainly existed — but to be entertained rationally it must be considered independently of any religious community, and above all in freedom from the dogmatic presuppositions and claims of the Catholic Church.

For an English-speaking student of the period, the empiricism of John Locke (1632–1704) and later of David Hume (1711–1776) which, along with the new physics of Isaac Newton (1642–1727), crossed the Channel in the flagship of Voltaire's *Lettres anglaises* (or *Lettres philosophiques*, 1734), seems the most likely source of Enlightenment naturalism. But an intellectual attack on the Church which was primarily philosophical in character could also arise from a metaphysical starting-point as different from empiricism as chalk from cheese. Seventeenth- and eighteenth-century rationalism had learned from René Descartes (1596–1650) the possibility of establishing truth-claims in terms of arguments formulated a priori rather than by inference from experience. Under the inspiration of Cartesianism the perfect science would be a universal 'mathematics' in which the 'Absolute' (that on which everything depends for its understanding, but whose own understanding is not dependent on anything else) becomes the ground of the 'relative' (the non-absolute) by a process of systematic deduction. Forgetting that the ordered connection of ideas is not necessarily the same as that of things, and turning all finite realities into their own concepts, the Amsterdam-born Jewish philosopher Baruch Spinoza (1632–1677) — regarded by many Enlightenment churchmen as the archetypal atheist — took the universe to be necessary, infinite, and eternal. It could be spoken of indifferently, Spinoza thought, as God (*Natura naturans*) inasmuch as it causes, or as nature (*natura naturata*) inasmuch as it follows by necessity from the existence of God. That ambiguity would later allow the German Romantic poet Novalis (Friedrich Leopold von Hardenberg, 1772–1801) to treat Spinoza as no atheist but a 'God-intoxi-

4

cated man'; the God in question was not, evidently, that of orthodox Christians. The possibility of regarding the entire development of the organic cosmos, and of human life within it, as an expression of an underlying divine activity can count as the Spinozist root of German Idealism, as that philosophy would soon be found in Johann Gottlieb Fichte (1762–1814), Friedrich Wilhelm Joseph von Schelling (1775–1854) and, above all, Georg Friedrich Wilhelm Hegel (1770–1831).

The notion that infinity and 'eternality' belong to the universe by right could also be reached by another route – not this time a 'universal mathematics' but the 'universal mechanics' of a speculatively developed experimental science. As the Anglican bishop-philosopher George Berkeley (1685–1753) had objected to Newton, either the 'absolute space' of the new physics was God, or something else beside God is eternal, uncreated, infinite and immutable. In point of fact, Newton – a Christian, though a heterodox one by Anglican as well as Catholic standards in matters of the Trinity – did not regard the world system as eternal. (The necessity of periodic divine correction of the naturally recurring irregularities that threatened it was, he believed, a 'proof' of Providence – something whose demonstration St Thomas Aquinas (c 1225–1274) had regarded as impossible.) Newton did, however, treat 'absolute' space (and time) not as created effects of God's action but as constituted by his very existence, in its ubiquity. The system of the world required an intelligent Agent as that primordial form of 'impressed force' which alone could originate the cosmos and give it structure. Not for nothing was Newton's root metaphysical concept for God that of dominion. The triumphs of Newtonian physics added imaginative power to the idea of the eternal necessity of an infinite world – an idea whose dislodging was itself a necessary condition for bringing home the Christian doctrine of gratuitous divine creation to men's minds.

2 | Catholics and unbelievers

Although wider factors, such as the negative image attached to confessional allegiance by the religious wars of the seventeenth century, and the imperfect ethical and professional competence of the clergy, played their part, the origins of the rejection of Catholicism by the mainstream of the French Enlightenment are, then, chiefly intellectual in kind. A leading modern historian of the movement, Peter Gay, has argued that the Enlightenment became ever more radicalised as it ran its course. In the early eighteenth century, the leading *philosophes* were deists who used the language of the natural law. After mid-century they tended to be atheists, favouring the vocabulary of utility. By the Great Revolution of 1789, most were still deists (and in America would remain so), but a certain progression into atheism is undeniable — as the career of the editor of that omnium-gatherum of Enlightenment criticism the *Encyclopédie* suggests. Denis Diderot (1713–1784) had considered a call to the Jesuit Society, but moved via the classically deistic position of the *Pensées philosophiques* (1746) on the sufficiency of natural religion to one of outright atheism. With his fellow materialist, the Baron d'Holbach (Paul Heinrich Dietrich d'Holbach, 1723–1789), he came to regard the world as nothing but matter in spontaneous movement: thus their

(probably) joint work *Le Système de la nature* of 1770. They are the foun-
tainheads of modern atheism for, as Hegel recognised in his rumina-
tions on the meaning of history in *Vorlesungen über die Philosophie
der Geschichte*, something new happened in the Paris of the *siècle des
Lumières*. Hitherto 'atheistic' had usually meant (as the early Christians
had discovered) holding a different view of God from one's own. Now it
meant exactly what it said, even though, as its name indicates, atheism
remains conceptually parasitic on the theism it denies.

Catholics (as other Christians) were suddenly faced with a programme
subversive not only of their Gospel, but of many of the assumptions
about the cosmos, man and his destiny taken for granted since classical
times and considered by the Church to be eminently congruent with its
foundational doctrines of creation and redemption. Here was a nature
to be mastered, not, in the first instance, contemplated. That its struc-
tures could be rendered in mathematic form was not, perhaps,
disturbing: such luminous evidence of intrinsic intelligibility was, after
all, also evidence for design. Much more serious was the materialist
view of nature's dynamism, where 'chance and necessity' (still to be
lauded in the late twentieth century by the biologists Jacques Monod
and Richard Dawkins) replaced final causes in explanation. And where
specifically human life was concerned, a classical view of the ends to be
achieved by knowledge, where those goals were arranged in an ordered
hierarchy surmounted and governed by wisdom, was replaced by a
more 'realistic' picture, where health, pleasure, and freedom from pain
were paramount. Expectation of the social blessings to be lavished by
the unimpeded development of scientific knowledge, belief that the
chief cause of injustice was a (thoroughly remediable) scarcity, and
confidence in the 'progressive and politically ever more enlightened
course of human history' could hardly leave unaffected the place of
religion in human hope.[1] The opinion that interest in religion entered
into irreversible decline with the invention of the water closet (so beneficial for public sanitation) lay close to hand.

But, as R B Pippin has pointed out, eighteenth-century ideologues who
proposed that the 'modern project', so defined, corresponded to what
any 'enlightened' example of a 'rational agent' would 'naturally' desiderate opened themselves to the accusation that such notions of enlightenment, reason and nature begged precisely the questions at issue —
and hence threw wide the door for a variety of countervailing responses.

3 | Response to the philosophes

Catholic writers were not tardy in their efforts to stem the tide of infidelity in what was still, after all, a Christendom society, as the Bourbon alliance of throne with altar testified. In the middle decades of the century they felt able to collaborate, if critically, with the deists in the writing of articles for the *Encyclopédie*. That work had originated, after all, from Descartes' claim that the sciences so clarified each other's deliverances that in principle human intelligence could make an accurate judgement on anything, and Descartes, who had, to his own satisfaction at least, proved God's existence to be not only certain but the foundational certainty which alone warrants confidence in the non-deceitfulness of human powers in perceiving and knowing, could hardly be termed an unbeliever: he had received his project from his spiritual director, the greatest theologian of France's golden age, Cardinal Pierre de Bérulle (1575–1629).

Subsequently, as the *Encyclopédie* became ever more the brainchild of anti-Catholicism, Catholics went on the defensive — generally by rehearsing once again those apologetic arguments for the truth of the Christian religion which were as old as the Church itself: commending the truth of Christian revelation by reference to the fulfilment of prophecy, the incidence of miracle (provocative, since the incredibility of the miraculous was a topic where atheists and deists were agreed), and the extraordinary moral excellence of the divine legate and founder of the Church, Jesus himself.[2] Here was a narrative better able to found interpretation of history and cosmos than the self-legislating reason or, alternatively, brutish empiricism of the *philosophes*. If, on the eve of the French Enlightenment, Pierre-Daniel Huet (1630–1721), bishop of Avranches, had already set the tone of such 'objective apologetics' by his (not especially distinguished) *Demonstratio christiana* of 1679, the style continued in, for instance, *La Divinité de Jésus Christ prouvé contre les hérétiques et les déistes* (1751), from the pen of the Maurist Benedictine Prudentius Maran (1683–1762), and found its echo across the Rhine in the work of the philosophically eminent German Jesuit Benedikt Stattler 1720–1797). Stattler's *Demonstratio evangelica*, subtitled 'The Certitude accurately demonstrated in methodical fashion, of the Religion revealed by Jesus Christ, against the Deists (*theistas*) and all the anti-Christian Philosophers of both the ancient and our own Age, as well as against Jews and Muslims' (1770), distinguished carefully between the moral necessity of a revelation *supernatural in its manner of communication* if the vagaries of natural religion were ever to be sufficiently clarified for human beings to trust religious guidance at large and the unconditional need for a revelation *supernatural in its substance* if the actual goals of creation – the glory of God and the felicity of man – were to be attained. Stattler's interest in why it is that men need divine revelation (and not simply the evidence that it has happened) was paralleled in yet more focused fashion by the Lorrainer Nicolas-Sylvestre Bergier (1718–1790). Bergier's emphasis on Christian truth as uniquely fitted to meet the demands of human subjectivity would influence the theologians of the early nineteenth-century Catholic Revival, and anticipate the 'apologetics of immanence' of the lay philosopher Maurice Blondel (1861–1949).

The atheistic question, after all, was not exclusively a philosophical one, though sixteenth- and seventeenth-century theologians like Leonhard Lessius (1554–1623) at Louvain and Marin Mersenne (1588–1648) – a one-man Parisian clearing-house for the correspondence of philosophers and scientists – had begun the tradition of treating it as though it were. The resources of Catholic Christianity – and the eighteenth-century Church in its preaching, liturgy, spirituality, and the saints these produced was far from being simply a philosophers' club[3] – were not to be exhausted by arguments from the world's design to its mighty Architect, whether by way of a Stoic-type reasoning from the intelligibility lodged in the nature of things, or in terms of that Platonic mindset for which the large element of order the world contains is inexplicable if the divine Orpheus does not constantly stroke the strings of the universe's lute.[4]

And if the Catholic apologetics of the Enlightenment lacked the thoroughgoing Christological and Pneumatological (and not simply theistic) content which was desirable, its authors could rarely compete with the literary skills of a Voltaire, who turned the weaponry of ridicule against the Church, its tenets, history, members, to devastating effect. Not till after the Revolution, with François René de Chateaubriand (1768–1848), would a prosist of comparable power be found to state the defence's position.

None of that is to say, however, that well-argued attempts to meet the *philosophes'* case in reasoned, if not rhetorically persuasive, terms were beside the point. And these, though rarely adverted to in intellectual histories of Europe, were readily forthcoming. Bergier, whom the archbishop of Paris brought to the capital for the purpose, wrote twice against d'Holbach: his 1769 *Apologie de la religion chrétienne* assesses the latter's *Christianisme dévoilé* (1767), and the *Examen du matérialisme* of 1771 unpicks the *Système de la nature* of the previous year. Bergier's *Le déisme refuté par lui-même* (1765) considers the very different thought, at once sentimental and totalitarian, but equally alienated from historic Christianity, of Jean-Jacques Rousseau (1712–1778). Like Stattler, the Savoyard cardinal Hyacinth Sigismond Gerdil (1718–1802) defended the Church's corner against all philosophic comers, not only Locke and Rousseau but also the Baron de Montesquieu (Charles Louis Joseph de Secondat, 1689–1755), whose naturalistic *Esprit des lois* (1748), though less hostile to the Church than the earlier *Lettres persanes* (1721), anticipated Hume's 1757 *Natural History of Religion*, and the atheist Pierre Bayle (1647–1706), whose *Dictionnaire historique et critique* (1695–1697) proved invaluable to his Enlightenment successors. Though Gerdil's enthusiasm for the spiritualising philosophy of Nicolas Malebranche (1638–1715) – who held that the human idea of the infinite is the very presence of the infinite God in our minds, which themselves are more closely united to God than they are to our bodies — would be seen by later Catholic thinkers as unfortunate, this polyglot writer did his best to counter a form of atheism which, unlike its predecessors, would soak through the high culture of the West and, by saturation, acquire adherents to be numbered, by the late twentieth century, in their millions.

4 | The history men

The question marks set by historical critics against the truth-claims of the Judaeo-Christian revelation in its Catholic edition were second only to those of philosophers. It was fortunate that the later seventeenth and the eighteenth centuries witnessed a remarkable renaissance of historical scholarship in the Church. Though the foundations of critical judgement are often laid in prejudices (in a neutral sense of that word) of a wider kind, it was helpful to have to hand, against those who poured scorn on the historical authenticity of Scripture, the detailed investigation of the letter of the biblical text by Augustin Calmet (1672–1757), president of the Benedictine Congregation of S Vanne, as found in, for instance, his 1719 *Dictionnaire historique de la Bible*. More epoch-making for future scholarship was the work of his fellow black monk Jean Mabillon (1632–1707), who by his account of the principles of documentary criticism, the *De re diplomatica* of 1681, created single-handed scientific 'diplomatics', though his work was taken further, in the full glare of Enlightenment sunshine, by the *Nouveau traité de diplomatique*, brought out by the Maurists Charles-François Toustain (1700–1754) and René-Prosper Tassin (1699–1777) in the years 1750 to 1765. That followed on the great monument to the corporate activity of the

Maurist Benedictines (a 'Congregation' destroyed in the French Revolution): the nine-volume *Spicilegium veterum Scriptorum et monumentorum ecclesiasticorum* of 1724–1733.

In Italy too, much was afoot. Giovanni Domenico Mansi (1692–1769), founder of an academy of church and liturgical history at Lucca, assembled all known materials relating to the history of the Councils before 1440. Two Verona patrologists, Pietro Ballerini (1698–1769) and his brother Girolamo (1702–1781), produced critical editions of the Fathers, most notably the still standard text of the writings of Leo the Great (c 400 to 461), which replaced that by Pasquier Quesnel (1634–1719) with its Gallicanising notes, for Gallicanism, so called from its origins in the work of French jurists, emphasised all those factors in the Church's life — Councils, sacramentally ordained bishops, and Christian civil rulers or the populations over whose territorial circumscriptions they presided — which could possibly be regarded as limiting the freedom of action of the Roman bishop, the pope.

If a gentler note is struck in the career of Ludovico Antonio Muratori (1672–1750) — librarian of the Bibliotheca Ambrosiana in Milan, and the scholar who best saw the significance of inscriptions for historical research (thus the *Novus thesaurus veterum inscriptionum* of 1739–1745) — with his plea for a due freedom in the Church for science and scholarship, Muratori was not for all that free of *parti pris*. He scanned the religious sources through the lenses provided by 'good taste', 'regulated devotion' and 'moderation of spirits', thus signalling his attachment to a Catholicised version of Enlightenment, and in the spirit of Newton rejected all metaphysical theories in favour of the pure documented datum — the historian's equivalent of the scientific 'fact'. By keeping scientific history in clinical isolation from religious faith, he paid the inevitable price in terms of a rupture between methodological naturalism and revelation itself.

No such scruples were shown by the Dominican cardinal Giovanni Agostino Orsi (1692–1761) whose 21-volume history of the early Church was not at all disinterested in its desire to correct the tendencies to Gallicanism in the influential *Histoire ecclésiastique* of Claude Fleury (1640–1725). In the history of the canonical sources, vital as these were in dealing with the challenges to the role of the Petrine office in the Church as mounted by Gallicanism and its Germanophone counterpart

Febronianism, the Venetian Jesuit Francesco Antonio Zaccaria (1714–1795) was especially active.

5 | Catholic Enlightenment, Catholic identity

As references in the preceding section may suggest, the eighteenth-century Enlightenment, as its moment faded to be overtaken by the harsher light of the Great Revolution of the West (1789–1815), did not find Catholics particularly united. On the contrary, in matters of Church structure and the shape of Catholic theology their Communion found itself in a crisis of identity. Its themes — the claims of the temporal; the autonomy of national churches; the relative independence of the pastoral from the dogmatic; ecumenism, authentic and otherwise; the adaption of catechesis and theology to the contemporary mindset; *los von Rom* ('away from Rome!') — are uncannily reminiscent of another period of disorientation to follow two centuries later in the aftermath of the Second Vatican Council.

Throughout Catholic Europe, in an age, in the wider Continent and its overseas dependencies, of 'enlightened despotism' where the indispensability of regalian rights for any effective, rationalising and modernising, prosecution of the common social good was ever more stressed, it seemed increasingly unsuitable that a nation should be bound to the leading-strings of an international Church. The suppression of the Jesuit Society was a major triumph for regalian nationalism over against ecclesial internationalism, and in the hue and cry which brought the Society low, the *philosophes*, with the honourable exception of Voltaire, showed that their righteous resentment of fanaticism was distinctly limited when the fanaticism in question hurt the Catholic Church.

In the German-speaking lands, the Enlightenment, though kinder, shared in much milder form the *Tendenzen* to be observed in France. It left its mark in, most notably, Austria, Bavaria and the electoral dioceses (the 'prince-bishoprics'), and in the last quarter of the eighteenth century spread to the Habsburg possessions in Tuscany where the combination of grand-ducal support and episcopal sanction won it short-lived vindication – theological, liturgical and disciplinary – at the 1786 Synod of Pistoia, quashed by the bull *Auctorem fidei* (drawn up by Gerdil) in 1794. The German Enlightenment would bring a new professionalism to theological studies, and a greater differentiation of specialisms within the circle of the 'sacred sciences'. Homiletics, catechetics and pastoral theology emerged as disciplines in their own right, and not just virtualities of dogmatics, while Church history began to go its own way in independence of theological doctrine: these developments, while bringing gains, were not entirely unmixed blessings if revelation is to be regarded as furnishing the formal perspective in which all Christian thinking is pursued. Moreover, the more positive impulses of the German-speaking Enlightenment were crossed by others as governments tempted by the national-Church idea and episcopalian regimes in the prince-bishoprics sought that autonomy at the expense of Rome (and hence, in certain respects, of the Church universal) which Gallican and Febronian scholarship and propaganda had urged. Furthermore, the contacts of *Aufklärung* Catholics with similarly minded Protestants, who were themselves on a slippery slope towards deism, accepting revelation as confirmatory, merely, of natural religion, would lead later Ultramontanes (those who stressed the primatial teaching and governing activity of the bishop of Rome *ultra montes*, 'beyond the mountains') to tax them with subversion of Catholicism's distinctive life. These critics had in mind such things as the dislike of 'enlightened' Catholics for monasticism (socially unproductive), their wish for reduced emphasis on Eucharistic adoration and the cultus of the Mother of God and the saints (too unacceptable to Protestantism), the pressure for vernacularisation of worship and a more biblical spirituality, joint Catholic-Protestant prayer meetings and the common formation of priests and pastors.

In point of fact, the Catholic Enlightenment (as in central Europe we may term it) left little mark on the central issues of Christian theology, though its agenda was disclosed in its pastoral products. Its Catechisms, for instance, tended to truncate earlier accounts of the chief mysteries of revelation, or rest content with allusive reference to them, emphasising instead the ethical and rational aspects of Christianity. Intellectually, its contribution lay in issues of method, where its representatives insisted on the need for constant recourse to Scripture and Fathers — in, however, a *wissenschaftlich* rather than fully ecclesial spirit. A certain reliance in positive or historical theology on Reformed and Jansenist books (Jansenism, a seventeenth-century movement both pastoral and scholarly, was thanks to the papal condemnation of its ultra-Augustinianism in matters of grace by now practically identical with Gallicanism) confirmed that displacement of dogmatics from its centrality to which the proliferation of new branches of theology was in any case leading.

All of this was manifested with peculiar clarity in the Habsburg monarchy. In line with the 1774 'Project for Re-organizing the Theological Schools in the Hereditary Imperial and Royal Domains', the Bohemian abbot Franz Stephan Rautenstrauch (1734–1785), director of the theological faculties of both Prague and Vienna, devised a new schema of studies emphasising the need for adaptation to advances in secular scholarship not only in Catholic universities but also in seminaries. His hostility to Scholasticism was well marked, but any disintegrative effect of his reform on the unity of theological understanding appears to have been unintended: his own theology — a reading of the economy of salvation at once historical and 'kerygmatic', centred on the evangelical message — seems to have anticipated the concern with the organic unity of Christian truth in the later, post-Revolutionary, Catholic Tübingen school.[5]

That Rautenstrauch realised his swingeing reform not by papal or episcopal mandate but as a bureaucrat in the service of the Habsburg rulers Maria Theresa (1717–1780) and Joseph II (1741–1790) — something for which he claimed canonical sanction in his *Synopsis iuris ecclesiastici* of 1770 — testifies to the weakened ecclesial sense which Febronianism, when manipulated by civil authorities, inevitably produced. Johann Nikolaus von Hontheim (1701–1790), coadjutor bishop of Trier, had begun in 1742, at the behest of the archbishop-electors, an enquiry into the historical well-foundedness of the papal claims. Though his results, published as *De statu ecclesiae et legitima potestate Romani pontificis* (1763), correctly reported that some patristic and mediaeval documents supportive of a high doctrine of the primacy were no more than imaginative reconstruction, the wider conclusions 'Justinus Febronius' espoused did not gain the reception he hoped. For while in 1786 at a meeting in Ems the German episcopate as a whole rejected the attempt severely to prune back papal authority as serving only to inflate that of the regional primates (the archbishops of Mainz, Trier, Cologne and Salzburg), civil governments and above all the House of Austria used Febronian material to justify their own already formulated anti-Roman policies. In the wider context of *Staatskirchentum*, the law faculty of the University of Vienna spearheaded an assault on the independence of the Church under its God-given apostolic ministry. The background of 'Josephinism' (named for Joseph II, the 'crowned sacristan') was that ever since Ferdinand I (1503–1564) the German-Roman emperors had tried to emulate the regalian system of Habsburg Spain; what was new is the appearance in the German lands, Habsburg and otherwise, of figures trained in the main centres of Gallicanism (Paris) and schismatic Jansenism (Leyden, Utrecht). The Febronian ecclesiology whereby papal action is limited to surveillance of the execution of conciliar decrees, other laws promulgated by the pope having no authority without the consent of the episcopate, played into the hands of civil authorities who declared the necessity of their *placet* before any pontifical document were published in their territory; their right to be consulted before any Church decision lest it should harm the State; and, not least, their power of disposal of all Church property. For the State to be solidly united, the Church must be directed by the civil power, with a view not least to the preservation of its faith, catechesis, preaching and worship from all fanaticism. For Josephinism included a certain rationalism.

Most theologians of the Catholic Enlightenment — Sebastian Mutschelle (1749–1800) is an exception — considered the philosophy of Immanuel Kant (1724–1804) beyond redemption. But subterraneously

Kant's influence was widespread in a general tendency to identify religion with morals, treat the Church as essentially an instrument of ethical education, and the sermon as more important than the Holy Sacrifice.

The rebellion in 1789 of church students against unorthodox professors at Louvain led Joseph's successor, Leopold II, to begin a process of dismantling Josephinism, at least in Flanders. The arrival of the Revolutionary armies in the Low Countries engulfed all such issues in a crisis greater by far.

II | REVOLUTION AND RESTORATION

1 | The Revolutionary impact

The French Revolution, soon carried via its armies and those of the military caesarism of Napoleon I Bonaparte (1769–1821) to most of continental Europe and beyond, broke on the Catholic Church with the force of a cataclysm whose storm uprooted all familiar landmarks in a hitherto sacralised landscape. From out of the crucible into whose fires traditional society and *homo christianus* fell there would emerge, however, a renewed sense of the importance of history and language, community and authority, tradition and the unity of the Church. And these themes – not without some hesitations and indeed false steps – would permeate the Catholic theology of the first half of the nineteenth century.

Unsurprisingly, the Catholic Church reacted with hostility to the French Revolution – also called, in its spreading via the 'nation in arms' of the Revolutionary armies and subsequently through the military monarchy of Napoleon with his grand design for the unification and rational administration of Europe, the 'Great Revolution of the West'. The Revolution's initial phase was characterised by a deliberate subverting of the Church's influence, as what was hitherto public belief became private opinion (as the *philosophes* had wanted), millenarian cults thrived (not least the cult of the Revolution itself), and a conviction gained ground that political change of a radical kind could install the good life on earth (or at least in France). The pillaging of ecclesiastical (as aristocratic) libraries and the systematic image-breaking led commentators to coin the word *vandalisme*. If at Notre Dame de Paris the Gothic figures of biblical royalty were hacked away, the very edifice of Chartres survived only because the burghers did not know what they would do with the rubble. In 1790 the Civil Constitution of the Clergy reduced the Church, already deprived of its property, to a state agency with the priesthood as its functionaries. After 1792 all clerics who failed to take the oath of submission to the Civil Constitution were punished by deportation and began to be hunted down; north of the Loire Catholic Partisans — *les Chouans* — came out, not least to give them protection.

A quarter century of carnage at home and abroad left its mark on French demography as Dr Guillotin's invention made possible decapitation in cartloads and the Terror re-introduced religious war (an estimated two million dead in the rising for king and Church in the Vendée) to a country which had almost forgotten it. Eighteenth-century Europe, with its small professional armies, was unused to bloodletting on the scale that resulted. Meanwhile police and espionage systems expanded, notably at the expense of bodies the State did not control, like Church and guild. It was, as Simon Schama has remarked, the Revolution's paradox that it invented the juridical entity of the 'citizen', only at once to surround it by the powers of a police state.[6] Economically, the Revolution hardly fitted the description of bourgeois-industrial transformant of a feudal-agrarian regime which Karl Heinrich Marx (1818– 1883) said it must. The country of its origin had developed its economy faster in the eighteenth century than it would under Revolutionary or Imperial rule. However, if the massive expansion of the peasantry through the distribution of land parcels strengthened that class which through customary benison and the cycle of the feasts was most attached to the Church, the humanism of the Revolutionary 'Declaration' of 'rights' that did not belong simply to the citizen, by the positive law, but also to man as such, enshrined nuggets of theological anthropology (for who gave men these rights if not God?) which Catholics could later retrieve by way of such markedly different media as the literary criticism of G K Chesterton (1874–1936) and the social encyclicals of the later nineteenth- and twentieth-century popes. A Catholic Christian can hardly say 'Yes' to the Revolution, but neither can he or she in all respects say 'No'.

What moves could be made, on the chessboard of intellect, to counter those forces which had unmade a Christian culture, the Christian society, the Christian State, and even — to the degree that they were able — the Christian Church itself in its Catholic form? They were respectively theological Romanticism (for culture), traditionalism, in a technical sense of that word (for society), what may be called theological counter-revolutionism (for the State), and neo-Ultramontanism (for the Church). These are movements which, though interconnected at many points, can also usefully be distinguished.

2 | Romantic theology

In literature and the arts, the norm urged by 'Romantic' aesthetics against what were regarded as the rationalist excesses of a universalising classicism was fusion of finite and infinite, matter and spirit, real and ideal. Romantic theologians would regard those cultural media as highly pertinent to religious philosophy for that very reason. A Romantic artwork seems by the sheer force of imaginative passion to press against the boundaries of the finite in evocation of the ineffable. The Romantic aesthetic gives preference to the particular and distinctive, and the art it favours will be markedly personal and subjective. Rather than conform to an inherited pattern imposed from without, it appears as the organic outgrowth of the artist's inward consciousness. Romanticism deems conceptual language to be secondary in comparison with the truth conveyed in symbolic images. It is tempted to worship human creativity. Romanticism views man as pure vital activity, whereby he generates both his own selfhood and the world itself, considered a significant environment. It sees man as a finite principle disclosing an infinite principle — the Absolute — which shows itself through an endless multiplicity of expressive forms. Over against the rationalising intellectualism of the Enlightenment mainstream,

Romantics emphasised the positive role of imagination in the human understanding of the real. Over against a mechanistic view of nature — for William Blake (1757–1825) Newtonian science partook of the Anti-christ — they stressed the spontaneity and purpose at work in the cosmos as well as in men. They awakened a new interest in history, the privileged locus of human freedom and creativity.

In the course of the nineteenth century, the European imagination would come to express itself in pervasively historicised forms; histor-ical thinking saturated the age. Imaginative interest in, and positive evaluation of, the past would be more marked in the century now opening than in any previous period.[7] While that was good news for Catholicism, inasmuch as the Catholic faith rested in good measure on an interpretation of history, and the Catholic religion pointed for its glories to the historical past, radical historicism would also raise problems as to how any truths transcending a time-conditional epoch of culture could be valid at all. A similar ambivalence afflicted the philo-sophical temper of Romanticism, to a Catholic judgement. Owing to the Romantic movement's origins in (amongst other things) Rousseau's elevation of spontaneous feeling, and the Kantianism which (on one reading, at any rate, of Kant's philosophy) severed mind from 'noumena' (things in themselves) leaving it but the scrapings of 'phenomena' (things as they appear), Romanticism necessarily wrestled with solip-sism, the sense that the human 'I', though it may claim to engage, in the various forms of its knowledge, with objective reality, is really only contemplating the human subject, through a series of mirrors, differ-ently angled. The viscosity of social and cultural experience on such presuppositions accounts for the discontentedness of the secular intel-ligentsia in the nineteenth century, as well as the homesickness for what is abiding and eternal which haunts Romantic art. The more meta-physically gifted of the theologians thrown up by the Romantic move-ment would seek, accordingly, to meet the epistemological needs of Romantic scepticism by assuring mind, world and human artefacts of their reality through finding for them a transcendent ground in God.

The Romantic notion of 'the people' was also flawed — though by no means valueless — in the perception of the Church. Nations are one way of circumscribing governable portions of humankind. The ethnic nationalism that was a characteristic product of Romanticism saw the nation as, more specifically, a community unified by genealogical descent, vernacular culture and its native history, and its people to be mobilised if necessary for the goal of constructing new sovereignties from existing states. But – quite apart from the grave inconveniences which follow when two or more ethnic populations share the same territory yet demand their own state apparatus – did the *Volksgeist*, the 'spirit' of the people, so define distinct ethnic kinds of human being that the common essence of humanity – and thus the unity of the species to be redeemed by Christ and incorporated in his Church – disappears? Was it to be the criterion against which all life together – and thus the Catholic Church with its faith, morals and discipline – should be measured, and perhaps found wanting.

For the time being, however, these dangers seemed more than offset by the newly propitious condition of the Romantic revival. Suddenly Catholicism, whose intellectual life – owing to the sweeping away of its institutional base by secularising governments – had sunk to so low an ebb as scarcely to be visible, acquired new attractiveness (and notable converts). Here was a religion where tradition and history were held in honour, and whose communal life, permeated by mystical values, embodied that 'vital principle' which Romantics sought. In Germany, Karl Wilhelm Friedrich von Schlegel (1772–1829), converted to Catholicism in 1808, was the foremost representative of the religious turn that Idealism and Romanticism were taking: anticipating the Christian Existentialism of a century later, he sought from religion meaning for existence and history. Precisely because he regarded the poetic as the positive representation of a totality of being which philosophy could only indicate negatively and by indirections, Schlegel's discovery of the biblical revelation (in the *Geschichte der alten und neuen Literatur* of 1815) as a peerless poetic resource had far-reaching implications. The poetic reason at work in divine revelation is the supreme condition of possibility for the transformation of culture which the Revolutionary cataclysm had made necessary. What Schlegel attempted for Germany, Chateaubriand, with less speculative power (Voltaire and Rousseau were hardly stimuli to thought of the order of Fichte and Schelling), would carry out – in his *Génie du christianisme ou beautés de la Religion chrétienne* (1802) for France. Whereas the Revolution – as also the philosophical system of the eighteenth century – had proved impotent to make men better – this was the burden of his earlier *Essai sur les révolutions* (1797) – the Church had renovated the moral basis of culture by giving man a higher idea of nature, of himself, and of the divine. Chateaubriand's four-volume work was a theological apogetics of culture: the incomparable civilising potential of the Church, attested in Christian art and literature, cannot, *qua* perfect effect, arise simply from ourselves, an imperfect source. Catholicism was divine universal truth in persuasively symbolic form.

Not all such writers were loners; there were centres of Romantic theology where laymen and clerics collaborated. A group of disciples of Johann Michael Sailer (1751–1852), bishop of Regensburg, whose eclectic *De idea theologi christiani* (1781) urged the theologian to incorporate within his work the historic sources of Catholic spirituality and liturgy, established a school at Lucerne in German Switzerland. Joseph Heinrich Alois Gügler (1782–1827), by presenting the Church-body as a supernaturalised organism which the Breath of the divine Spirit animates (thus his *Geist des Christentums und der Literatur* of 1810), and in 'The Sacred Art' (*Die heilige Kunst oder die Kunst der Hebräer*, 1814–1818) and 'The Cyphers of the Sphinx' (*Die Ziffern der Sphinx oder Typen der Zeit und ihr Deuten auf die Zukunft*, 1819) portraying Old and New Testaments respectively as rehearsing in richly symbolic form a vision of human history in its God-oriented rhythmic development, provided the key themes for the most important non-Scholastic Catholic theology of the nineteenth century, that of the Tübingen School. Theology, history and philosophy could all be compendiously brought together in the version of the idea of the Kingdom of God most appealing to Romantic sensibility – a reunion of all creatures in harmony under God: here was the most 'contemporary Catholic dogmatics' as in the sub-title of a work from another diffusion point of Romantic theology, Bamberg: the *Freie Darstellung der Theologie in der Idee des Himmelreiches oder neueste katholische Dogmatik*, published between 1815 and 1817 by Friedrich Brenner (1784–1848).

And in Munich the Bavarian king Ludwig I (1786–1868), having transferred to the capital the University of Landshut, took the opportunity to re-catholicise a number of its chairs (though Schelling taught philosophy). There were thus brought into constellation luminaries of Catholic Romanticism of varying magnitudes. Franz Xaver von Baader (1765–1841), as professor of speculative theology, influenced before his re-conversion by the Protestant mysticism of Jakob Böhme (1575–1624), produced a (highly unsystematic) 'system' where human knowledge has as a condition of its possibility participation in the divine. Faith and knowledge are reciprocally necessary in a *con-scientia* ('co-awareness') of God and man. Philosophy, which arises as the self-explication (or catharsis) of religious tradition, cannot survive divorce from the latter — not the least reason that in Baader's Christian sociology religion is treated as the true fount of civil society, practical embodiment of philosophic wisdom as the latter should be. Johann Joseph von Görres (1776–1848) as professor of history, though sharing Baader's intense concern with Christian mysticism — something evidenced in his *Die christliche Mystik* of 1836–1842 — re-pristinated the Christian interpretation of history, most notably in *Grundlage, Gliederung und Zeitenfolge der Geschichte* (1830). While his plea for the re-creation of the German-Roman empire with its mutually limiting jurisdictions (he opposed all ascription of omni-competence to the state power) went unheeded, his defence of the liberty of Catholics, and the rights of their hierarchs, especially via the *Historische-politische Blätter*, a periodical founded in 1838, was much more effective. Johann Joseph Ignaz von Döllinger (1799–1890), professor of canon law and Church history, the youngest by far of the Munich trio, was early influenced by the Traditionalism of Félicité Robert de Lamennais (1782–1854), but his mind, as events proved, was of a scientific and data-collecting rather than philosophical or theological and speculatively interpretative kind. Hostile to the rise of Neo-Ultramontanism and suspicious of Scholasticism, his enormous learning in the Church history of the patristic, mediaeval and Counter-Reformation periods did not prevent his rupture with the Roman see after the declaration of the juridical primacy and doctrinal infallibility of the pope at the First Vatican Council (1869–1870). Indeed, he cited his reasons as at once historical, theological and political, even though the maximal interpretation of the papal prerogatives which before the Council ultras desired by no means imposed itself in the actual wording of the dogmatic constitution concerned.

3 | Traditionalism

The metaphysical uncertainties of the Romantic self, combined with the anxieties generated by the anarchy that the Revolution, its constitutional phase passed, had precipitated, stimulated the formation of Traditionalism — at once a philosophical-theological and political-ecclesial movement. For the Traditionalists of whatever ilk, man has misappropriated a place that belongs to God, to whom traditional dues must be restored. But the strategies adopted by the Catholic Traditionalists, though varying among themselves, were rarely as philosophically innocent as those of the cognate Anglican Conservatism embodied in the work of Edmund Burke (1729–1797). Some words of the critic George Steiner on Counter-Revolutionism sum up the Burkeian ethos better than they do the Catholic Traditionalists, though they pick out elements in Catholic Romanticism well enough.

> The psychological and stylistic components of the counter revolutionary sensibility are those of an ardent remembrance (often embellished and arcadian) of things past; of a profound distrust of voluntarist, cerebrally inspired innovations in the inherited weave of communal life; they are ... those of instinctive *pietas*

and ... an intuition of the organic in the very pulse and structure of history.[8]

Typical of the Catholic Traditionalists was distrust of individual reason, not of reason *tout court*; what they rejected was hermeneutical suspicion of human tradition at large, not the abandonment of all critical sense whatsoever. Their shared *tenenda* were two interconnected theses, namely that unassisted individual reason cannot attain — at any rate with any certainty — religious and moral truths, for the latter have their origin in a primordial revelation transmitted to successive generations of the human race by its universal consensus or 'common sense'. While individual reason slumbered, corporate reason could be awake. What the *philosophes* had stigmatised as obscurantism and prejudice could well be society's tried and tested intelligence. In the name of emancipation, the Enlightenment philosophers had deracinated their fellow men and women, stripping them of 'prior judgements' (which after all is what the word 'prejudice' literally means) that represented the 'we' in every 'I'. Inherited beliefs, in the ethical and spiritual realm, should be thought of as the past as present: corporate judgements carrying memory rich in sifted experience from age to age. Testimony as such must carry some epistemic weight — for to attempt to show the reliability of testimony in general simply by examining one's own experience would be an impossible undertaking.[9] For Louis Gabriel Ambroise de Bonald (1754–1840), if, negatively, the competing variety of philosophical systems up for hire shows the incapacity of one man's reasoning to impose itself on all and sundry and points the way to an individualism whose final bitter fruit is atheism and anarchy, then, positively, the ubiquitous medium of language (which no man has created) points to the existence of God. And if, then, a First Cause gave the gift of language to the first human family on earth, it is unthinkable that God should have deprived that society, in whom, as in a nucleus, all subsequent humanity was pre-contained, of the truths indispensable to social existence. The ideas of which we stand in most need are innate, but not to individuals, only to society as a whole. The laws which ensure society's endurance are transmitted to us with, in and by language, and to oppose such truths as are guarded by universal human consensus (even if to individual reason they are but postulates or hypotheses awaiting proof) is to act against society, and against nature.

The dynamism which gave life to human communities could be

called divine precisely because of its anonymity, precisely because it was a 'process without a subject'. In the fact that behind languages and societies there is, properly speaking, no one, the traditionalists saw an irrefutable proof of the existence of God.[10]

But as the reference to 'communities' in the plural in the last citation suggests, the Traditionalist appeal to humankind at large could be adapted by Romantic nationalists to their own needs. On which view, the blossoming of national identities is also the work of the Creator, and it is above all when cut off from the influence of national idiom that the human *cogito*, so far from finding liberation, shrivels up. The Enlightenment had been a genuinely international phenomenon, but one of its offspring was exacerbated secular nationalism. The *philosophes* agreed with Spinoza – who was passionately devoted to the institutions of the Dutch Republic and whose demythologising reading of the Hebrew Bible had made of Scripture a book of rules, paradigms and rituals for the governance of a state according to nature: when the state is destroyed, no good can flourish. Political piety is, accordingly, the highest virtue. The French Revolutionaries, concerned to transform a state they considered archaic (theocratic, monarchical, aristocratic) gave a new charge to the term 'nation' or 'fatherland'. Stripping lawful authority from monarch, Church, nobility, they defined legal status as whatever the representatives of the nation might choose to confer. But Church authority, having learned the lessons of a Europe in upheaval, regarded national awakenings and visionary politics as (in the common or garden sense of the word) romantic illusions incapable of providing the due liberties and settled values that civilised institutions should house.

And this was Lamennais' painful discovery. In the 1818 *Essai sur l'indif-férence en matière de religion*, Lamennais, though not placing the same emphasis as de Bonald on the philosophy of language, agreed with the latter's *Législation primitive* (1802) that to an absolute scepticism which was both impracticable and a doctrine of death there could only be opposed, in the first instance, an instinctive faith in the witness of the race. Such faith in the authoritative consent of humanity, from which acceptance God's existence at once follows, is the very principle of human knowledge and certitude. Lamennais' defence of his philosophical doctrine, published in 1821, received the *imprimatur* of the pope's household theologian, the 'master of the sacred palace', but controversy mounted since for other critics, from Gallicans to Jesuits, Lamennais had overthrown the distinction between natural and revealed religion; acceptance of his tenets logically implied that the natural theology taught in the Catholic schools should be rejected as productive of atheism and the overthrow of Catholicism as such. Lamennais' Ultramontanism − if the historic revelation confirmed the instinctual faith of humanity and added to its general consent the new consensus of a universal Church, then the pope, the universal pastor, must be the organ of this enhanced *sens commun*, the voice of the tradition of the people − was unacceptable to Gallicans at home. His dislike of Scholastic philosophy, necessarily including the eclectic Scholasticism of Francisco de Suarez (1548–1617) to which the renascent Society of Jesus was committed, made his thought unpalatable to Jesuits abroad.

On completing in 1829 his *De la Religion considérée dans ses rapports avec l'ordre politique et civile*, at his school of La Chesnaie (recognising that the intellectual needs of the Church, which had lost its universities, monasteries and religious study houses, exceeded what individuals could provide, he had created a remarkable *atelier* with departments for history, philosophy, theology, languages and Christian literature),[11] Lamennais broke with Legitimism, declaring he could no longer support any system that united Church with State.

A truly integral Catholicism, Lamennais now thought, would more plausibly be constructed on the power of popes to overawe emperors and kings − in the name, not least, of those outside the 'political nation'. Here the idea of a Catholic society making few (if any) concessions to secularity or pluralism was married with a democratic and socially utopian hope for a new world. Renaissance, Reformation, Enlightenment and Revolution were stages in the decline of the spiritual power's ability to resist the rise of political tyranny. As he told Pope Leo XII della Genga (1760–1829), princes began this rebellion, making themselves judges of the divine law and hence undermining the salutary authority of the Church. In Emile Poulat's persuasive thesis, Catholic counter-revolution and Christian democracy spring from the same root: the first 'liberty' to be established must be that of the Church to influence society.[12] Lamennais' call on the French bishops to shake off the throne's emasculating hold and hazard the Christian regeneration of society by reliance instead on the dual support of the chair of Peter and the people met with no welcoming response. In 1832 Pope Gregory XVI Cappellari (1765–1846), a Camaldolese monk with a high view (even for popes) of the primacy and personal infallibility of the Petrine office-holder, condemned the Liberal theory of the Church's relation with civil society in the encyclical *Mirari vos*; Lamennais' forthright reply provoked the further papal rocket of *Singulari nos*, which blasted the Mennaisian denial of the preamble of faith, and the way supernatural revelation lost all gratuity if reason could not ensure society's most minimal survival without faith.

Though Lamennais passed then from Catholic history, the influence of his communitarian thinking survived among his disciples, and notably Philippe Olympe Gerbet (1798–1864) who, impressed by the work of the Tübingen ecclesiologist Johann Adam Möhler (1796–1838), translated Lamennais' vision into Möhlerian terms of the Eucharistic cultus, finding the true means of uniting the human community in the Eucharistic communion of the Church.[13] The school of Chesnaie played its part not only in mediating the knowledge of Möhler to France (the first account of his *Die Einheit der Kirche oder das Prinzip des Katholizismus*, 1825, would appear in the Mennaisian journal *Mémorial* for 1828).[14] It also helped give the theological understanding of the act of faith the fruitful prominence it enjoyed in the later nineteenth and early twentieth centuries.[15] The popularity of Traditionalism at Louvain, in the period when the future Pope Leo XIII Pecci (1810–1903) was papal nuncio to Belgium, would be a factor in the Roman encouragement of a Thomist revival by way of antidote. The problem could be viewed in concentrated form slightly further south in the Alsatian capital of Strasbourg where the abbé Louis Eugène Marie Bautain (1796–1867) mixed the spiritual intuitions of the contemporary mystic Magdalena-Luise Humann (1766–1836), Lamennais' Traditionalism, the German Idealism flourishing across the river that washed his city, and elements of Platonism into a heady brew. But its name was fideism, as emerges from the promise exacted from him by the Roman Curia in 1844. He would not in future teach that the existence of God, the spirituality and immortality of the soul, the principles of metaphysics, and the motives which make revelation credible, lie beyond the range of human reason, and reason 'unaided' at that. The act of faith may be supra-rational, but it leaves reason — and so the human creature — its own dignity. This the popes, like the schoolmen, knew.

4 | Theological Counter-revolutionism

The de-Christianisation of culture and society to which Catholic Romanticism and Traditionalism attempted to respond could also take the form of theological Counter-revolutionism, a political theology unashamed of the name. The lay theological writings of Joseph Marie de Maistre (1753–1821) followed on fifteen years as minister-plenipotentiary of the king of Sardinia in the Russia of Alexander I (1777–1825). De Maistre's *Soirées de Saint-Pétersbourg, ou Entretiens sur le gouvernement temporel da la Providence* (1821) rehearses various themes of Traditionalism (the inseparability of thought and language and the divine origin of the latter, the horror of a 'separated philosophy', appeal to the consent of the wise of all times and places, continuity and tradition as pre-conditions of progress) but gives fewer hostages of fortune to the possible charge of fideism. Even before his sojourn at the Romanov court, with its opportunities for reading and reflection, de Maistre had begun to lay the foundations of his theological politology. Writing in the 1790s, de Maistre treated the Revolution as the providentially ineluctable outcome of the frivolous irresponsibility of the *ancien régime* in tolerating, and conniving at the fashionableness of, the *philosophes*, with their atheism or at least deism. By demonstrating how in a society deprived of God, and the crown that, tutored by the Church, mediates the law of God to men, the centre cannot hold, the Revolution has proved the necessity of both religion and legitimate monarchy, and no adherent of either will wish it had never been. He would be disappointed by the concessionist spirit of the first Bourbon monarch of the Restoration: what was needed was, rather, absolutism tempered by mercy, and rendered just by devotion to God and attention to the historic vocation divine Providence had allotted to the nation.

The foundations of de Maistre's 'theological counter-revolutionism' lie in his acute understanding of the practical correlates of the dogma of original sin. Given the ineradicable quality of human culpability (this side of the Eschaton), the attempts of temporal revolutions to anticipate the final judgement can only intensify man's 'dis-grace'. Offending against both human nature and the plan of Providence they incarnadine the hands of historical agents. Creation will mean destruction, liberation tyranny. If de Maistre's writings anticipate the papal critique of radical liberation theology in the 1980s, they are more powerfully echoed in the work of a Russian Orthodox counterpart in the decades when dialogue between Christianity and Marxism, and an accommodationist *Ostpolitik* were officially approved ventures of the Catholic Church of Paul VI Montini (1897–1978).

> The conception of revolution as a divinely occasioned act of political self-chastisement, the summons to the restoration of a religious-political *auctoritas* in a fundamentally theocratic State and society, are those of Solzhenitsyn. His total rejection of the Russian Revolution in the name of the Christ of Byzantine majesty and suffering, his detestation of the uprooted intelligentsia which brought on the crises of 1917, his incomparable image of the cannibalism, of the self-devouring, which are the iron law of a Bolshevist utopia, make of Solzhenitsyn a close counterpart to Maistre.[16]

But de Maistre knew perfectly well that no divine guarantee validated the performance of the Christian dynasties, whose sphere was in any case bounded by the particularities of the statehood to which each belonged. For men to be united, the civility of ordered life under traditional institutions no longer suffices, if ever it did. Instead, to unite where so much divides, there must be a spiritual sovereignty unlimited in sway to the earth's bounds because stemming from above. In *Du pape* (1819) he argued accordingly that the temporal authority committed to kings will never be secure without the concomitant recognition of the spiritual authority vested in the Roman pontiff. In the age after that Revolution which for the first time presented secular history as (endlessly?) transformative of the conditions of human possibility itself, no less a power would serve on the global stage of the human spirit to recall with effect the basic sanities available to life with others before the Kingdom.

5 | Neo-Ultramontanism

Lamennais' influence on attitudes to a universal primate endured even when crucial aspects of Traditionalism and Liberalism suffered censure. This was because many Catholic Churchmen in the first half of the nineteenth century were increasingly estranged from regalian notions of the Church-State relation. Frequently indeed, local bishops themselves appealed to Rome for help to struggle free from such encumbrances. And this tendency facilitated the triumph of Ultramontane ideas. The metaphor may be apt. The future Gregory XVI's treatise on the subject was entitled precisely *Il trionfo della Santa Sede*, 'The Triumph of the Holy See' (1799) — though his creation of missionary bishoprics and vicariates brought his office more real influence than struggles with the Powers. While before the 1830s the development of Neo-Ultramontane principles and aspirations had been left to go its own sweet way, the Papacy now began to support overtly what it had earlier merely looked upon with distant benevolence. The destruction of Catholic universities in the Revolution and the passing of the ecclesiastical principalities as decreed by Bonapartist reorganisation in Germany made it likely that resistance would be weak.

Let us also note the role of converts from Christian bodies like the Anglican which, though episcopal in structure, lacked for want of the Petrine office (or some analogate thereof) clearly enunciated doctrine and firm, state-free, leadership. William George Ward (1812–1882), Fellow of Balliol College, Oxford, arrived at his theological position with a mind not warmed by history (it left him cold) but sharpened by encounter with the *Logic* (1843), at once syllogistic and inductive, of John Stuart Mill (1806–1873). Ward abandoned Canterbury for Rome so as to escape from what his mentor John Henry Newman (1801–1890) called the 'channel of no-meaning between the Scylla and Charybdis of Aye and No'. The (epistemological) need for a religious authority empowered to promulgate a clear and explicit rule of faith, and a recognition that conscience can intuit the higher ethical standard which the plenitude of Christian doctrine promotes in asceticism and sanctity – truth in its relation to holiness – brought Ward first to Tractarianism, the 'Catholic Movement' in the Church of England, and then, in 1845, on deprivation of his degrees at Anglican Oxford for writing *The Ideal of Christian Church* (1844) to Catholicism itself. In *The Ideal*, the necessity of an external guide for faith and religious practice is declared paramount, and none (Ward adds) can be authoritatively offered if such a living voice be fallible: it must, if it exists (and inspection of the Church of Rome shows it does exist), be divinely assisted. 'Wardism', as the troubled High Churchman William Ewart Gladstone (1809–1898) called it, pre-announced its author's Neo-Ultramontanism by its tone – no longer the early Tractarians' attraction to the mystical theology of the Fathers, their patriotic love of the Church of England, and large indifference to the social problems of the day, but, on the contrary, admiration for the Scholastic system, coolness towards anything specifically national, and zeal for the imposition of norms, and inculcation of virtues, suited to repair the failings of a *laisser-faire* society. It was hardly to be expected that Ward would *not* rally to the new Ultramontanism typified by Lamennais and de Maistre – despite his lack of enthusiasm for their (in any case mutually divergent) politics.

> The Ultramontane doctrine – the infallibility and prerogatives of the Roman see – became in their hands the symbol of that principle of unity and effective authority, which had enabled the Church to stand immovable amid a society whose structure had been shaken to its foundations.[17]

In the aftermath of the European 'Year of Revolutions', 1848, when political Liberalism in the States of the Church turned to bite the hand of the pope — Pius IX Mastai-Ferretti (1792–1878) — who had briefly fed it, and hopes of a *rapprochement* between the Catholic Church and Liberal or republican rule foundered on the issue, to be conceded neither by the bourgeoisie nor by the Church, of education, the positions of Liberal and Ultramontane Catholics simultaneously hardened. If in France the Neo-Ultramontanism of the satirist Louis Veuillot (1813–1883) opposed the Liberal Catholicism of the historian Charles René Forbes Montalembert (1810–1870) chiefly over the issue of the Church-world relation (for Veuillot the Church would flourish if Catholics behaved as a compact phalanx, intransigently resisting the inroads of modern secularism), in Germany it was primarily questions of critical scholarship and its freedom which set at loggerheads Döllinger and the Tübingen *Theologische Quartalschrift* on the one hand, and on the other hand Matthias Joseph Scheeben (1835–1888) and the school of Mainz. That is true even though as early as the Vienna Congress (1815) Catholics concerned to pre-empt any resurgence of Febronianism, or development of Protestant or Masonic hegemony in the former *Reichskirchlich* territories, entered into concert, and to that end adopted Neo-Ultramontane positions. Just so, for that matter, was Montalembert concerned not only with the civil ethos but for the due freedom of Catholic scholarship as well.

For Ward, convinced that the outcome of modernity would be a choice between atheism and a Catholic theism seated in the chair of Peter, there could be little hesitation. Sharing the distinctive emphasis of Neo-Ultramontanism on the utility of papal interventions in doctrine and discipline both numerous and broad (the more the merrier), he favoured a maximalist definition of the scope of the Petrine office. Made editor of the episcopally owned *Dublin Review* by Cardinal Nicholas Patrick Stephen Wiseman (1802–1865) of Westminster, his remit was to offset the influence of the Liberal Catholic *Rambler* (later *The Home and Foreign Review*).

> The *Rambler* appeared to restrict its Catholic principles to the acceptance of the definitions of faith, and to set aside as unimportant and often untrue the whole mass of ethical and doctrinal teaching which makes up the practical life of Catholicism. This amounted, in Mr Ward's opinion, to the denial of the

41

Catholic ideal — which had a unity of its own — the definitions representing only the fixed points and outlines of a large system, and the outcome of a mass of energising principles.[18]

The terms of that controversy would be highly germane to the debate on the scope of papal infallibility which preceded and accompanied the First Vatican Council.

The debates over culture, society, State, in the epoch of Romanticism, Traditionalism, Counter-revolutionism, would also have their relevance: for how else, asked Neo-Ultramontanes, than by a strengthened Petrine office was the freedom of the Church to stand secure in the face of the emergent omnicompetent nation-state? In thus safeguarding its own freedom would it not then be able to defend others' freedom too?[19] They could not have guessed that a pope with universally primatial jurisdiction would one day face not the competing moral culture of a Protestant super-power, or the manipulative Catholicism of inadequate leaders in a South American republic, but the systematic ruthlessness of Stalinist Russia or Nazi Germany.

III | VARIETIES OF REASON

1 | Semi-rationalism

The Catholic theology of the Enlightenment and Restoration periods was evidently not unacquainted with disagreement as to the nature of rationality, and the contribution that reason, not least in its formal academic mode, philosophy, should make to the life of faith (or, come to that, the life of faith make to reason and philosophy). That issue of the varieties of reason and how most judiciously to select among them for the Gospel's sake remained highly *aktuell* in the Catholic thought of the nineteenth century.

With the 'Semi-rationalists' Georg Hermes (1775–1831) and Anton Günther (1783–1863) we find Catholic theologians attempting to respond to the challenge not only of Kant (Hermes) but also (Günther) of Hegel — the mightiest figure of the Idealism which philosophically dominated their age. Hegel had argued that, despite its widespread cruelty and folly, human history exhibits in its developing course man's potential for rationality. In his *Science of Logic* (1812–1816) he claimed that his own logic, as the intellectual penetration of the immanent dialectic of becoming, is itself 'the thought of God before the creation of the world'. This claim, if well founded, entailed that philosophy, not religion, is the source of the ultimate coherence available to life and thought. Based as philosophy is on reason, not revelation, it is (in Hegel's hands) conclusive and universal, and on both counts superior to faith. The prophetic intellectual, not the priest, holds the crystal ball where the meaning of reality can be read. Hegel's over-ambitious system, and the inflated concept of the services philosophy can offer it embodied, belongs with a series of efforts by post-Kantian thinkers in Germany to close the gap between appearance and reality, phenomenon and noumenon, which Kant's philosophical revolution had opened up. Such writers as Johann Gottfried Herder (1744–1803) and Johann Georg Hamann (1730–1788) censured Kant for his fragmentation of human understanding into three (as it might seem) unrelated varieties in his three 'critiques': *Der Kritik der reinen Vernunft*, on 'pure reason', or speculative philosophy (1781 and 1787); the *Kritik der praktischen Vernunft*, on 'practical reason' or morality (1788); and the *Kritik der Urteilskraft*, the '*Critique of Judgement*', on aesthetics (1790). They proposed instead that 'sensibility' or sensation gradually transforms itself into 'ideality' or intelligibility. Subsequently, taking up the clues offered by Kant's critics, the Romantic Idealist philosophers from Fichte to Hegel elaborate a system of reason that is simultaneously a phenomenology of spirit. They see reality as a living process that embraces both the self and the world, and aims at spirit's complete transparency to itself through its self-expression in the world. Here the search for systematic unity indicates that the Romantic movement proper is being left behind.

In Catholic theology, 'Semi-rationalism' is a portmanteau term for writers who, whatever the differences among them, share what is deemed to be an exaggerated view of human reason, both in demonstrating and in explaining revealed truth. The disordered state of Catholic intellectual life in the early decades of the nineteenth century, combined with the extraordinary prestige the new philosophies enjoyed, made it *a priori* likely that some Catholic theologians would follow down the primrose path where a number of their Protestant counterparts had led. Hermes and Günther were simply the most exposed of the divines who, in Germanophone Catholicism, drew on post-Kantian philosophy so as to ground Church dogmatics speculatively, harmonising faith and knowledge: thus, for instance, Patrizius Benedikt Zimmer (1752–1820), who taught dogmatic theology at the

Universities of Dillingen and Ingoldstadt-Landshut, made use in turn of Fichte and Schelling to repair the breaches opened up by Kantianism in the defence walls of a rational metaphysics (chiefly supplied by the Lutheran philosopher Gottfried Wilhelm Leibniz, 1646–1716, and his systematising disciple Christian Wolff, 1679–1754) supposed to serve as a propadeutic for Christian belief.

Hermes, a Westphalian, gained his spurs at the University of Münster where, exercised by the challenge to supernatural religion that the philosophies of Kant and Fichte represented, he wrote his enquiries into Christianity's inner truth, the *Untersuchungen über die innere Wahrheit des Christentums* (1805), which earned him a chair at the relatively *parvenu* University of Bonn. The services he rendered there (ironically, as things later turned out, in mediating between the Prussian king — to whom the University, with its background in the Catholic Enlightenment, had appealed against the local bishops — and the bishops themselves) were compounded by the wide welcome given to his two-part 'introduction' to 'Catholic Christian theology': the *Philosophische Einleitung in die Christkatholische Theologie* of 1819, and its historical-dogmatic counterpart, the *Positive Einleitung in die Christkatholische Dogmatik*, which, though based on his lecture courses, appeared posthumously in 1834. Hermes proposed to overcome both the critical philosophy of Kant and Fichte's idealism by re-instating the methodical doubt of Descartes, while at the same time furnishing a new criterion of certitude for any truths that systematic doubt may leave us still believing: the criterion, namely, of *necessity*. A metaphysical truth is certain when the understanding thinks it as necessary and the reason supplies that necessity's rationale. That could have an application to Christian apologetics where, ever since Stattler, fundamental theologians had tried to prove revelation's necessity as well as possibility. But what then of the truths of history, on which turned the other main question of Enlightenment apologetics — the factual happening of a revelation judged both possible and necessary. Here Hermes argued that an alleged historical truth is itself 'necessary', with the necessity which belongs to practical (as distinct from pure) reason if it is required for our moral action. And of all the experiences deposited in history that might be considered indispensable to moral events today, those given with the historic revelation are the most crucial. The practice of the Judaeo-Christian virtues, essential as these are to the truly good life, presupposes the credibility of the Jewish-Christian God. Hermes' conclusion was that authentic faith depends on demonstration, just as real virtue turns on faith thus founded. All faith, if not credulous and so vicious, results from some necessity, whether metaphysical or moral.

The welcome given Hermes' thought, signalled as this was by the creation of the *Zeitschrift für Philosophie und katholische Theologie* for the diffusion of his ideas, found no answering echo among the German episcopate, and in 1835 Pope Gregory XVI submitted his writings to the judgement of two Roman theologians, Carl von Reisach (1800–1869), the Rector of the German College and a future cardinal of enormous influence in the Curia of Pius IX, and the Jesuit Giovanni Perrone (1794–1876), a main pillar of the historically minded if fundamentally scholastic theology of the Collegium Romanum in the same pontificate. The Prussian government, persuaded by Hermes' disciples, declared illegal the publication of the Brief announcing the negative verdict which ensued, thus precipitating an imbroglio that led, among other things, to the temporary imprisonment of the Cologne archbishop. Attempts to gain a retractation of the Roman action, basing themselves on the 1844 inhibition of Bautain's Traditionalism, show the problems Catholic theology experienced in swimming a straight course between rationalism and fideism; they came, however, to a definitive end with the promulgation of the dogmatic constitution *Dei Filius*, on faith and revelation, at the First Vatican Council. It could never be Catholic to deny that faith's formal motive is the authority of God revealing, or to strip the act of faith of its free and supernatural character.

Hermes, however, had never tried to suppress the fact that in revelation come, and in abundance, mysteries impenetrable to reason. (It was the fact, not the content, of revelation he considered demonstrable.) Reason was not for him our only principle of knowledge as Christians (the sole *Erkenntnisprinzip*); rather was it our only principle of discernment as to where knowledge may be found (our unique *erkennendes Prinzip*). Indeed, as the title of the *Positive Einleitung* implies, dogmatic theology meant for Hermes the study of doctrinal sources (in Scripture, Tradition, magisterium): the patristic as well as Scholastic attempt to interrelate doctrines to each other and to natural truths he considered an abuse of thought. In this he could have no sharper antithesis than Günther, a fact which shows that their lumping together as a pair is but a convenience of theological history.

Günther was one of the many Bohemians (until the Sudetenland crisis of the Hitler period) of German tongue; his studies at Prague of modern German philosophy shook his Catholicism, but his faith was restored by contact with St Clement Maria Hofbauer (1751–1820), the Redemptorist priest, a former baker's apprentice, who in his opposition to the minimalism of Josephinist and *Aufklärung* Catholicism gained the title of 'apostle of Vienna'. Apart from short periods in Hungary and Habsburg Galicia, Günther would spend the rest of his life in Vienna as a freelance ecclesiastic, who supported himself through his writings, and until 1848, ironically for one who was to fall foul of Church censorship, as a State censor of books for the imperial government. A highly original mind who spurned the use of even the literary forms of previous theology (the titles of his works in their ingenuity and indeed bizarreness are reminiscent of his Danish Lutheran contemporary Søren Aaby Kierkegaard, 1815–1855) his theology took as its aim what he believed had been Schlegel's: by philosophy to raise the faith which simply accepts revealed truths on divine say-so to the rank of genuine knowledge by the penetrating comprehension of those same truths.

Günther attempts to combat the Hegelian and Schellengian systems by stealing a number of their conceptual tools. Considered as a thinking organism, man is a unity-in-duality. The psyche, *Seele*, which belongs to the natural order, is the subject of the conceptual function, the interpreter of appearances; mind, *Geist*, is the subject of the ideal thinking whose primary object is the ego's own conditions or states. By way of 'meta-logical' inference from the powers of receptivity and spontaneity exhibited by the ego, the psyche arrives, through mind, at the idea of its own being, and, by contradistinction to itself, the truths that nature and God are also real. As to God, in its dependence and limitedness the soul must have as its antecedent condition what is absolute and infinite. Can that divine Being be described? If nature, the endlessly multiple and so comparatively undetermined, stands over against mind, which is always a unitary substance, that rational apprehension of the bipolar character of reality (mind-nature) enables us to speak of the being of God — with the difference that what in ourselves in the world is process is in God consummated from all eternity, as the Father brings into being the 'substantial emanation' of the Son, and there issues from both the Spirit who synthesises them as does our ego nature and mind. (Are we not told in Scripture that we were made 'in his image'?) The created universe, as the realised idea of the non-divine being and life (the divine 'non-ego'), has its epitome in man, the synthesis of nature and spirit, from which Günther further deduces the rational basis of the dogmas of the Incarnation and Redemption whereby the triune God realigns with himself a race where these relations have gone recklessly awry.

Günther's system was influential: his disciplines included numerous university and seminary professors, and the founders of the Congregation of Beuron, who recreated German Benedictinism on the model of the Solesmes of abbot Prosper Louis Pascal Guéranger (1805–1875), the greatest figure of the monastic revival in post-Revolutionary Catholicism. But in 1857, despite powerful supporters in both Empire and Curia, the Congregation of the Index censured Günther's Trinitarian theology, Christology, anthropology and theology of creation, and above all the theological rationalism which held these together. Günther himself respectfully submitted in the external forum, but when after his death his fundamental theology was anathematised in a canon of the 1870 General Council, a number of the intellectuals who had supported him leaked away into the 'Old Catholic' churches.

2 | The Catholic Tübingen School

The story of the Catholic Tübingen School opens in South Germany soon after 1800. In the territorial re-structuring of Germany which followed the Revolutionary and Napoleonic Wars, a large part of Catholic Swabia was handed over to the Protestant king of Württemberg. That prince, anxious to demonstrate his liberality to his newly acquired Catholic subjects, founded at Ellwangen a school of Catholic theology which settled in 1812 at Tübingen in the Black Forest. From its inception the Tübingen School was typified by two main features. First, it was marked by devotion to Catholic tradition in a wide sense: to the Liturgy, the Fathers, and Catholic thought and literature down the ages. Second, it was open to the diverting (in both positive and negative sense of that word) philosophical culture of early nineteenth-century Germany, to those Romantic and Idealist strains of thought already touched on in this study. Romantic influence can be detected in the school's emphasis on human subjectivity as the point within creation where grace is principally active, and in the Tübingen theologians' ecclesiology, for they stressed the historical becoming of the Church rather than its enduring being. A bridge between Romanticism and Idealism already existed in the Protestant context in the person and work of Friedrich Daniel Ernst Schleiermacher (1768–1834)[20] who managed to reconcile in himself the simple Protestantism of the Moravian Brethren, among whom he had grown up, with Kantian agnosticism, Spinozist immanentism and Romantic sensibility, all of which influences conspired to lead him to his key belief, that religion's highest office is to serve a sense of union with the infinite.

The two principal concerns of the Tübingen theologians were fundamental theology and ecclesiology. In the former by a 'naturalist supernaturalism' concerned to show the inter-weaving of the orders of reason and revelation, nature and grace, they argued that reason finds its absolute foundation not in its own intellectual quality but in acceptance of a revelation mediated by a salvation history where human nature is brought to transcendent fulfilment. Thus for Johann Sebastian von Drey (1777–1853), though Christianity is essentially a sacred history, it is not for all that a mere succession of empirical phenomena. Instead, it shares in the necessity of an eternal plan whose organic development it is. The reality of the Church, rooted as this is in the mystery of Christ and ushering in the divine Kingdom, reconciles the ideal and the real, the rational and the empirical, in itself. This is why, despite the crucial importance of history — and so in theology of the genetic method in studying the history of doctrine — Catholic theology cannot simply be the history of dogma, but must unite historical method with speculation in the service of theological science. And by the latter Drey meant a structure where the data are integrated into the elaboration of a single necessary idea from which all other relevant ideas can be deduced. This idea, however, is furnished by no philosophy but only by revelation, and it is, as Brenner had already noted, the idea of the Kingdom. Drey presented a programmatic statement of what theology should be in his *Kurze Einleitung in das Studium der Theologie, mit Rücksicht auf den wissenschaftlichen Standpunkt und das katholische System*, which appeared in the same year, 1819, as the first issue of the *Theologische Quartalschrift*, the school's journal, which he co-founded. The two sides, historical and speculative, of his genius were shown in such different works as his editions of early Christian texts, and the three-volume apologetics conceived as a 'scientific substantiation (*Nachweisung*) of the divinity of Christianity in its appearing'.

In ecclesiology, the most characteristic theme of the Tübingen School was that of the Church as supernatural organism. Möhler, for example, spoke of the Church as an organism whose basis is the supernatural life given by Christ. Since Christianity is a divine reality, it transcends any particular statement of its content. But as time goes on and the Church develops, we can glimpse different aspects of this revelation which the various phases of the carrier organism show us as they unfold. The Church, both as institution and as sacramental life revolving around the Mass, reflects the mystery of the Incarnation, for this divinely constituted society is the mystical Body of Christ, the manifestation in efficacious sign of God's saving mercy. Here Möhler's account was both descriptive and prescriptive: in theological fact, the objective community of the Catholic Church is, through its symbols, that finite-infinite union which Schleiermacher had sought in the individual subject,[21] but it will not be this effectively for its members unless in each generation they re-find that spirit of *agapê* which characterised the community of the early centuries — for whose somewhat idealised evocation Möhler relied on the researches of the Church historian Johann August Wilhelm Neander (1789–1850), a Jew converted to the Schleiermacherian Gospel.

3 | Newman

Möhler's ideas had some affinity with those of Newman, a largely self-taught theologian who, after his conversion from Anglicanism to the Catholic Church, worked largely on his own. Just as the more philosophical side of the Tübingen theologians (and notably their debt to Schelling) aroused anxiety in less adventurous Catholic circles, so the ideas of Möhler and Newman on the Church and doctrinal development would be suspected of too hasty a surrender to the spirit of the age.

An account of the spiritual aeneid which took Newman from the Anglican to the Catholic community ('Oxford made us Catholics') belongs with a history of Anglican, rather than Catholic, theology.[22] But as his fellow convert, fellow cardinal, Henry Edward Manning (1808–1892), archbishop of Westminster, complained, he did not leave his Anglican inheritance entirely behind; the 'old Oxford patristic tone' continued to be heard within the Catholic Church. It was the subtle, delicate temper of Newman's intelligence, with its ever-shifting vantage points, rather than any particular conclusions to which it came, which was most alien to such seekers of forthright principle as (Ward and) Manning. Newman's legacy lay in four areas: the nature of reason's approach to God's existence and self-revelation; the implications of conscience; the idea of doctrinal development; and the inter-relations of the prophetic, pastoral and priestly offices in the Church. We can consider each of these in turn.

If Samuel Taylor Coleridge (1772–1834) had preceded Newman, in the English context, in drawing attention to the importance of a priori principles in fruitful philosophising (here Coleridge's acquaintance with the Germany of Johann Christian Friedrich von Schiller (1759–1805) – that most intellectual of dramatists – Schelling and Schlegel was crucial), another Anglican, Joseph Butler (1692–1752), bishop of Durham, had impressed him with his view that moral certainty constituted sufficient grounds and more for the guidance of life. Whereas Ward would group systematically a priori, intuitively grasped, principles that philosophy must, on pain of paralysis, presuppose, principles that would locate inductive logic context in a wider context where belief in God forms part (thus the *Essays on the Philosophy of Theism* of 1884), Newman, with his acute psychological gifts, spoke rather of antecedent dispositions which reason cannot create yet must judge not unreasonable, dispositions that incline us so to sift the evidence for faith as to arrive at true assent both to God's existence and to his self-revelation. In his (Anglican) *University Sermons* on faith and reason (1839–1841) Newman had also proposed that, as between 'implicit' and 'explicit' reason, the former is the more fundamental, and in the 1870 *Essay in Aid of a Grammar of Assent* he would lay out more fully the case for the primacy of implicit reason, collating as it does the evidence for a conclusion in terms of an entire experiential field or flow, where many considerations occur to the mind that are lost to view when explicit reason takes over, isolating items of evidence and submitting them to a formal process of investigation. In all major areas of human reflection, imagination and reason work in tandem: here Newman brings together the inheritance of Coleridge and Butler, those milder English variants on European Romanticism and Enlightenment respectively.

Among the experiential materials germane to an account of religious belief Newman gave the palm to conscience. It is in the presence of God as all-holy Ruler and Judge not only in the depths of the human heart but as a phenomenon of history, forcing itself onto the public stage by way of breakthroughs of moral perception, most strikingly of all in and through the Jewish-Christian tradition, that we know the scene of life to be not as it first appears: a spectacle of Godlessness where man is spiritually alone in the world.

The exercise of conscience took Newman into the Roman Catholic Church. The 1845 *Essay on the Development of Christian Doctrine*, published on the morrow of his reception into the Catholic Church, was written not so much to explain that action – as Newman wrote, people could not 'get' his reasons:

> ... except at the cost of some portion of the trouble I have been at myself... Moral proofs are grown into, not learnt by heart.[23]

– as to clear away a difficulty. The *Essay* uses the notion of antecedent probability to disengage the way revelation retains its distinct identity, in new situations, and faced with new questions, through historical time. Just as revelation itself developed as, through Old Testament and New, it pursued its course, so, Newman thought, we can expect the Church's understanding of the finished Gospel of God to develop likewise. And by a variety of analogies – logical, biological, psychological – he set out to show how doctrines, practices, traits in contemporary Catholicism are coherently interrelated not only with each other but also with the primitive deposit. The complex yet unitary impression left on earth with the apostolic preaching can be and is elucidated by the subsequent doctrine of the Church, since the Redeemer himself has equipped it with organs that discern with unfailing reliability what does or does not belong to the faith once delivered to the saints.

Not that the whole picture of what Catholicism is can be gained simply from looking on the ground, to see how in parish with its pastor, the faith is practised by – normatively – the devout faithful. No more is it to be found in its entirety in the writings of doctors and theologians. Nor do the sovereign judgements of that bishop who holds the keys of Peter provide a complete panorama of the saving revelation. In the Preface to *The Via Media of the Anglican Church* (1877) Newman described these three 'offices' – sacerdotal, prophetic and regal – as functions that operate by continuous interaction in the body of Christ. The idea that for the health of Catholicism the 'mystical', 'intellectual' and 'institutional' elements in the Christian religion must all be encouraged to flourish simultaneously would be taken further by the cosmopolitan but London-based philosopher-theologian Friedrich von Hügel (1852–

1925), and the wider notion of the 'triple office' — sanctifying, teaching, shepherding — which the Church exercises in mediation of the Christ who is himself Priest, Prophet, King would pass, through the encyclical *Mystici Corporis Christi* of Pope Pius XII Pacelli (1876–1958), into the official documents of the Roman Church.

4 | Rosmini

Meanwhile, south of the Alps, a very different kind of theological epistemology had taken shape. Antonio Rosmini-Serbati (1797–1855) was only
just a geographical 'Ultramontane': his home town, Rovereto, now in the
Italian province of Trento, formed part of Südtirol, Austria, below the
Brenner Pass. But his heart was not with the dynastic inter-ethnicity of
the Habsburgs; in 1848 we find the *arciprete* Rosmini an ambassador
extraordinary of the king of Piedmont to the still liberal Pius IX and, on
the outbreak of the Roman Revolution, taking unceremonious refuge
with the Bourbons of Naples at Gaeta, where intelligence of his support
for the pope's short-lived constitutional nationalism, and of his unusual
theology, made him an unwelcome guest.

If Rosmini's *Sull' unità dell'educazione* (1826) announced the need for a
counterblast to the educational programme of Enlightenment rationalism, an unpublished manuscript of 1850 shows him dividing out his
(three hundred) books and essays so as to make of them an orthodox
response to Diderot's *Encyclopédie*: ideology and logic; metaphysics;
morals; pedagogy and methodology; political science; the philosophy
of supernatural realities; and pastoral and ecclesial writings.[24] In this

ambitious project, Rosmini hoped to meet the triple threat to Catholic intellectual life posed by Enlightenment influence, Kantianism and the decadence of much contemporary Scholasticism — for without an intellectual life as comprehensive as it is metaphysically invigorated, the claims of the biblical revelation about God and his re-ordering of human destiny cannot be thought through. Recourse to Aquinas — whom Rosmini considered a genius comparable only to Newton — might have saved the situation, but his school had misinterpreted his mind by a narrow Aristoteleanism; Rosmini himself would offer the renewed metaphysics of a 'personalist ontology', drawing on the ancient Fathers (Augustine, 354–430) and mediaevals (Bonaventure, 1221–1274) as well as such early modern writers as Blaise Pascal (1623–1662) and Malebranche.

If philosophy is to lead the sciences to theology, it must serve as the common guide of them all, and for this its own object must be universal (since no particular truth could generate so comprehensive a principle) and objective (for subjects, in their particularity, do not create effects more exalted than themselves). The idea of being (being's 'ideal' or undetermined form — being at large) is, for Rosmini, the 'divine in nature', the mirror of God's subsistent Being, the 'light that enlightens every man coming into this world', of which the Johannine Prologue (1,9) had spoken. And this suggests the possibility that, far from conflicting, reason and faith may be at one. The first truth, Rosmini held, is not only the principle of philosophy. As supernatural light — the Word in person — it (or rather he) is needed for understanding the 'real' being which exists in all its subsistent vitality and, moreover, the 'completion' that marries the indeterminate possibility of ideal being to being's form as real. Rosmini thus followed up the 1830 *Nuovo Saggio sulle origine dell'idee* by writing a two-part anthropology devoted to the 'sciences' of, this time, not the object so much as the subject. He declared the trinity of forms of being to re-appear in the intellectual, sensitive and volitional aspects of human nature, united as these are in the human person who is their ordering principle: thus the *Antropologia naturale* of 1838. And in the posthumous *Antropologia sopranaturale* (1884), Rosmini described the Word, who 'bears the very stamp of [the Father's] nature' (Hebrews 1,3), as acting for man's renovation in his intellect and through the Spirit in his will. That is how incorporation in Christ constitutes the very principle of Christianity itself. The differentiated order of the sciences of the object, reflected in the science of the subject, becomes practical action in the ordered perfection of love, to which the *Massime di perfezione cristiana* (1830) and Rosmini's 'Institute of Charity' (the religious Congregation he founded) bear witness. For the good, which is as universal as being, requires attention to our neighbour's intellectual, temporal and spiritual or eternal wellbeing.

Under the influence of the Thomist revival of Leo XIII's pontificate, a number of theses of Rosmini's 'system of truth' were judged temerarious: to affirm that we know nothing unless in knowing we also, and primarily, know God, is not this an epistemic version of pantheism?[25] Neo-Scholastic critics unsympathetic to Augustinian illuminism regretted that Rosmini had not considered how the problems of modern epistemology, like that post-Cartesian discipline itself, had largely been generated by the cultural anxiety that accompanied the fracturing of the mediaeval tradition.[26] Rather than content himself with saying that beliefs are warranted when the cognitive faculties of human beings, duly aimed at truth, are working properly in the kind of circumstances for which they were designed to function, he produced an elaborate epistemological system which continued to worry theologians long after the audacities of his pleas for the radical reform of Church and civil society were forgiven by Pius IX.[27]

5 | The Roman School

The better fortune with which Rosmini's work met under the reputedly arch-conservative Pius IX when compared with his more liberal successor Leo XIII should alert students of Church history to the difficulties inherent in fixing such labels. The 'Roman School' under Pio Nono was not 'know-nothing'. Rather were its members positive theologians, far from hostile to the new German theology,[28] and largely indifferent to Scholasticism considered as a coherent, integrated system — in all of which respects they differed markedly from their most prominent Leonine successor and fellow Jesuit Joseph Kleutgen (1811–1883), with whose rise to influence an era passes.

In 1824 Leo XII had returned the Roman College to the Jesuits, in the hope that it would become an intellectual centre of excellence for the entire Church. But it was only with the arrival in 1830 of Giovanni Perrone that it took on a distinct and corporate cast of mind. Twenty years before Döllinger's plea for a fuller recognition of the role of historical scholarship,[29] Perrone had divined that theology must use as her handmaids not just philosophy but history too. His model was the erudite seventeenth-century historical theologian Denis Pétau (1583–

1652), even if the re-edition of the great work of 'Petavius' on Christian doctrine in its historical development was the doing of Perrone's colleagues Carlo Passaglia (1812–1887) and Clemens Schrader (1820–1875). Though Perrone crossed swords with Newman over a celebrated paper on development, an encounter often presented as the Italian Scholastic at odds with the English historian, that episode was atypical, for, according to a modern German student of both, in all essentials their thinking agreed.[30]

Roman school theology was favoured high and wide. Both Perrone and Passaglia helped in preparing the dogmatic definition of Mary's original righteousness — the 'Immaculate Conception' — in 1854. Despite a reserved attitude to the question of the pope's temporal sovereignty (Passaglia, indeed, caught in the dilemma of papal *pietas* and nascent nationalism, fled the camp to the Turin of the *Risorgimento*'s architect, the anti-clerical Count Camillo Benso Cavour 1810–1861), members of the school contributed to drafting the *Syllabus of Errors*, a summary of Pius's criticisms of ideological and social modernity in thirty-two documents of his pontificate so far (1864). Their school formed future bishops and budding theologians from and for all parts of the Catholic world. It possessed in Perrone's *Praelectiones theologicae* (1835–1842, nine volumes), a model statement of Catholic theology, several times revised and many times reprinted, not only in Rome but also in Louvain, Turin, Vienna, Regensburg, Naples, Barcelona, Prague, Milan, Madrid and Paris, and circulated in *précis*, translation, part edition.

The influence of the *Collegio Romano* was especially marked in the German-speaking Catholicism of the later nineteenth and early twentieth centuries. The school's emphasis on the exact investigation of the historical development of doctrine, rather than philosophical speculation about its corollaries, was displayed in a galaxy of talent in the Franconian university city of Würzburg. One should mention first Joseph Dominicus Denzinger (1819–1883), Orientalist and editor of mediaeval theological texts, whose name is still a byword thanks to his *Enchiridion Symbolorum, Definitionum et Declarationum* (1854), a much-used manual of creeds and conciliar and papal statements on doctrine, currently in its thirty-seventh edition (1991). Next comes Joseph Hergenröther (1824–1890), patrologist, expert historian of the Photian schism, and erudite apologist for the Petrine claims vis-à-vis not only theological and historical critics (*Das unfehlbare Lehramt des Papstes*,

1871) but also political ones (*Katholische Kirche und christlicher Staat in ihre geschichtlichen Entwicklung und in Beziehung auf die Gegenwart*, 1872, with English and American editions in 1876 and 1889 respectively). Leo XIII appointed him Cardinal Prefect of the Apostolic Archives in 1879 as his chosen instrument in throwing open the hitherto 'secret' archival collections of the Papacy to the scholarly public – a mammoth task of establishing research facilities which did not, however, prevent him from undertaking the continuation of the exhaustive 'History of the Councils' initiated by the Tübingen Church historian Karl Joseph von Hefele (1809–1893), made bishop of Rottenburg in 1869. The third of the trio was Franz Hettinger (1819–1890), at whose hands the apologetics of Romantic theology received for the first time disciplined doctrinal and historical control: thus his *Apologie des Christenthums* (1863–1867), and *Lehrbuch der Fundamental theologie oder Apologetik* (1879). His discovery of the theological potential of the *Commedia* of Dante Alighieri (1265–1321) looks ahead to the exploitation of classics of Christian literature by such writers as Romano Guardini (1885–1968) and Hans Urs von Balthasar (1905–1988).

The losses to the school entailed by Passaglia's defection and Schrader's transferral by the Jesuit Society to Vienna were made good by the advent of the Tyrolese Johann Baptist Franzelin (1816–1886), who professed not only Arabic, Syrian and Chaldaean but dogmatic theology likewise. Among treatises on all the chief theological subject matters his *De divina traditione et scriptura* (1870) retains classic status. His work synthesised the tendencies of his school, where positive and speculative theology could fructify each other, and philosophy and history, Christian experience and systematic theology sit down together to drink. Perhaps because of the subtlety of their methodology, and despite the gift of a cardinal's hat to Franzelin in Pius IX's last years, the influence of the *Collegio Romano* ebbed in its finest hour: Minerva's owl, as Hegel remarked, takes flight at dusk. The divorce of historical studies from speculative theology – the price paid for the metaphysical and epistemological gains of Neo-Scholasticism[31] – would weigh heavily on the Catholic Church when the Modernist crisis broke.

6 | Pius IX and his Council

The crisis of conscience which affected Passaglia over the pope's temporal power and the adjudication sought from Perrone over Hermesianism sum up the two issues which led Pius IX to summon a General Council of the Church in 1869: the nature and implications of the Petrine office; and the interrelation of faith and reason. Since the Enlightenment these questions — the autonomy of the church under an international head, the relation between revelation and rationality — had proved singularly conflictual, both within Catholicism and without.

Cismontane feeling had been exacerbated by two facets of Pius's rule: his insistence, after the débâcle of 1848, on the necessity of the States of the Church (or at least the civil rule of the City of the Popes) to the freedom of action of the Roman pontiff, and the promulgation of that compendious challenge to liberal shibboleth, the *Syllabus of Errors*. The Piedmontese monarchy, supported by Liberal-national feeling throughout Italy, was bent on the unification of the peninsula, an aim that entailed the absorption of the millenial civil 'patrimony of Peter'. Though a lengthy government enquiry of 1857 showed a fundamental acceptance of the papal régime except on the part of a minority of intellectuals and bourgeois, the economic development of the Pontifical State was, by nineteenth-century standards, painfully slow — even if, by compensation, it avoided the worst social ills, like the industrial employment of children, endemic elsewhere. Reliant for defence on the military aid of friendly powers in an age where literate opinion counted, winning a battle of ideas was as vital as it was unlikely. The consolidation of what remained of the so-called 'Donation of Constantine' (in reality, the transfer of central Italy to papal jurisdiction was the work of the eighth- and ninth-century Frankish kings) took its place as part of the papal attempt to gather all the forces of a besieged Christendom under the leadership of the bishop of Rome. The primacy of the city of Rome, so Manning explained, does not lie in its claim to be capital of a re-united Italy but , through its church and pastor:

> ... in its apostleship to the whole human race, in the science of God with which it has illuminated mankind, in its supreme and worldwide jurisdiction over souls, in its high tribunal of appeal from all the authorities on earth, in its inflexible exposition of the moral law, in its sacred diplomacy by which it binds the nations of Christendom into a confederacy of order and of justice — these are its true, supreme, and — because God so has willed — its inalienable and incommunicable primacy among the nations of the earth.

No wonder the anti-Christian energies of contemporary civilisation were exerted against the temporal power, to wrest away the 'only spot of ground on which the Vicar of Christ can set the sole of his foot in freedom'.[32] The year following Manning's address, Pius IX promulgated the *Syllabus of Errors*, with its culminating anathematisation of 'progress, liberalism and modern civilization' — not, however, a condemnation of chloroform, gas lighting and the secret ballot, but of a society falsely emancipated from revelation by various forms of naturalism and rationalism (sections I–II), become indifferent to religious truth (section III), alienated from the salvific role accorded the Catholic Church and its supreme pastor by the Redeemer (section V), not least in regard to the civil order (sections VI, IX and X), and from right moral thinking, both on questions of nature and grace (sections IV and IIII), notably in connexion with the institution of marriage (section VIII). In other words, the Promethean tendencies of an aggressive humanism

— in different guises, Idealist in Germany, Positivist in France, Utilitarian and eventually Social-Darwinist in England — had become harnessed to the socially re-constructive project of a progressive bourgeoisie which, by means of these philosophies, was 'liberating' civil society from the moral codes and institutions — Church, family, local community, artisanal workplace — which had hitherto empowered its members, as groups first of all, but then as individuals — something clearer to such late twentieth-century commentators as the American sociologist Christopher Lasch than to many contemporaries.

To Liberal Catholics, anxious to reach accommodation with the more sympathetic successors of the *anciens régimes*, this was indeed a bitter pill to swallow. And need they swallow it? The aftermath of the Gallican and Febronian controversies of the seventeenth and eighteenth centuries, and such more contemporary *causes célèbres* as Pius IX's 1863 letter to the archbishop of Munich on the occasion of Döllinger's congress of Catholic scholars in that city, left room for manoeuvre in fixing the limits of the pope's pastoral rule and teaching authority, as well as the — not unconnected — boundary-lines between faith and reason (including the practical reason of statesmen). The bull of convocation of the First Vatican Council, issued in 1868, spoke of the Council's terms of reference as pastoral (the remedying of the evils of the age), but an article by the French correspondent of the journal of the Roman Jesuits, *Civiltà cattolica*, unleashed the dogs of theological war when it proposed that the bishops' time would be better spent on the definition of papal infallibility and the dogmatisation of the doctrine of Mary's Assumption, together with a rendering of the content of the *Syllabus Errorum* as the definitive teaching of the Church, to be held by all the faithful. Supported by Veuillot's *L'Univers*, the idea was as quickly denounced by Liberal Catholics in the German universities and in France, where they made common cause with the remaining old-style Gallicans. Greek-Catholic bishops, subjects of the Ottoman sultans, sensed shipwreck ahead, and in their archiepiscopal palaces the holders of the great metropolitan sees of the Danube monarchy shuddered at the affront to their traditions and those of the Catholic courts. Bishop Alexander Goss of Liverpool, on the other hand, decided, *more anglico*, to sit out the Council at the Hôtel Beau-Séjour in Cannes.

Such reactions were, as events proved, like the theological journalism that triggered them, only partly warranted. After many trials and tribulations (the level of passion made Vatican I more reminiscent of the patristic Councils than of its predecessors in Florence and Trent), the dogmatic definition of the Petrine office, in the Constitution *Pastor aeternus*, taken together with its own authoritative interpretation by the 'deputation *pro fide*' charged with the exposition of the text to be voted by the Fathers, did justice to the legitimate concerns of majority and minority — even if a small but articulated body of clergy and lay faithful, chiefly in *Mitteleuropa*, proved irreconcilable. For while in matters of the primary of jurisdiction, the majority were intent that no canonical limit be placed on the power of governmental intervention by the first see (which holds, in the keys of Peter, the fulness of apostolic power), the minority insisted that the use of those keys shall be for the upbuilding, not the destruction, of the local churches of the *Catholica* under their sacramentally ordained episcopal heads. And whereas, in the realm of doctrinal teaching, the same minority attested that binding doctrinal determinations by the church-in-primacy shall consist in interpreting the *sensus fidei* in the communion of churches, the majority made clear that this moral obligation to consult the episcopate (and through them the wider Church) be not misconstrued as a legal condition of valid doctrinal interpretation. In Peter's role in the episcopal college (and so the communion of the whole Church) a charismatic impulse plays — not, however, arbitrarily but for the furtherance of Tradition's life and mind. And if the extent of the subject matter to which the Petrine 'charism of truth' applied were less clearly defined than its conditions of exercise, the natural sense of the 'faith and morals' the Council spoke of was to exclude the wider purview of political, historical and scientific questions (save where these are logically entailed by truths of faith and morals) that Neo-Ultramontanes like Ward had in mind. *Pastor aeternus* was in any case a fragment, a part of a draft *De ecclesia* to have contained a rich theology of the Church organism (articulated not least by its episcopal members) under the inspiration of that ecclesiology of the 'Body of Christ', meta-historical yet incarnated in history, common to both the Roman and Tübingen Schools. The seizure of Rome by Italian troops left the Council prorogued in confusion.

Not, however, before it had dealt with the prior question of revelation and reason in the Constitution *Dei Filius* — logically as well as chronologically prior since it established the grammar by reference to which the explicit truths taught propositionally by the Church and the implicit truths contained within the imperatives of her authoritative action must be construed. That document, drafted by Franzelin and Schrader but episcopally modified with the aid of Kleutgen, sails serenely through waters much of the religious philosophy and fundamental theology of the previous century had found hard to navigate. Reason can of its own created power know God and his chief defining attributes, and know him with certainty (so much for 'absolute' or unconditional traditionalism), and yet (here comes the corresponding censure of not only rationalism but semi-rationalism too where the cap fits) revelation is nevertheless needful — necessary without qualification for truths of the supernatural order, but morally prerequisite also in the fallen condition of mankind for any stable grasp even of the existence of God and the incidence of his law. *Dei Filius* added precision to how Catholic theologians should understand divine authorship of the scriptural Canon, vehicle of biblical revelation,[33] and reiterated the Tridentine teaching that no Catholic exegete can so interpret Scripture as to make it conflict with that sense of the text which Holy Mother Church puts forward in her doctrine — a portent for the struggle over Scripture between bishops and scholars in the not too distant future. Created reason is obliged to follow uncreated truth, when revelation strikes it, not from any fresh perception of inner-worldly realities, merely, but by the impact of the authority of God, furnishing us in his wondrous self-attestation through the incarnational narrative with motives of credibility ample enough, yet not for all that (*pace* Hermes) detracting from the freedom of the act of faith, even when considered as intellectual assent. *Dei Filius* looked ahead to its sibling soon to be born, when it speaks of the divine Word's foundation of the Catholic Church that all may recognise this saving truth — not least through the 'sign of credibility' which the Church itself — one, holy, catholic and apostolic — constitutes on earth. Within the Church's teaching, the mysteries strictly so-called are (against Günther) never the proper nutriment of natural reason, yet with reverence and discretion reason can usefully apply itself to their study. Relating these truths to their natural analogues, and exploring their internal nexus, or inter-connexions, theological rationality can contribute to a process of doctrinal development whereby, however, graced understanding does not transform its materials heterogeneously into something else (doctrine does not change), but deepens that judgement (*sententia*) of them which the

Church has already possessed (the understanding of doctrine develops). Here would be, for a new century, not only a conclusion to the theological debates of the old, but also a fresh beginning.

7 | Scheeben

The emphasis of the First Vatican Council on the understanding of the mysteries via the 'analogy of faith' — that is, their own reciprocal illumination — provides the key to the thought of that *sui generis* product of the Roman School, Scheeben, the most gifted dogmatician of the late nineteenth-century Church, herald of the theologic aesthetics, one hundred years later, of von Balthasar. A Rhinelander, much of whose life was given to the formation of priests at the seminary of Cologne, Scheeben reacted in healthy fashion to the German and Austrian Semi-rationalists. From his earliest work on the concept of the supernatural (*Natur und Gnade*, 1861), which he defined as a sharing in the very being of God, he set himself to recover the mysteric character of the Catholic Gospel, a truth made known through revelation, unattainable by rationality, and even when achieved through faith not measurable by concepts formed through reason alone. At the same time as the Prussian philosopher of history and theoretician of culture Wilhelm Dilthey (1835–1911) was proposing a new discipline for the 'sciences of the human spirit' (*Geisteswissenschaften*), on the ground that even in the natural sphere human life was so rich a mystery that it escaped adequate description as an empirical object, Scheeben, by an analogous enterprise in the realm of theology, was discovering the need for a meta-empirical, indeed supra-natural, language of mystery.

Scheeben's most comprehensive use of the word 'mystery' serves to denote the entire life of Christians as poured forth from Christ and the Spirit to become, in human freedom, a growing unity of divine-human truth and action. But he also disposes of the term in a narrower setting, to signal the way in which the mystery — this same saving divine revelation in its transformation of human thought and practice — illumined as it is by faith, appears at one and the same time dark and light, obscure and radiant, to our knowledge. From the basic assumptions embodied in such language Scheeben reached his peculiar idea of a theological 'system': not, as with the Idealist-influenced Tübingen divines, a matter of the unfolding of some basic concept (albeit a revelationally given one) into an order of ideas as comprehensive as a world, for, to Scheeben's mind, such a structure would rather imprison the Word of God than suit it. For him the articles of faith, and the consequences that can be deduced from them, are *Stammglieder*, or constituent members of the organism of Christian belief, inasmuch as they find their meaning in the totality of that belief, open upon it, and share its mystery-character; it is in this mode that they can be laid out in ordered fashion by the theological mind.

In Scheeben's *Mysterien des Christenthums* (1865), accordingly, the revealed truths constitute a system just insofar as they form aspects of what he terms a 'mystical cosmos' whose coherence can be exhibited only by the analogy of faith. Its character he had earlier evoked in *Die Herrlichkeiten der göttlichen Gnade* (1863), which presents the splendour of the Holy Trinity as its incandescent centre, re-orienting the world to glory by uniting creaturely being 'nuptially' (that is, both intimately and fruitfully) — through Christ, Mary and the Church — with the uncreated being of God himself.

8 | Leonine Neo-Thomism

While Scheeben's lyrical Scholasticism was unusual, he welcomed the Thomist renaissance pioneered by Leo XIII: and in the *Handbuch der katholischen Dogmatik* (1873–1887) married its principles to his own passionately purposeful erudition. What underlay the meteoric rise of Neo-Scholasticism in the middle to late decades of the century was the fear that Catholic intellectual life would dissolve into chaos under the pressure of the myriad philosophical movements of the time. As its name suggests, Neo-Scholasticism was an attempt to revive the methods and conclusions of the mediaeval Schoolmen, and notably St Thomas, in a new age. Not till 1838 did Thomas's Order, the Dominicans, take steps to reinvigorate their flagging tradition. Re-establishing the study pattern of the pre-Revolutionary period led to the creation of the Parma edition of Thomas's works, the revival of the teaching of Aquinas at the Roman College of the Minerva and, by the 1870s, the emergence of a new light: Tommaso Maria Francesco Zigliara (1833–1893), a Corsican who entered the Roman Dominicans in 1851, was ordained by the future pope Leo XIII at Perugia in 1856 and, after many years of mutual admiration, raised to the cardinalate at the latter's first consistory in 1879. It was to Zigliara, celebrated for his widely received *Summa Philo-*

sophica (1876), that Leo would entrust the superintendence of a more exigently critical edition of Thomas's works (the 'Leonine'), 'for whose first volume the Thomist cardinal supplied the commentary.

One swallow does not, however, make a summer. Parallel to the Dominican revival of Thomism, interest in his thought, the pope well knew, was blossoming elsewhere. As early as 1810 the Collegio Alberoni in Piacenza had become a cradle of Neo-Thomism, using Thomas-inspired manuals. In 1824, the newly restored Society of Jesus had made a 'closet Thomist', Luigi Taparelli d'Azeglio (1793–1862), director of the *Collegio Romano*, though he had perforce to organise his study-group in secret, for insofar as the Society had a house-theologian it was not Thomas but the eclectic Baroque Scholastic, Suarez. In Spain, Suarez' homeland, Ceferino Gonzales (1831–1894), later Dominican bishop of Malaga, founded the first explicitly Thomistic journal, *La Ciencia tomista*. Meanwhile in Rome itself the arrival of the Neapolitan Thomist Matteo Liberatore (1810–1892) at the Roman College, and the rising of Kleutgen's star, led to the internal transformation of the earlier Roman school — even if the epistemology and metaphysics of the newcomers were, despite their best intentions, still more Suarezian than authentically Thomist. Liberatore would convert the influential *Civiltà cattolica* to the Thomist cause, his own writings so interrelating epistemology, anthropology, ontology and ethics as to be their own advertisement, if what was required was a

> ... coherent, integrated system better suited than the post-Cartesian systems of philosophy to deal with the problems of truth, reality, and human conduct.[34]

Kleutgen, who left Rome under Pius IX, was brought back to 'house-clean' the Gregorian University (as the *Collegio Romano* had become) as well as its cadet, the *Apollinare*: his influential blockbusters, *Die Theologie der Vorzeit* (1853–1874) and *Die Philosophie der Vorzeit* (1860–1863) argued that nineteenth-century German theologies (which earlier members of the Roman School had found partly criticism-worthy, partly persuasive) were systematically faulted by the influence of post-Cartesian philosophy and thus were congenitally incapable of defending the Church's teaching on faith and reason, nature and grace.

And this opens the box that is the rationale of the Neo-Scholastic programme. Neo-Thomists held that an epistemology of intuitive reason, the claiming of an *a priori* grasp of God, was the philosophical source of the ills of nineteenth-century theology. More specifically it lay, they said, at the root of two seemingly opposed evils, (semi-) rationalism and traditionalism. As the First Vatican Council so resoundingly declared, neither of these systems could preserve a proper balance between faith and reason or distinguish adequately the supernatural from the natural knowledge of God. In the interests of orthodoxy – not least that of the First *Vaticanum* – Catholic theology must abandon forthwith the subjective starting-points of the philosophies which saw intellectual day after Descartes and return to the sane metaphysics of St Thomas, grounded as that is on a grasp of the conceptualisable in finite reality, attained through the happy co-operation of the lowly human senses and the busily exploring 'agent' or 'abstractive' intellect of the Aristotelian theory of knowledge. (In any case the plurality of opposed systems had undermined philosophical wisdom, and bred scepticism in its place.) And furthermore, just as the natural and supernatural orders might be successfully distinguished at the level of a theory of knowledge with the help of Aquinas, so the same was true at the level of an account of being. For, drawing on the Aristotelian metaphysics of substance and accident, the source of a being's flowering and the flowering itself, Thomas had presented the order of grace as a supernatural supervention through whose causality the order of human nature was raised up to a realm beyond itself. Sanctifying grace modified the essence of the soul while the theological virtues of faith, hope and charity transformed the soul's faculties, mind and will. It was not surprising, Neo-Thomists argued, that Catholic theologians who had abandoned Thomas's metaphysics were no more able to describe satisfactorily the relation between nature and grace than they were that between reason and faith. A mark of true philosophy will be its willingness to share house and home with the truth of Christ, neither denying revealed truth nor interpreting it rationalistically, but accepting help from the Gospel in its own intellectual enterprise while retaining nonetheless its own autonomy, and characteristic arguments and methods. Nor is this mediaevalism in some pejorative sense, for just as Aquinas had absorbed the best contemporary thinking into his own presentation of truth, so a revitalised Scholasticism can do the same. All this was signalled in the sub-title of Leo XIII's encyclical *Aeterni Patris* (1879): 'the establishment of Christian philosophy in the tradition of St

Thomas Aquinas, the Angelic Doctor, in our Catholic Schools'.

And if Liberatore were the chief architect of that letter, the key player in the movement was undoubtedly the pope himself. A member of D'Azeglio's circle, on becoming archbishop of Perugia he had determined to introduce Thomism to his seminary there; at Vatican I he had, significantly if unsuccessfully, proposed the formal condemnation of Rosmini's ontologism. Elected pope in 1878 he grasped the unique opportunity to shed the light of the Thomist revival on the wider scene.

So grandiose a scheme (for, as the encyclical makes clear, no area of thought or culture is to be untouched) was naturally not to be realised overnight. Arguably, if it ever stood forth in the world of letters in the culture-transforming way Leo had imagined, it would be in the work of the French lay theologian and polymath Jacques Maritain (1882–1973). But was it not stymied from the outset by three factors: its disassociation from the development of historical scholarship; its excessive identification with the doctrinal office of pope (and episcopate); its unworthy literary style? In point of fact, the new Scholasticism, whose official reception was marked, after all, by the initiation of critical editions not only of Thomas but of Bonaventure, had its own historical scholars. Franz Ehrle (1845–1934), ordained a Jesuit priest in Cambridgeshire on account of the *Kulturkampf*, co-founded with the Dominican Heinrich Seuse Denifle (1844–1905) the scientific study of the history of Scholasticism, to which their *Archiv für Litteratur- und Kulturgeschichte des Mittelalters*, begun in 1885, soon became an indispensable tool. Yet such erudition did not mean that historically minded Neo-Scholastics considered theological history to be launched on a boundless adventure. Ehrle was prefect of the Vatican Library, Denifle Prefect of its Archive, and such linking of Neo-Thomism with the magisterium of Church hierarchs was far from fortuitous. It suited both sides that Rome should defend doctors portions of whose writing had passed into the very definitions of the Church. As for the unattractive literary style, when, in *Die Theologie der Vorzeit* Kleutgen proposed to show how Scholastic theology's relation to positive might be fruitful, he urged an analytic method that would reduce doctrines to their constituent elements for the purposes of comparison with the ancient sources. It was just such relentless dismantlement and piecemeal examination of the component parts of the theological mechanism (here the metaphor of organism seems out of place) which explains the uninspiring nature of manualist Scholasticism on the even of the Modernist crisis and beyond.

IV | MODERN AND ANTI-MODERN

1 | Blondel

Among the charges that might be entered against the 'Third Scholasticism' (that second reflorescence, after the sixteenth- and seventeenth-century Baroque, of the mediaeval springtime of the Schools), hostility to the modern has not been considered in the foregoing, for considered as a criticism either of a philosophy or of revelation-dependent thinking, it must be accounted remarkably weak. Modernity must be content with being, definitionally, in fashion; to add an assertion of epistemic privilege goes too far. However, the members of the Church are in the world, and pastorally attention must be paid to its *Weltanschauung*, to what the papers say. The late nineteenth century was, as any age must be which combines rapid technological innovation with a feeble grasp of the doctrine of creation, a time when *homo faber* ruled. It was an epoch of pragmatism, of the predominance of action. The philosophy of Maurice Blondel was an attempt to gain a hearing for faith in a pragmatist milieu.

Blondel's philosophy of action, lengthily expounded, subtle, highly wrought, would provide some hostages of fortune to that variety of Modernism which interpreted dogma as a function of human needs.

Insisting that his 'method of immanence' was not a 'doctrine of immanence', this deeply loyal lay Churchman from Aix-en-Provence would devote much of his later writing to the excision of the ambiguity. Blondel could have echoed (the still Anglican) Chesterton when the latter wrote:

> I agree with the pragmatists that apparent objective truth is not the whole matter; that there is an authoritative need to believe the things that are necessary to the human mind. But I say that one of those necessities precisely is a belief in objective truth... Pragmatism is a matter of human needs; and one of the first of human needs is to be something more than a pragmatist.[35]

But a professional metaphysician desirous of defining his position vis-à-vis his forebears cannot be so swift.

Blondel took the idea that the central problem of metaphysics is really human destiny and its investigative method a method of immanence from his reading of Spinoza – who after all had entitled his main metaphysical treatise the 'Ethics'.[36] Blondel looked to human action for the 'substantial bond' (a key phrase in the ontology of Leibniz, Blondel's earliest enthusiasm) which could constitute the concrete unity of each by assuring their communion with all. Although Thomists would accuse Blondel of excessive obeisance before the shade of Kant (and Kant's thought had indeed become influential in France notably through the work of Charles Bernard Renouvier, 1815–1903), he considered himself to have overcome the irreconcilable Kantian dualisms of pure and practical reason, sensibility and understanding, the phenomenon and the thing itself, not by the speculative route of the Idealists but through the idea of action itself – a synthesis of willing, knowing, and being which re-makes the bond that had once (in the mediaeval era) held together physics, metaphysics and ethics. Defending himself against the charge of pragmatism, he wrote in a letter of 1902:

> What I am proposing is fundamentally a kind of panlogism... If I have seemed to be anti-intellectualist, it is because I wanted to recover for rationality areas which the philosophy of the idea – not to be confused with intelligence or intelligibility – excludes...[37]

Spinoza had been right to say that human destiny has no rational solution unless it is founded ultimately on the Absolute — but wrong to suppose that man must solve his destiny by thought alone. Locating man's destiny in bliss through intellectual love of (a pantheistic) God, Spinoza tried to conquer the Christian heaven by pagan reason. Blondel's position is: *in operibus, lux* (light comes with acting). The rational and practical orders must be re-related: in that reunion the division between realism and idealism will disappear. So also will the Prometheanism for which, through his own powers, man can integrate himself in absolute reality. For Blondel's conclusion from his study of action — notably from the disparity between the will in its transcendence of all possible finite objects and the choices of such objects in which its life here below consists — was that no natural state of affairs can be the ultimate term of action. If action (and so our relations with the world of objects) is ultimately intelligible, this can only be the gift of God.

The philosophers of the Thomist renaissance were disquieted. If God's supernatural fulfilment of human life is 'indispensable' even to the philosopher, then what becomes of the gratuity of grace? If, moreover, all just assessment of the objective world, all knowledge, turns, as Blondel alleged, on a spiritual act of acceptance of *l'Unique nécessaire*, God himself, then is not this a form of fideism, subversive not only of the *philosophia perennis* but of all sane philosophy? To the first question Blondel replied that he could hardly be naturalising the supernatural, rationalising faith, since the philosopher's concept of *le surnaturel* was precisely that of something inaccessible though needed (and so the question becomes, his critics responded, Can a 'need' be a demand, *exigence*, on the justice of God; and will not *this* be indeed the abolition of the freedom of grace?). And on the epistemological issue, Blondel retorted that he was not speaking of the objective value of our representations of the world around us, but of the spiritual value of our concrete knowledge in the context of our concrete destiny. He distinguished between the knowledge of being, possible even to an atheist, and the being of knowledge: those who refuse to open themselves to God do not become ignorant of all truth, but the truth instead of saving them condemns them, and this must affect the quality of their knowledge. Here Blondel's thought found a continuator of genius in the dramatist and philosopher Gabriel Marcel (1889–1973) for whom the being that gives value to existents is, beyond all the problematics of objectivity, a mystery which discloses itself only to the freedom that is ready to welcome it.

In his later writings, Blondel showed more appreciation of Thomism, and a certain regret for his earlier criticisms. His own philosophy — which is not, of course, by definition a theology — could in any case hardly claim to replace the divinity of the Schools. At the same time, his work was intended to be an apologetics, a new evangelisation, as the 'Letter on Apologetics'[38] (1896) makes clear. It was the distance of the language of Christian Scholasticism from that of a dechristianised high culture which alarmed him — that and the gap between history and dogma which he would address in the work of that title. Here, on the eve of the Modernist crisis, he shared some of the anxieties of those soon to be dubbed by that sobriquet, as his correspondence with Alfred Firmin Loisy (1857–1940), von Hügel, and Lucien Laberthonniére (1860–1932) bears witness.[39]

2 | Modernism

The quintessence of Modernism is the willingness to surrender to the
Liberal Protestant assault upon the citadel of traditional dogmatic belief
— but to insist on doing so in a specifically Catholic way. The difficulty
created by Protestant scholarship dates back to the demolition-work on
biblical historicity of Hermann Samuel Reimarus (1694–1768), above all
in his posthumously (and in the first place fragmentarily) published
Apologie oder Schutzschrift für die vernünftigen Verehrer Gottes (1774–
1778); to the argument of the latter's editor, Gotthold Ephraim Lessing
(1729–1781), that universal truths are not in any case the sort of proposi-
tion which should be made to depend on historical arguments[40] and
the consequent attempt of the exegete David Friedrich Strauss (1808–
1874) in his *Leben Jesu* (1835–1836) to show that the real value of the
New Testament portrait of Jesus Christ lies in its creative mythology.
The distinctive feature of Catholic Modernism lies in the concomitant
claim of the right, nonetheless, to retain the entire fabric of the traditional and devotional practice of Latin Christendom — reinterpreted,
however, as an apparatus of beautiful and psychologically effective
symbolism, and justified on the basis of a subjectivist philosophy

which introduced a cleavage between devotional value on the one hand and intellectual or factual truth on the other.

The ambiguity of Modernism (and Counter-Modernism) to the Catholic historian of theology lies in the fact that, to a degree, the Catholic Modernists were reiterating genuine advances in nineteenth-century theology and philosophy in the Church, just as anti-Modernists were unnecessarily fearful of them. First, there were the massive gains of historical studies as such, and in particular the bid of positive theology for accommodation within the building of speculative theology proper. Second, there was the idea of doctrinal development found in Newman as in Tübingen. Both themes were no strangers to the Roman School itself, in its Pian form. And third among such benevolent factors can be placed the 'new' apologetics of Blondel — new, yet with such forerunners at the end of the *ancien régime* as Bergier — with its attempt to find the intellectual justification of the Gospel in the felt needs of the human spirit: the key of the faith fits the lock of human existence as such.

But Modernism was not just the sum-total of various legitimate movements in Catholic theology, just as anti-Modernism was not simply partisan reaction by the supporters of Neo-Scholasticism. Lines of reflection in earlier and unimpeachably orthodox writers were projected and taken to conclusions their original authors would not have recognised (in Blondel's case, *did* refuse to recognise). For first, in the matter of history, Modernists typically had exclusive resource to historical science so as to determine the theological meaning of biblical and other texts, rather than accepting a role for tradition in the hermeneutical process. Instead of saying that there is an important place for historical study within theology, history becomes everything.[41] Second, on dogma, the Modernists gave the impression that doctrine was simply a vehicle for the response of a given age to the divine. A doctrine well suited to the time-spirit of one generation might be gawkily out of place in another. Instead of saying that there is a historical dimension to the explicitation of doctrine, evolution becomes everything. And third, in revelation the Modernists appeared to be claiming that the orientation of the human spirit to transcendence was the entire explanation of the Christian religion. Scriptures, sacraments, dogmas, Church institutions become so many symbolic forms thrown up by the movement of the human spirit toward God in history.

Instead of saying that the intrinsic ordination of humankind to God is a necessary complement to the external signs and teachings of divine revelation, interiority becomes everything – not unassisted by Kantian subjectivism and Schleiermacher's sentimentalism. It was, for the latter schemes of thought, axiomatic that neither God nor the effects of his action can be grasped, since human knowledge, limited as it is to the realm of appearances, cannot reach the transcendent realm of what lies beyond phenomena. It was not always realised that to be counted a critical historian subscription to Kantian (or sub-Kantian) philosophy can hardly be made a necessary condition.

The problem of methodological naturalism was central to the stormy petrel who most made the engagement of the doctrinal magisterium of the Papacy with the Modernist scholars and thinkers into a 'crisis', Alfred Loisy. Loisy proposed to vindicate the accumulated history of a bi-millenial Church against the claim of the Liberal Protestant historian of dogma Adolf Harnack (1851–1930) that Catholicism bore little if any resemblance to primitive Christianity, while at the same time treating many of the conclusions of German liberal exegesis as scientifically established truths: thus L'Evangile et l'Eglise of 1902. In his explanation of the principles involved, Autour d'un petit livre (1903), Loisy made clear his view that a protean Gospel, whose fluid essence can be moulded into many shapes in different periods, is appropriately carried by a Church endowed with an endless capacity for adaptation from age to age. He presented his work, accordingly, in his own words:

> ... firstly, as an outline and historical explanation of the develop-
> ment of Christianity and then as a general philosophy of religion
> and an effort to interpret the dogmas, the official creeds and the
> definitions of the Councils, the purpose of which is to reconcile
> them with the realities of history and the mentality of our
> contemporaries, by sacrificing the letter to the spirit.[42]

If that self-description is unusually revealing in its admission that entailed in the Loisyiste project was not only the turning of some tools forged by German Protestants against their makers but a re-conceiving of Catholic doctrine on a massive scale, Loisy's loss of faith in Christ as the Word incarnate was at this time a private grief, concealed from the authorities of the Church. It was in blissful ignorance thereof that such Christian Democrats as the secular priest editors of La justice sociale

(Paul Naudet, 1859–1925) and *La vie catholique* (Pierre Dabry, 1862–1916), as well as the outstanding lay activist Marc Sangnier (1873–1950), with his organisation *Le Sillon*, appealed to Loisy's example by way of proposing that, just as theological scholarship could be in responsible fashion independent of Church authority, so too could the lay involvement of Catholics in politics. The term 'political Modernism' would soon be born.

Meanwhile in England the Anglo-Irish Jesuit George Tyrrell (1861–1909), convert from Anglicanism, early enthusiast for the Thomist revival, and spiritual writer of genius, had been introduced by von Hügel to both Blondel's philosophy and Loisy's exegesis. Tyrrell would construct, in such broadsides against the union of Neo-Scholasticism and official doctrine as *A Much Abused Letter* (1906) and *Through Scylla and Charybdis, or The Old Theology and the New* (1907), a novel theological programme from out of the bricks laid somewhat randomly by Loisy in the course of his biblical writings. In its central thesis:

> Christ did not present himself as the teacher of an orthodoxy and Catholic theologians would be very wrong to understand faith as the assent of the intellect to the historical and metaphysical assertions of a 'revealed' theology marvellously preserved from errors, since theology — by which he meant in fact dogma — was only a human effort to grasp in intellectual terms the divine force working in man.[43]

Christian revelation is directed not to the mind but to heart and will. At least until his last months, when in *Christianity at the Crossroads* (1909), his 'system', as he (in part ironically) described it, disintegrated under the impact of a rediscovery of New Testament apocalyptic, Tyrrell had a clear vision of his aims and the means with which to achieve them. The affective power of Catholic symbolism in texts and ritual must be placed at the service the only deity likely to be recognised in the cultural space of Late Victorian and Edwardian England, the 'Power that makes for Righteousness' of the (consciously post-Christian) poet and critic Matthew Arnold (1822—1808).[44] Catholicism redefined in the interests of a missionary and pastoral purpose will lose its intellectual scandal but retain its emotional — and thus moral — potency. Though across the Channel the philosophers Laberthonnière and Edouard Le Roy (1870–1954) did not go so far, the former, as Oratorian editor of the

Annales de philosophie chrétienne, stressed the primacy of the ethical corollaries of dogma ('moral dogmatism'), while the latter, a layman, and successor of the Jewish intellectual Henri Bergson (1859–1941) — by whose evolutionary thinking he was influenced — in a chair at the Collège de France, proposed that while dogmatic statements have the negative function of inhibiting error, their positive role is the practical one of engendering religious attitudes and action. Here Le Roy's religious thought reflected his wider epistemology: for him, theoretical science itself does no more than manipulate symbols; it cannot penetrate reality.

Chiefly through the agency of that great broker of contacts the Baron von Hügel, the Modernist current began to lap Italian shores likewise. Though French- and English-derived notions of exegetical method, doctrinal development, and the epistemic status of dogma, as well as philosophical immanentism, played their part, the chief concerns of Italian Modernism were Church reform (given unforgettable expression in the novel *Il Santo*, 1905, of Antonio Fogazzaro (1842–1911), though his recipe of holiness and mysticism included an ingredient of sensuous aestheticism as well), and social issues, on which the journal of the priest-sociologist and politician Romolo Murri (1870–1944), *Cultura sociale*, took a line, under the name of 'social Modernism', cognate with the French Christian Democrats in their desire for an emancipation of the Catholic laity in their capacity as citizens from the tutelage of the Church hierarchy. The German *Reformkatholizismus* of Franz Xavier Kraus (1840–1901), professor of the history of Christian art in Strasbourg, differed from the Modernism of the South by its Statism and cooler, *bürgerlich* tone. Its pastoral proposals renewed the demands of the German Catholic Enlightenment, and anticipated the construction put on the documents of the Second Vatican Council (1962–1965) by Curial liturgists and post-Conciliar Catholic radicals. Intimately linked with the rise, fall and rebirth of European Modernism was 'Americanism', a championing of greater independence of thought and action among Catholics in that country where the rhetoric of freedom was potentially all-absorbing, the United States.

The magisterium of the Catholic Church (that is, the pope and bishops in their character as guardians of doctrine) reacted disproportionately to Modernism when one considers the quantity of the Modernists, but not when one thinks of the quality of their teaching. A tiny scattered handful, the Modernists' voluminous correspondence argues little more than their belonging to an era when postal services had improved and the telephone was as yet uninvented. Yet if not conspirators they did indeed hope to provoke a revolution in theological studies, and so in the culture from which doctrine and preaching are shaped. The Roman response, despite the presence of a canonised saint on the chair of Peter (Pius X Sarto, 1835–1914), left something to be desired. The decree *Lamentabili* (July 1907) of Pius X's Holy Office, preceded by a number of pastoral letters against Modernism from residential bishops in Italy, attempted to deal with the movement on a European scale through the condemnation of a pot-pourri of citations, taken, without context or commentary, chiefly from Loisy's work but with some use of that of Tyrrell, Le Roy and the historian of exegesis (and future biographer of Loisy) Albert Houtin (1867–1926). Such identification of *sententiae*, key-statements, was perfectly customary, but functioned better with classical theologians who thought in theses. By contrast, the pope's encyclical *Pascendi* (September 1907) was a brilliant attempt to identify the logical direction in which Modernism tended – summed up in the catchwords 'historicism', 'immanentism', 'agnosticism'. Although a number of books by Modernist authors had already been censured, it was the public rejection of Rome's negative adjudication of 'sentences' in *Lamentabili* and the pope's authoritative intervention in *Pascendi* that led to the excommunication of the priest-theologians among the Modernist writers. The truly regrettable aspect of the reaction – otherwise the healthy production of anti-bodies by an organism in its own defence – was the semi-official connivance at the creation of a veritable Counter-Modernist espionage ring by Mgr Umberto Benigni (1862–1934), no 'Curial hack', however, but a professional historian who had founded the first journal for social issues in Italian Catholicism (*Rassegna sociale*) and was currently engaged in writing a seven-volume social history of the Church. But the 'social Gospel', so Benigni thought, need not be what social Modernists threatened to make of it: the reinvestment of energies intended for the service of a supernatural institution aiming at salvation in work for a temporally better world. As the related debate over Liberation Theology in the 1980s would show, the Church's salvific mission could not simply be re-described as a social task. Looking back from 1927 von Hügel came to consider the various Modernisms closely interrelated after all:

The main and decisive difference now appears to me to be the difference between Religion regarded as a purely intra-human reality, its only evidence being confined to the aspirations of the human race; and Religion seen as manifesting its own evidence, metaphysical, the effect in us of something; more than us — of more than any purely human facts and desires.[45]

3 | The Social Catholics

The rough ride which the social Modernists endured should not be taken to mean that the Catholic Church of the nineteenth and early twentieth centuries disclaimed, at the highest levels of its leadership, a social mission. The question was, how best should the Church intervene in the temporal order, and by what connexion was that temporal task linked to the Catholic community's supernatural calling.

Throughout the nineteenth century Catholics had been involved in the work of recreation of political and social order (however defined) in the wake of the Great Revolution and the agrarian and industrial changes that partly preceded and partly accompanied and followed that cataclysmic series of events. The ability of capitalist industrial production to undermine traditional social arrangements would in due course present Catholicism with both a threat and an opportunity. The threat would take the form of Marxist revolutionary activity, for despite the theoretical Marxian disapproval of 'Jacobinism' — which represented to scientific-socialist orthodoxy the heresy that human will, not economics, shaped history, and thus symbolised the much-despised romantic subjectivity, the Jacobins, as Catholicism's most ruthless enemies during the Revolution in France, had a profound influence on Marxist mythology. The lesson they taught was twofold: the (socialist) revolution must seize hold of the central state apparatus, or, if there hardly be one, then create one: and it must show no mercy to either actually or even potentially counter-revolutionary elements. But the Church, if faced with a menace more mortal than any known under the *ancien régime*, also looked out on fresh opportunities. In France, Germany, Austria, stirrings of opinion and aspiration among the farming population, the lower middle class and modest professionals led to the formation of popular movements, simultaneously religious and social in character, to which the anti-papalism of thrones, aristo-cracy and *haute bourgeoisie* of the pre-Revolutionary period was alien. This would give Leo XIII and his successors the chance to form a distinctively Catholic social conscience on the basis of the social reflec-tion and action of, in particular, the century's central decades. In that context it is useful to distinguish between 'political Catholicism' – the defence of the freedom of the Church against its enemies; 'charitable Catholicism' – the prosecution of the works of mercy practised from apostolic times for the direct succour of the poor (even though with the crisis of many traditional forms of livelihood such works might in the modern period undergo considerable reorganisation); and 'social Catholicism' strictly so called, which took the characteristic evils of social modernity as its target. Among these, proletarian misery, the pauperisation of the labouring classes under industrialism, was in the period before 1914 the chief.

The aim of Social Catholicism was the reconstitution of a just city, though views of what was *debitum*, 'owed', to various social groups, and beyond these to the vocation of humanity itself, in the light of created reason and the divinely revealed Gospel, could differ. As early as Adam Heinrich Müller (1779–1829), a Romantic period convert to Catholicism in north Germany, three themes are sounded which will recur in many variations. The first was the appeal to the family as not only the fundamental unit of society but the model for its diversity of functions within interdependence of life. The second (and in Müller's case this betrayed the influence of Burke) was respect for those struc-tures of common life which had developed under the aegis of Christian civilisation, and notably the estates and corporations which focused duties, loyalties and the making of decisions. The third motif already found in Müller's lectures on statecraft to the Saxon diplomatic corps and court was the danger to the social weal found in an alliance between liberal economics and political aims of an absolutistic sort.

The co-presence of such concerns made it difficult to place Social Catholics on a conventional Left-versus-Right analysis of politics. Whatever their internal differences, they were agreed that the Church had the duty not only to defend the poor but to moderate the social consequences of inequality; liberty would only be possible when it ceased to be individualism and sought the welfare of all. This might mean (as with Müller) an emphasis on the responsibility of the propertied to take steps to adjust the social order in the interests of the disadvantaged, or, as with Alban de Villeneuve-Bargemont (1784–1850), who took the opportunity of the overthrow of the restored Bourbons in 1830 to retire from public life and write his treatise on Christian political economy,[46] the attribution of a direct role to the State itself, not just in alleviating distress but in ensuring that, as in the days of cottage industry, labourers could conduct their own economic activity, assisted by credit unions, mutual aid societies and the like. Such men hardly shared the proto-Chestertonian vision of the revolution as a great might-have-been of evangelical history entertained by Philippe Benjamin Joseph Buchez (1796–1865) – whose forty-volume history of the Revolution was ransacked by the Scottish moralist Thomas Carlyle (1795–1881) in his own more celebrated work.[47] Yet Buchez's proposals (made through the instrumentality of his journal L'Européen, his global study the Essai d'un traité complet de philosophie au point de vue du Catholicisme et du progrès [1839–1840], and his short-lived presidency of the Constituent Assembly of 1848) for the establishing of co-operatives for skilled artisans, state regulation of working conditions and the operation of a minimum wage, had common features with their programmes. Christian socialism and Christian conservatism touched each other even if they did not always embrace. For both, 'modern' could mean 'antimodern'. To deal with the new kind of poverty now stalking the land both practical initiatives and a new (or was it old?) social ethos would be necessary. Such was the shared conviction of the Rhinelander Adolf Kolping (1813–1865), priest-creator of a chain of hostels with educational as well as religious facilities for a new class of rootless, unmarried journeymen, and of Wilhelm Emmanuel Ketteler (1811–1877), intellectual leader of mid-century Social Catholicism, bishop of Mainz.

Ketteler, though not a Thomist, thought that clues to a solution might be found in Aquinas' view of sociality; in any case the Liberalism that acknowledged no bonds to one's fellows beyond the decision to respect their freedom would have to be displaced by the recovery of a more potent alternative tradition where freedom and dignity for human beings rested on God's will, goodness, and power. To Ketteler's mind, the social problem raised the issue of the Church's deposit of faith inasmuch as modern societies tacitly affirmed a principle of materialistic egoism, opposed to the doctrine of the universal destination of goods. It was in this formal perspective that the Roman magisterium would pronounce on such topics — though, as Paul Misner has pointed out, the prudential arguments of a pastor were also prominent in Ketteler's thinking.

> The Church can provide long-term remedies in traditional ways: charitable institutions for the sick, poor and aged; Christian marriage and home life; education not only in economic skills but in the realm of culture and values; and associations of every kind, prompted by the innate Christian communitarian tendencies. Only genuine Christian devotion can maintain such forces and institutions in the long run, as the liberals will find out. Their efforts to supplant Church organizations with secular ones can draw on natural human inclinations up to a point, but is it not the residual Christian selflessness in their members that accounts for such life as they enjoy?[48]

The benefits of a Christendom society, thus extolled in Ketteler's *Die Arbeiterfrage und das Christentum* (1864) were equally at issue in the (exactly contemporary) *Syllabus of Errors*. These texts constituted the dual inspiration of Albert de Mun (1841–1914) and René de la Tour du Pin (1834–1925), two aristocrats in whose tireless activity — the first organisational, the second ideological — the message rang out clearly that the Revolution of 1789 represented the absolute freedom of labour, and thus delivered the weak, defenceless, to the mercy of the strong. Though a Christian social order could hardly exist without a Christian government, there remained the possibility of creating occupational guilds and professional associations, and of wresting from even an anti-clerical Republic (the '*de facto* government' as de Mun called it) the mede of justice it was capable of measuring out.

In Austria-Hungary, Karl von Vogelsang (1818–1890), student of Müller and Ketteler, was persuaded by de Mun's advocacy of a régime of labour where owners and workers had rights and duties spelled out by corporations, but situated this within a wider vision of an 'organic commonwealth' culminating in a 'social monarchy'. Through the *Oesterreichische Monatschrift für christliche Socialreform* and his position in the imperial Parliament, and assisted theologically by two Dominicans, the Bavarian Albert Maria Weiss (1844–1925), professor at Freiburg-in-der-Schweiz, and Andreas Frühwirth (1843–1933), later Master of the Order of Preachers and cardinal, Vogelsang campaigned for the de-centralisation of economic power in favour of self-managing enterprises both urban and rural, while political order should, he maintained, rest not on the representation of mere numbers but on natural vocational groupings better able to oppose statist pretensions and defend public freedoms in civil society.

In the 1880s these intellectual impulses reached mature form via the Catholic Congresses of Liège (1886, 1887, 1890) and the annual meetings, from 1885 onwards, of the 'Fribourg Union', an international study group of Catholic social reformers drawn from, especially, France, Austria, Germany, Italy and Switzerland. In a period of intensified industrial unrest, the second volume of Marx's *Kapital* appeared, after that worthy's death in 1883; in the same years Manning, whose interest in these questions was deep, realistic and effective, was declaring that the Church could no longer simply rely, for the communication of her social ethos, on the favour of princes. In 1894 Leo XIII published his great social encyclical *Rerum novarum*, which drew most heavily on Ketteler's work ('my great predecessor') though the Pope's attempt to rally French Catholics to republican legitimacy in the interests of peace between Church and State met with less response. Indeed, the anti-Liberalism of many Social Catholics, their dissatisfaction with parliamentary plutocracy, would open them to alliance with authoritarian movements of the Right, like the *Action Française* of the Positivist (yet royalist) Charles Maurras (1868–1952), or, in the post-Second World War world, with authoritarian movements of the Left, above all with the (equally atheistic) communistic socialism of Marxism-Leninism. In each case, the philosophical and social sanities of Thomism (as well as fidelity to the biblical inheritance) helped save the Church from a fatal *mésalliance*.

4 | Rousselot and Maréchal

Even more fundamental than the material order, however, was that of the spirit: that indeed — the 'primacy of the spiritual' — had been a major point at issue in the dispute of first Blondel and then, after the Roman condemnation of Catholic collaboration in the *Action Française*, Maritain with Maurras. If Thomas, like Maurras, had stressed (as Aristotle before them), the priority of the *polis* over the individual, he had also, unlike Maurras, regarded the salvation of each unique person as the ultimate goal. A collectivism careless of individual dignity was avoided in the one case, but not the other. While Maurras, hostile to statism, wished for limited, de-centralised government, the rationale of his desire was not the flourishing of individual liberties since, on the contrary, he emphasised the State's right to a discretionary power in their regard. And here he was supported by the influential Regent of the Toulouse Dominicans, and populariser of Aquinas' thought, Thomas Pègues (1866–1936).

If, in an era of official support for the Thomist revival, much turned on the interpretation of Aquinas' thought, the same was not less true in philosophy, theology's preamble and handmaid. Pierre Rousselot

(1870–1915), Jesuit, professor at the Parisian Institut Catholique, tragically cut down on the Great War battlefield of Epargnes, took the view that Blondel (and Bergson) were right in regretting an excessively conceptualist reading of Thomas that risked making of him a rationalist *avant la lettre*. Given that theology must be informed by a philosophy both coherent and true, that of St Thomas was an answer to prayer — but it must be freed from that excessive conceptualism with which such masters of Leonine Neo-Thomism as Liberatore and Kleutgen had saddled it, and from which the thinkers of *Annales de philosophie chrétienne*, and notably Laberthonnière and Blondel, would disencumber it. Thomas's epistemic ideal was not the rational but the intellectual meaning, a grasp of the intelligible as penetrating as it was unified or single. Without a grasp of Thomas's view of divine and angelic understanding, what he takes human knowing to be does not appear. Without some assistance from that Idealism which the early Neo-Thomists had spurned, the genuine thought of Thomas could not be re-appropriated, or so Rousselot believed. As Fr Gerald McCool sums up the latter's *L'Intellectualisme de saint Thomas* (1908):

> *Ratio*, the distinctive form that characterises man as the lowest of the spiritual creatures, is a drive to *intellectus*, the intuitive intelligence that man shares with the angels. Its discursive unification of the world through science, art, history and the symbol is an effort to 'mime' the insight into the real which, in comprehension of the whole and penetration into the singular, *intellectus* alone can furnish. That is why St Thomas, as an intellectualist, held discursive knowledge in low esteem.[49]

And in any case, as a theological (and not simply philosophical) interpreter of Aquinas, Rousselot acknowledged the concrete goal of the life of the mind to be the beatific vision of God himself. Given the ontological condition of possibility for that union which the eager openness of mind to the intelligible unity of being creates — and this was the major theme disclosed in explorations of the psychology of mysticism by Rousselot's Louvain confrère Joseph Maréchal (1878–1944), the supernatural grace of God opens the eyes of our intelligence to 'see' through Jesus Christ the transforming self-offer of the triune God. Not only enlightened but moved by charity — here Rousselot's investigations of the mediaeval doctrine of love (*Pour l'histoire du problème de l'Amour au moyen-Age*, 1908) and his reading of *Annales* philosophers came into play, man acquires a sympathetic, connatural attitude towards the supernatural order, whereupon the stem of his natural intellectual powers produces its glorious flower in the life of revelational faith. Only in the Age to Come, in heaven, however, shall we perceive the world as it really is, unified in God's absolute perspective, since we shall at last understand it through the medium of his infinite existence.

Rousselot was an opponent of conceptualism, but not of the concept. Unlike the Bergsonians, he regarded representation in concept as the matured fruit of spiritual perception. Again, he was suspicious of a realism defined over against Idealism in all respects, but not of the primacy of being vis-à-vis the subject: unlike the Kantians, he treated the analogy of being — that keystone of Thomist metaphysics — as foundational to all description of reality. In neither respect was Maréchal, his exact contemporary, so circumspect.

Though both thinkers underlined the importance of 'final' or purposive causality (the natural drive, *érôs*, of each spiritual creature moves it to 'return' to God by becoming like him), Maréchal gave this factor unique weight and, attempting to outdo Kant, acclaimed it as the way to render Thomism the truly 'critical' philosophy. While Maréchal continued to hold that the repertoire of the mind's ideas is received by 'abstraction', from the senses (else he would not have been a Thomist at all), he maintained that the dynamic finality of the mind itself 'referred' these objects to the Absolute (and so unified them) in the moment of the judgement that affirmed them as mediations of the real. It was in this way that Maréchal became the founder of that 'transcendental Thomisn' of the middle and later twentieth century of which Karl Rahner (1904–1984) was to be the most celebrated exponent. While agreeing with Kant that man enjoys no intuition of noumenal realities, Maréchal disputed the Kantian conclusion that a speculative metaphysics is impossible. Fichte had already shown how vital to Kant's critiques of practical reason and of judgement (his ethics and aesthetics) is man's spiritual striving, his will, and had found there a key to the nature of the Absolute, since God for Fichte is the infinite Ground of spiritual will. Yet the acceptance of such a pantheism is not an inevitable price to pay for overcoming the disjunction between practical and speculative reason in Kant's system. To know the Infinite it is not necessary to be the Infinite oneself. It suffices to say that, striving as the finite human intelligence does for the Pure Act of Being, it at once unifies the objects of its own discursive activity (coming to know things, as common-or-garden Thomism had in more empirical style asserted, as recognisable wholes) and also refers them to the noumenal Absolute, the infinite God. If Kant had grasped the logic of his own philosophical corpus in its entirety, he would have seen where it was taking him — not to the overcoming of speculative metaphysics but to its confirmation in a new, 'critical' and thus epistemologically improved, manner.

5 | Maritain and Gilson

But just this was what the two leading lay Thomists of the Third Scholasticism, Maritain and Etienne Gilson (1884–1978), disputed. The notion that one can accept the insistence of modern philosophies of subjectivity on the massive character of the mind's own contribution to its account of reality, so long as one also emphasises the dynamic tendency of the human spirit towards the real, in a continuous dissatisfaction with its own — insufficiently unified — conceptions, was itself unacceptable to these two figures, Maritain from a philosopher's vantage-point, Gilson from an intellectual historian's. The question as to whether transcendental Thomism does justice to the traditional realism of Catholicism (owed ultimately to the doctrine of creation) in matters of philosophical theology remains a lively one, thanks to their interventions — as the critical studies of Cornelio Fabro of the University of Perugia demonstrate. Yet all these thinkers — whether 'critical' or 'classical' — would be united in regarding the restoration of Thomism as salvation from the twin errors which followed on Scholasticism's collapse — rationalism, ultimately the 'geometric pantheism' of Spinoza, and empiricism, in the last resort the 'sensism' of Locke and Hume.

Regarding epistemology as a boom industry ready for deflation, Maritain and Gilson were in any case free to devote their energies to the positive construction, on sites laid out by philosophy, ethics, aesthetics, science and politics, of that spacious neo-mediaeval city for which Leo XIII had hoped.

The France of the inter-War period, when Maritain and Gilson came to their intellectual maturity, was undergoing a major religious revival.[50] It housed a culture where the literary imagination — in, for instance, the novels of François Mauriac (1885–1970) — could still function in a recognisably Catholic way. Graham Greene could write of Mauriac in words betokening immunity to the ontologically disorienting effects of cultural Modernism in the first half of the European twentieth century:

> He is a writer for whom the visible world has not ceased to exist, whose characters have the solidity and importance of men with souls to save or lose, and a writer who claims the traditional and essential right of a novelist to comment, to express his views ... M. Mauriac's characters exist with extraordinary physical completeness (he has affinities here we feel to Dickens), but their particular acts are less important than the force, whether God or Devil, that compels them ...[51]

Only, perhaps, in the confidence bred in such a climate was so comprehensive an achievement possible. If the shift of sympathies under the Third Republic in favour of the Catholic Church was owed more than anything to the behaviour of priest-conscripts (like Rousselot) in the trenches of the Great War, the Catholic renaissance had its literary roots in the years immediately preceding August 1914, and it was through two gifted imaginative writers, the poet Charles Péguy (1873–1914) and the novelist Léon Bloy (1846–1917), that the technically Protestant Jacques Maritain and his wife Raïssa, an equally unbelieving Jewess, came to Catholic faith.[52] Maritain, already set for a philosophical career, made of his first published work, La philosophie Bergsonienne (1913), a manifesto of the Thomist revival, consequence of, and further stimulus to, contacts with Francophone Dominicans which he would never entirely abandon.

Knowledge for Maritain begins with the intellectual intuition of the act of being of concretely existing things; in a curt dismissal of post-Cartesian, and especially post-Kantian hesitations (even more summary when echoed by Gilson), he stigmatised the refusal to grant such a starting-point as a malaise of perception, a turning away from light. Not that Maritain's philosophical thought was crude: in *Distinguer pour unir, ou les degrés du savoir* (1932) he offered what he termed a 'critical realism' (Gilson would dislike the phrase precisely for its whiff, however faint, of Kant) whereby one could set forth the 'great types of knowledge' — those of natural science and metaphysics, first of all, but also those of faith, 'wisdom' and mystical contemplation, exemplified for him in the writings of the Carmelite doctor St John of the Cross (1542–1591). These ways of knowing must be kept distinct, but so as eventually to unite them by an analogy-thinking which reflects the ordered differentiation of reality itself.

Over against an individualist subjectivism, which he believed had over-taken European culture in three great stages marked by three 'refor-mers', Martin Luther (1483–1546), Descartes and Rousseau, Maritain proposed the remedy of a Christian personalism where 'person' (unlike 'individual') is relationally defined, and so deprived of all antithesis to the common good (thus *La personne et le bien commun*, 1946). Where ontological analysis primed by Trinitarian theology could produce so illuminating a conclusion, Maritain was encouraged to sketch out in *Humanisme intégral: problèmes temporales et spirituels d'une nouvelle chrétienté* (1936) the vision of a new Christendom where Catholicism, by the plenary ('integral') character of its theocentric humanism, could provide a positive framework for the flourishing of other, non-Christian groups, untying the tragic knot which in the era of combined scientism and nihilism in the two ideologically propagandist super-powers of Bolshevik Russia and Nazi Germany was keeping humanity bound. Maritain's notion of a Christian commonwealth which unifies yet respects autonomies within it could be taken as the *Leitmotiv* likewise of his ethics, for which theological determinants are ultimately crucial but without occluding the significance of historical, existential and rational factors; the moral philosophy of good pagans finds its due place within a wider whole.

Maritain's extension of the Neo-Thomist tradition not only to include but to give privileged status to questions of aesthetics, if largely innova-tory, was fully in line with Leo XIII's programme. The insistence in *Art et scolastique* (1920) on artistic making as a form of practical reason was decisive for those artists who like Eric Gill (1882–1940) wished to realign an increasingly elitist and *déraciné* world of fine arts with the common sense and respect for skill which ordinary people shared with their mediaeval forbears. Yet this was no Philistinism: Maritain stressed the nature of beauty as a 'transcendental' determination of being, one that exceeded all limiting categories and reflected the creative originality of reality's divine Source. If the emphasis here lay on the form inherent in the artwork, Maritain would do full justice to the imaginative subjectivity of the artist himself in *Creative Intuition in Art and Poetry* (1953), an important milestone in the discriminating reception by Catholic thought of post-Romantic art — 'discriminating' because Maritain also sought to identify work that through narcissism, surrealism and titanism rejected not just rationalism or imprisonment within a canon whose possibilities were now exhausted, but reason and reality themselves.

Gilson complemented Maritain's work chiefly by lending the philosophical culture he was in process of creating greater historical sharpness, but also by taking further many of his more genial insights. He came to his subject by way of investigating the Scholastic sources of Descartes — yet another example of the fascinated ambivalence of Catholics towards that seminal and controversial figure. At the Sorbonne, and despite his positivist teachers, Gilson soon discovered the strengths of Thomism — which was for him the work of a theologian, first and foremost, albeit a theologian whose faith — the faith of a saint — enabled him to bring the rationality of a subjacent philosophy to its fulfilment. In all the great Christian thinkers — and not just with the Church Fathers for whom (arguably) the distinctive claims of philosophical reason do not yet stand out — we are dealing with a 'Christian philosophy', in which such doctrines as creation, the Trinity and the hypostatic unity of Christ act as midwives to fresh advances in rational truth itself. (Here Gilson salvaged the nugget of truth in Güntherianism.) Whereas the early twentieth-century Papacy had somewhat optimistically lumped together Thomas with Bonaventure and other luminaries of the Middle Ages, celebrating their centenaries as the common triumphs of a *philosophia* (and *theologia*) *perennis*, Gilson made it perfectly clear that they must be admired for different things — Thomas for the proto-Existentialist quality of his notion that existence (the divine act of communicating being) precedes essence (the 'whatness' of things that limits existence in receiving it as potency does act): thus

Le Thomisme. Introduction au système de S. Thomas d'Aquin (1919);
Bonaventure for his synthesis of Christian mysticism: this was Gilson's
line in *La philosophie de saint Bonaventure* (1924). And as for Scotus,
while admiring his subtlety and dialectical power, Gilson found his
world where existence becomes a mode of essence one in which he
could not breathe (*Jean Duns Scot. Introduction à ses positions fonda-
mentales* [1952]). However, these discoveries did not lead Gilson to
acclaim a facile pluralism, ushered in without forethought as to implications. In *The Unity of Philosophical Experience* (1937) he proposed to
show that the entire history of philosophy falls into place as exploration
of partial truths with piecemeal methods if only the student has
grasped (with Thomas) that the ontological mystery *par excellence* is
that of the being of beings — to which all other aspects are tributary.
Whether Catholic intellectual life could survive, in flourishing fashion,
the collapse of such a unitary view of metaphysics by the acceptance of
an irremediably radical pluralism in philosophy was the question that
contemplation of the theological scene, from the inter-War years to the
Second Vatican Council, inevitably raised.[53]

V | BACK TO THE SOURCES

1 | Casel and the liturgical revival

Up to the end of the nineteenth century, Catholic thought since the Enlightenment (it seems safe to say) had been dominated by philosophical issues — in which it reflected, *malgré lui*, the agenda set by the Enlightenment itself. This did not mean that the themes of the Trinity and Christology, salvation and grace, the Church, the Mother of God, the saints, the Last Things, had ceased to be taught or written about in the theological schools. But the flash-points of debate were philosophical and fundamental theology; the principal protagonists worked on the interface between reason and revelation. The first half of the twentieth century, by contrast, was marked by the desire for a more theological theology, for an intellectual culture more pervasively saturated by dogmatic thought, for more direct influence from revelation's heartlands. The movement of *ressourcement* — *recursus ad fontes*, 'going back to the sources' of revelation in Tradition and Tradition's primary monument, Scripture — was the chief form which this desire took.

The Liturgy had always been a *locus theologicus* or authoritative source for Catholic theology. Its historical study had hardly ceased in Catholicism since the seventeenth century. From the mid-nineteenth century onwards, erudition stockpiled thanks to the industry of such liturgical scholars as the Tübingen historian Ferdinand Probst (1816–1899); Mgr Louis Duchesne (1843–1922), professor at the Parisian Institut Catholique where his bold views on doctrinal history aligned him in the eyes of many with the Modernists – though this did not prevent his directing the French School at Rome until his death; his more conservative counterpart at the Ecole de Sainte Barbe and the Toulouse Institut Catholique Mgr Pierre Batiffol (1861–1929), a pupil of the 'father of Christian archaeology', Giovanni Battista de Rossi (1822–1894); the south German Orientalist Anton Baumstark (1872–1948), who professed both in Germany and the Netherlands; his near namesake Suitbert Bäumer, (1845–1894), monk of Beuron, the Guéranger-inspired mother-house of a recreated German Benedictinism – though during the *Kulturkampf* launched by the German Chancellor, Otto von Bismarck (1813–1898), against the Catholic Church, he transferred his stability to the Belgian abbey of Maredsous; Fernand Cabrol (1855–1937), monk of Guéranger's Congregation who became abbot of its foundation at Farnborough, in England; his confrater there Henri Leclerq (1869–1945), who collaborated with him in editing – indeed, in largely writing – the multi-volume *Dictionnaire d'archéologie chrétienne et de liturgie* (1903–1953), and Edmund Bishop (1846–1917), a convert layman who worked not only on the indigenous sources of his native England, but also, like a number of the above, on the genesis and early history of the Roman rite. At the level of practice rather than scholarly theory (though the two never cease to exercise reciprocal influence), the Romantic movement had been accompanied by a re-awakening of minds and hearts to the theological riches of the *de facto* liturgical rites of Catholicism, in South Germany, France, England.

> The Benedictines, the Tractarians, and the Tübingen theologians proclaimed that religion unnourished by the visible Catholic Church with liturgical worship, the Eucharist or the Mass, at its heart could not long maintain vital spiritual life in an age of secularism and revolution.[54]

No influence here was fuller or more long lasting than Guéranger's. Despite the opposition of much of the French episcopate, wedded like a substantial portion of the clergy to the local Neo-Gallican uses of Troyes, Chartres, Lyons, and others, even if with the Napoleonic régime's insistence that diocesan boundaries must follow those of the new administrative units, the *départements*, such rites no longer corresponded as before to the local churches, Guéranger succeeded in winning his campaign for the superiority of the Roman-Gallican rite (the Mass rite of the papal curia and diocese of Rome) and the Tridentine-Roman breviary (for the liturgy of the Hours). An indefatigable writer, his *Institutions liturgiques* (1840–1851) and *L'Année liturgique* (1841–1866) opened the eye of thousands to the meaning of Catholic ritual. Though sometimes accused since, by more radical — if also anthropologically superficial — liturgists of a hothouse monastic aestheticism, Guéranger conceived his work precisely as a response to the social and cultural anomie and individualism of post-Revolutionary Europe. The question he faced was: How is Christian community to be re-created? His answer was a theory of social prayer of which the monastic congregation was to be the living exemplar. In the prayer of the Liturgy, that mysterious communication between heaven and earth where Christ aggregates human beings to the body of his Church, the supernatural unity of the many in the God-man is realised: thus Guéranger's last work, *L'Eglise, ou la société de la louange divine* (1875).

Such an ecclesial — rather than simply antiquarian — concern motivated those who, in Belgium and Germany, re-launched the liturgical movement in the wake of Pius X's spirited call for the people to pray the Mass more effectively,[55] assisted by frequent recourse to holy communion and the re-creation of Latin Christendom's specifically liturgical music, plainchant. At the Malines Congress on this topic of 1909, and in the monasteries of the Beuronese Congregation at Maredsous and Mont César (Louvain), a new impulse went out which would gradually transform the worship of parishes and religious communities and (despite a certain *insouciance* among *pastoral* liturgists towards the ritual and devotional dimensions of the historic rites) helped ensure that, by the time of the Second Vatican Council, the Liturgy be that resource for the energising and deepening of Catholic faith which Guéranger intended.

A quite special place belongs in the context of a history of modern Catholic thought in this connexion to the German-speaking Church of the inter-War decades, where a determined effort was made to give the Liturgy pride of place in shaping theological culture by thinking out a new account of why it mattered so much.

Odo Casel (1886–1948), monk of the Rhenish abbey of Maria Laach, argued that since the Liturgy is the Church's deepest response to divine revelation, it should be its principal stimulus to theological reflection. Moreover, once we consider the pattern of the Liturgy and the liturgical year as a guide to the Christian religion, we discover that the centre of it all is Christ in his death and resurrection: the *pascha Domini*, the Lord's 'passing over' from death to new life, celebrated in every mass, on every 'first day of the week', and at the climax of the year, Easter itself. Basing himself on the Letter to the Hebrews and the Johannine Apocalypse, Casel proposed that the paschal mystery is in some sense outside time, for until time's end the crucified and glorified Christ stands before his Father as mediator between God and the world. The point where this permanent paschal mystery of mediation touches the world is the Liturgy, which thus becomes not only the chief stimulus to theology but even its single most important subject matter. Everything crucial about Christ's saving work has passed over into the liturgical sacramentality of the Church. Odo Casel's life ended abruptly but with perfect sense of style in his collapse after intoning the solemn cry *Lumen Christi* as liturgical deacon at the Paschal Vigil of Easter 1948 at Maria Laach. Some months previously Pius XII had promulgated his encyclical on the sacred Liturgy, *Mediator Dei*, in which he had looked to Casel for illumination while simultaneously criticising (though not by name) a certain unilateralism in his writing. Casel had drawn on the phenomenology of comparative religion for an analogical description of the Gospel sacraments:

> The mystery is a sacred ritual action in which a saving deed is made present through the rite; the congregation by performing the rite takes part in the saving act, and thereby wins salvation...[56]

— a salvation which, in the Christian case, is the first-fruits of that definitive redemption of the creation the Father will accomplish in the glorious Parousia of the Son at the end of time. Though Casel exaggerated the historic influence of the mystery religions of the Greco-Roman world on apostolic Christianity, there is an ontologically suggestive parallel between the Church's mysteries and those ritual solemnities whereby primitive peoples celebrate a creation-like divine act so as to ensure the continued existence of the world.[57]

2 | Adam and the ecclesiological revival

One concern of more cautious Churchmen about the possible negative 'spin-offs' from the liturgical movement lay in its privileging of the mysteric over above (if not necessarily over against) the institutional nature of the Church. In point of fact, the Catholic Church can only be understood in Chalcedonian fashion, just as for that decisive Christological Council of 451 the Word incarnate is one person in two natures, divine and human, so too the Church is a unity-in-duality, an integrated mystery-society.[58] On the grounding premise of the 'ecclesiological revival', the mystery whereby the Church extends into the sphere of human living, the communion of the uncreated Trinity becomes present, by Christ's own will and testament, as an apostolically led (and therefore hierarchical) society. If in much (but by no means all) earlier ecclesiology the articles of the Creed on 'one, holy, catholic and apostolic Church' and 'the communion of saints' had been kept too far apart, for the Catholicism of the 1920s, so at any rate Guardini opined in *Vom Sinn der Kirche* (1922), the transcendent and immanent dimensions were interpenetrating again. In the idiom of his writing, a synthesis of Scripture, Scholasticism, literary allusion and the vocabulary of the contemporary philosophies of 'life' and 'existence', current since

Friedrich Wilhelm Nietszche (1844–1900), 'the Church is coming to life in the souls of men'.

> With the development of individualism since the end of the Middle Ages, the Church has been thought of as a means to true religious life — as it were a God-designed framework or vessel in which that life is contained — a viaduct of life but not as life itself. It has, in other words, been thought of as a thing exterior from which men might receive life, not a thing into which men must be incorporated that they may live with its life.[59]

That life, Guardini explained, is a life lived in Christ, through the Spirit, for the Father, and the Church which shares it solves the antinomy of building up community and perfecting personality — here, in a divinised organism, both are one. The Church is regaining that 'cosmic spaciousness' which belonged to it in the ages of faith, its true identity as the creation transfigured.

What Guardini meant is best consulted in the work of Karl Borromeo Adam (1876–1966), a Bavarian — indeed, sometime tutor to the Wittelsbach crown prince — ordained priest for the diocese of Regensburg in 1900 and enrolled as an advanced student in the University of Munich in 1902, by which act he began a theological career spanning the entire period up to the Second Vatican Council, which he attended as an octogenarian *peritus*, 'expert'.

The late nineteenth and early twentieth centuries in Germany saw a revival of Romanticism, eclipsed as that movement had been by Neo-Kantianism and a Positivism both scientific and historical. By way of reaction, people wanted to affirm the interconnectedness of all reality, to re-integrate emotion and intuition into understanding. *Lebensphilosophie* was a metaphysics of the pre-rational as well as the rational, and sometimes of the anti-rational too. If Nietzsche is its most celebrated, and definitely neo-pagan, representative, it took more moderate and Catholic form in the work of the mediaevalist and poet Stefan George (1868–1933), who counselled search for the deep springs of the affective life and intuitive understanding, a return to nature, and a spirited resistance to the banalising effect on culture of industrialism, bureaucracy and mass democracy of a levelling kind.

In Adam's ecclesiology the Church, as a communal organism at once human and divine, is invoked as the answer to the human longing for a fuller life and more meaning-filled existence. To this end the theme of the mystical body of Christ — already rehearsed in Möhler and the Roman School theologians who prepared the way for the First Vatican Council — is deployed to new effect. Adam dismissed the two reigning varieties of liberal Protestant theology — those of Harnack and Ernst Troeltsch (1865–1923) — as self-excluded from dealing with the mystery of the Church: Harnackianism because there

> ... the criterion by which all data are comprehended is not the living, streaming, historically tangible life of the Church and its own dynamics, but an a priori, historically unprovable idea of the Christ of Christianity,[60]

and the historicism of Troeltsch because Troeltsch's celebrated criteria of historiographic credibility (the ever-open 'revisability' of theses; the analogy of putative facts of faith with everyday experience; and their exclusive correlation with the operation of historical causes within the world-order) rested upon

> ... a tacit denial, antecedent to and prejudging all serious invest-igation of the supernatural character of [the Incarnation][61]

and so of the coming to be of Christ's Church-body upon earth. Adam challenged Protestant theological hegemony head-on by the counter-assertion that only the Catholic Church, in her 'life', her 'existence', could mediate the corporate yet personal salvation of which the Gospel speaks. Specifically,

> ... [that] Church was already, in the mystery of the Incarnation, established as an organic community. The 'many', the sum total of all who are redeemed in Christ, are in their inner relationship to one another, in their inter-relation and correlation, in their organic communion, objectively and finally the Body of Christ, for this Body is redeemed humanity, the 'reconciled world'.[62]

Yet any ecclesiology which would do justice to the witness of Scripture, Fathers and the subsequent Catholic tradition cannot be a theology of one idea alone. And in point of fact Adam presents the Church as not only Christ's Body but his Bride, and the embodiment, here and now, of the transcendent Kingdom he came to bring; he writes of it as not only an authorised teacher speaking in Christ's visible absence, but as the sacrament of God's presence in Christ (thus looking ahead to the notion of the Church as *Ursakrament*, the 'primal sacrament' of which the seven sacraments are the chief manifestations); he treats of a 'communion of the faithful' which extends beyond the boundaries of the visible realm to include the expectant, suffering souls of Purgatory and the exultant saints in heaven, with the Mother of God as their crown. Yet this whole fellowship in all its aspects is rooted in the life which streams from Christ the Head to his Body, for together they form, in the words of Augustine, the *Christus totus* – a motif laid out with a panoply of references in an encyclopaedic study *Le corps mystique du Christ* (1933) by Adam's Belgian contemporary, the Jesuit ecclesiologist Emile Mersch (1890–1940). And if Adam's principal study of ecclesiology, *Das Wesen des Katholizismus* (1924), struck more Scholastically minded theologians as too impressionistic, and in danger of downplaying, in favour of the inter-personal nature of the Church, the institutional features of its being which, not least, guarded that communion of inter-personality, Adam was able to satisfy Pius XI's Holy Office with the modest re-writing entailed in its 1934 edition, while the Hungarian Benedictine Stanley Jaki, in a comprehensive review of 'new tendencies in ecclesiology' carried out in the next pontificate, could remark that though an ecclesiology which consists solely of meditation on the great images for the Church left by Scripture and Fathers might prove modernistic, one which confined itself to the doctrinal definition of the Church's institutional structure would certainly be abstract.[63]

3 | Lagrange and the biblical revival

For Adam, although the 'living spirit of revelation' is found in the Church's mind rather than in any book (and hence, in different modes, in the hearts of the faithful and the apostolic teaching authority), it remains true that Catholicism affirms the whole of Scripture. With an eye on the hyper-modernising tendencies of liberal Protestantism, and the selective reading involved in classical Protestantism's hermeneutic, he declared that for the Church 'no thought in holy Scripture is antiquated or unseasonable, nor does she allow one truth to be obscured or garbled for the benefit of another'.[64] The intenser study of the Bible, both as a whole and in the detail of its multitudinous parts, formed the single most important element in 'going back to the sources'.

The career of Père Marie-Joseph Lagrange (1855–1938) was already perceived by contemporaries as a significant breakthrough of Catholics into that precise exegesis — so far as possible scientifically grounded: philosophically, archaeologically, and (what was more difficult) historically — which had taken its rise in the Protestant academies but was now to find a home, suitably modulated by the sense of Christian tradition, in the old Church. Studying with Batiffol at the Sulpician seminary at Issy, the young Lagrange was prophesied over by his master. He would form part of the

> ... new school, the school which will defend, by study and science, the holy ark of the Church.[65]

After preparatory studies in Egyptian, Arabic, Assyrian and *rabbinica* at Vienna, the idea arose in 1888 of taking over a pilgrim hostel founded by some enterprising Dominican in Jerusalem, and making it a centre of biblical studies. More especially it should be a 'practical school' of such studies, on the model of the Parisian *Ecole pratique des hautes études*, founded at the end of the Second Empire, with its *Quatrième section* for the historical and philological sciences, and its *Cinquième* for the religious. The need was to know the languages, the Land, and the Bible itself, so text and monument would be the keys.

To grasp the specificity of the reception of 'higher criticism' via Lagrange into the Catholic tradition it is necessary to appreciate the ardently spiritual temper of the ecclesial environment he created. The constant movement between 'oratory and laboratory' was crucial, and far from irrelevant to the concept of biblical study Lagrange represented was his decision to incorporate with the foundation stone of the *Ecole Biblique* a collection of devotional objects redolent of traditional piety.

> By way of difference from Loisy's case, the hermeneutic practised by Lagrange did not pertain first and foremost to sheer scientific curiosity, free of all religious influence. In his theological perspective, the faith that responds to revelation uses historical criticism exactly as with Thomas Aquinas it had used Aristotelian philosophy – as an instrument of intelligibility. Lagrange did not put faith in brackets. He did not practise a secularised reading of the Bible ... but a believing reading.[66]

But to those fearful of the innovations which acceptance of the historical-critical method might bring in its train – erosion of the historical bedrock of the Scriptures, denial of literary unity and authorial identity in the case of particular books, and for both of these reasons the advance of a purely Pickwickian concept of biblical inerrancy and so a lessening of confidence in Scripture's inspired quality, Lagrange's protestations seemed like camouflaged *Loisyisme*. Even Lagrange's *M. Loisy et le Modernisme* (1932), a rejoinder to Loisy's *Mémoires pour servir à l'his-*

toire religieuse de notre temps (1930–1931), did not suffice to allay episcopal anxiety about the *école large*, though he had written (so he
explained to the Dominican master-general) to 'point up the fact that
[Loisy] was justly condemned and that his intervention had hindered
the development of biblical studies as Leo XIII had conceived them'.[67]

For if Catholic scholars had largely confined themselves, till the late
nineteenth century, to the relatively 'safe' area of the study of the
history of the biblical text ('textual criticism'), Catholic exegesis had
largely consisted, between the Council of Trent and that same point in
time, in commenting the Bible with the aid of citations from the Fathers
and the mediaeval exegetes, the 'masters of the sacred page'. It was telltale that one outstanding example of such work, the commentary on the
canonical books of the Fleming Cornelis Cornelissen van den Steen
('Cornelius a Lapide', 1567–1637), received an English translation as
late as 1876–1886 for the Gospels, and 1896–1897 for a selection of the
Pauline Epistles. Leo XIII, however, conscious of the great possibilities
for enhancing understanding of the literal sense of Scripture (the
historically original sense) held out by nineteenth-century historiography and its auxiliary sciences, sought to further the application of
such study to the Bible. At the same time, the 'Biblical Commission' he
created in 1901 for this purpose also had the task of defending the
inspiration and inerrancy of Scripture as solemnly reaffirmed in the
pope's encyclical on the Bible, *Providentissimus Deus* (1893). The
Commission acted, in fact, as safeguard against too facile an acceptance
of fresh hypotheses. It insisted on the substantially Mosaic provenance
of the Pentateuch, the chronological primacy of St Matthew's Gospel
(not necessarily in Greek), the Johannine authorship of the Fourth
Gospel, a Pauline undertow to Hebrews. It warned against interpretation of books prima facie historical as non-historical (unless the *sensus
Ecclesiae* expressed in the Liturgy and elsewhere was not opposed to
this and, likewise, against over-ready a willingness to treat much of the
sacred text as 'implicit citation' for which the inspired authors did not
vouch). Such 'decisions', approved by the pope *in forma communi* –
that is, without invoking infallibility – bound, it should be said, only to
public respect; scholars were encouraged, indeed, to submit to the
Commission any solid arguments they encountered against them.

The Commission was never again so restrictive as under Pius X and his
successor, Benedict XV della Chiesa (1854–1922). Lagrange, who main-

tained that the Catholic exegete's duty to respect Church discipline in such matters imposed no arbitrary limit — because the believing reception of the Bible in the Church is an integral part of the constitution of the meaning of the Scriptures, to interpret the Bible by the Church is precisely to acknowledge the basic relation that joins the two — fell foul of the faint-hearted nevertheless. His study of critical principles, *La Méthode historique* (1902), was found too conservative by Duchesne, Laberthonnière and Blondel. Yet the Dominican master-general sought its re-writing; it was because, in the end, he asked Lagrange to abandon the field of Old Testament studies altogether (since there scientific criticism was at its most radical) that, providentially, the latter started upon his great quartet of commentaries (*Marc*, 1911; *Luc*, 1920; *Matthieu*, 1923; *Jean*, 1926).

The journal Lagrange founded, the *Revue Biblique*, was only the best known of a series of collaborative projects in which Catholics sought to satisfy simultaneously the demands of scholarship and theological tradition, for the benefit of the reading public at various levels of sophistication. These might take the form of reviews such as *Biblische Studien* and *Biblische Zeitschrift*; *Biblica* and *Verbum Domini*; the *Catholic Biblical Quarterly*; *Cultura Biblica*; *Revista Biblica* and *Estudios Biblicos*; *Lumière et Vie* and *Bible et Vie Chrétienne*, or again encyclopaedic aids like the *Dictionnaire de la Bible*, with its 'supplements'; or straightforward commentaries such as *Herders Bibel Kommentar*, *La Sainte Bible*, or the *Regensburger Neues Testament*. Gradually Catholics conceded the utility — if sometimes hedged round with caveats — of the methods employed by Protestant and Anglican scholars, though they insisted also on the need to contextualise such study in awareness of Church tradition (what would come to be called the text's *Wirkungsgeschichte*, the history of its after-life in the impact it had made). Pius XII's encyclical *Divino afflante Spiritu* (1943) recognised that Scripture contained many different genres of literature, thus easing somewhat the problem of historicity; the pope also spoke of the written or oral sources from which a book might be composed. If comparative literature and source criticism were thereby admitted with a smile to the charmed circle of sacred sciences, the application of form criticism (the investigation of possible oral units subjacent to a literary tradition) to the Gospels was fraught with more difficulty, and in 1964, while the Second Vatican Council was sitting, the Pontifical Biblical Commission issued a judicious 'Instruction on the Historical Truth of the Gospels' which admitted the possible influence of early Christian proclamation, liturgy and pastoral care on the Gospel tradition, but not to the extent of rupturing the reportage of Jesus' words and deeds. If thereby only a modest dose of form criticism was prescribed, the same was true of the 'redaction criticism' by which students sought to describe the theological creativity of the evangelists in re-working the materials they had received. The papal exegetes were evidently aware that academic Bible study has its own traditions (and indeed fashions), for good and ill. As in its own way just as much an interpretative community as the Church itself, the academy could not be allowed simply to impose its own (in any case internally controverted) canons of judgement. If the Church needed the historical critics to understand the making of Scripture, they could not substitute for it in questions of the content, doctrinal and spiritual, of what was thus made. It was Lagrange's role-modelling achievement to have kept hold of both ends of the chain, both dogma and criticism, for the Bible, though human discourse and therefore historically enacted, is nonetheless the Word of God.

4 | Daniélou and the patristic revival

Patristic scholarship was one of those areas that, like liturgical history and the textual criticism of the Bible, had enjoyed a continuous history in the Catholic Church since the pre-Enlightenment era. On the eve of the Great Revolution, the Oratorian Andrea Galland (1709–1779) had published in Venice in fourteen volumes a 'library of the ancient fathers and ecclesiastical writers' (1765–1781, re-printed in 1788) though Galland died before completing the authors of the seventh century. The Revolution itself, when its armies reached Würzburg in 1792, cut short a second promising attempt, accompanied by a helpful *Thesaurus rei patristicae*, earlier still. In a Church still struggling after the decima-tion of its institutional life to re-create its centres of learning (in France the Catholic Institutes, which, unlike the seminaries, could genuinely claim to function at university level, were not opened till 1875, and in the fifty years since the collapse of Lamennais's La Chesnaie, the only monastic school of scholarship was Solesmes), a unique contribution was made by the priest-publisher Jacques-Paul Migne (1800–1875) when he offered to the public from his own printing press, between 1840 and 1847, a 'Complete course of patrology or universal library, entire, uniform, convenient, economical, of all the holy fathers, doctrines and ecclesiastical writers both Greek and Latin who have lived since apostolic times up to Innocent III, 1216, for the Latins and to the Council of Florence, 1439, for the Greeks', intended, as the forty-nine remaining lines of its title indicated, to be useful, in its texts, indices, introductions and commentaries not only to scholars but to business men and indeed, 'if they have the strength', to the 'lazy and ignorant'. In an age when familiarity with the classical languages was widespread among the educated, Migne's *Patrology* had a far-reaching effect on positive theology. Supplemented from 1894 onwards by the *Patrologia Syriaca*, and from 1903 by the *Patrologia Orientalis* (both produced in Paris) and the *Corpus Scriptorum Christianorun Orientalium* (published in Louvain and Washington), the Migne *Patrology* preserved many of the pre-Revolutionary editions based on manuscripts available at the Renaissance and subsequently, but lost in that great conflagration of libraries and learning which the Revolution entailed.

Despite the Abbé Migne's hopeful advertisement, the massive tomes of his *Patrology* were not likely to reach the Parisian man (or woman) in the street. There also remained the question as to how the contents of his texts would transmute into theology — or even whether it was desirable that they should — since surely St Thomas, and the Scholastics after him, had integrated all that was essential in the patristic corpus into their own, intellectually more coherent, synthesis. And if the Fathers were to be a stimulus to the 're-awakening of the Church in souls' of which Catholics in Europe after the Great War seemed so confident, then a 'neo-patristic ' revival would have to free the patristic authors from their confinement in histories of dogma and question them as to their moral and ascetic teaching, their spirituality and mysticism, doctrine of monasticism and the Religious life, social and economic ideas, theology of history.[68]

It was to this juncture that the Jesuit and future cardinal Jean Daniélou (1905–1974) belonged. Stemming from an unusual background in that, though his parents were passionately Catholic (his mother was a moving spirit behind the creation of the 'free' — that is, Church-run — *Ecole Normale* at Neuilly-sur-Seine when state anti-clericalism led to the expulsion of the teaching Religious in 1906), his father had several times occupied a cabinet post under the Third Republic. Daniélou managed to marry a lifetime's absorption in patristics to an enthusiasm (not always shared by more conventional brethren) for an opening of French Catholicism to a wider world. His experiences of life at the Maison de la Jeunesse, an international student hostel; the work of the Compagnie-Saint-Paul, where he was lay warden; ecumenical contacts at the home of the Maritains; friendship with the future editor of *Esprit*, Emmanuel Mounier (1905–1950), initiator of the radical-Catholic dialogue with Marxism; the co-founder of a 'Cercle Péguy' for the theological exploitation of the grandiose epic poetry of that master in the interests of a typological theology of history of a patristic kind – all this had made its mark before Daniélou ever entered the Society of Jesus in 1930. These large sympathies were further expanded by his studies on the Jesuit scholasticate at Lyons-Fourvières where he heard Père Henri de Lubac (1896–1991) lecture on Islam and Buddhism and forged links with the abbé Jules Monchanin (1895–1957) – the 'hermit of Saccidânanda' (a Sanskrit rendering of the Trinitarian names as 'Principle', 'Logos', 'Bliss') – whose life-work would be the installation in India of an ascetic Catholicism so constituted as to be intelligible to Hindus.[69] At the same time, de Lubac confirmed his interest in patristic exegesis (notably as practised by Origen of Alexandra (c 185 – c 254), and Balthasar – a precocious fellow student – Daniélou's love of the Cappadocians, of whom Nyssa was at the time the least studied.

In a short period of twenty-four months, and despite all the difficulties imposed by residence in German-occupied France, Daniélou was made professor of the history of Christian origins at the Parisian Institut Catholique (succeeding Duchesne at one remove); became editor of the prestigious Jesuit journal *Etudes*; defended at the Sorbonne, and published his doctoral thesis under the title *Platonisme et thologie mystique. Essai sur la doctrine spirituelle de saint Grégoire de Nysse* (1944); brought out as the first volume of a series, *Sources Chrétiennes*, intended to put the texts of the Fathers into the hands (or even the pockets) of clergy and laity without funds for purchasing vast extensive tomes, a translation with introduction of Gregory's *Life of Moses*; created a missionary cell of high intellectual quality, the Cercle Saint-Jean-Baptiste; became director of the review *Dieu Vivant*, at once outward-looking to contemporary culture yet 'neo-orthodox' in its emphasis on the absolute primacy of God and his revelation and the fecundity for human thought of the doctrines of Incarnation, salvation and eschatology; and published his globally oriented theology of history *Le Mystère du salut des nations* (1945).

This capacity for tireless work at a consistent level of excellence made Daniélou the outstanding figure in the neo-patristic revival in mid-century Catholic theology. At the same time, while in no way indifferent to the classical doctrine of the Church, he realised that, if the Fathers were to make their mark on the pastoral renewal of Catholic culture as a whole (in the service of that overall missionary conception which is the connecting thread in his life and work), their writings must be investigated for more than their immediate contribution to the making of the conciliar dogmas. Here his doctrinal thesis — on Nyssa's spiritual doctrine — was emblematic, and the same concern for the wider inspirational value of ancient Christianity (in, this time, its pre-Nicene remains) encouraged him in the three-volume *Histoire des doctrines chrétiennes avant Nicée* 1958–1967, either to re-order well-known material in stimulatingly novel fashion, or to explore byways (notably among the Jewish-Christian writings somewhat marginalised by the Great Church) that led to unusual vantage-points. The faith of the Church, Daniélou was implicitly saying, needs many cultures and epochs for its full (which can never mean inexhaustible) expression. The questions this raised — the theological meaning of history; the way to establish theological norms for the governing of changing intellectual styles; and the implications for the Church's doctrine if a unitary philosophical culture (constructed with so much effort since Leo XIII) should be abandoned — lie close to the surface of the chapter that follows.

VI | HISTORY AND META-HISTORY

1 | Christopher Dawson

Though the migration of Maritain to the United States and Gilson to Canada had its own explanation in their individual biographies, it could also be taken as a sign of the heightened role that North America would play in Catholic thought in the later twentieth century. The move to Harvard of Christopher Dawson (1889–1970), most prominent, in the period, of Catholic interpreters of historical meaning, fits the same pattern. Dawson, the offspring of minor Yorkshire landowners and clerical patricians from the Welsh Marches, was an Anglo-Catholic influenced, while at Edwardian Oxford, by the religious philosophy of von Hügel (with its integration of institutional, theological and spiritual elements) as also by the historian of mediaeval political and social ideas Ernest Barker (1847–1960). His conversion to the Church of Rome in 1913 was precipitated, however, by reading the concluding volume of Harnack's history of dogma, where the great Protestant scholar described Luther's attack, from the angle of his doctrine of justification by faith alone, on the Catholic understanding of Christian perfection. What to Harnack was a return to the primitive Gospel was to Dawson an irreparable breach with the Christian past.

Dawson's earliest professional work was for the *Sociological Review*, the journal of Le Play House, a 'think-tank' inspired by the pioneering French sociologist Pierre Guillaume Frédéric Le Play (1806–1882) whose six-volume *Les Ouvriers européens* (1855) analysed social structures — from the Steppes of Russia to the North of England — in terms of 'work, place and folk'. To these Dawson would add 'religion', for he had already accepted the dictum of the Liberal Catholic John Emerich Edward Dalberg Acton (1834–1902), Regius Professor of Modern History at Cambridge, that 'religion is the key of history'.[70] Academically brilliant but unplaceable — history, religion and literature were all, with sociology, grist to his mill — a post was created specially for him as 'Lecturer in the History of Culture' at the University College of the South-West (later Exeter University) in 1922. The modest demands of his slight audience enabled him to begin work on a mammoth cultural history, provisionally entitled 'The Life of Civilisations': this was, after all, the age of Oscar Spengler (1880–1936), author of *Der Untergang des Abendlandes. Umrisse einer Morphologie der Weltgeschichte* (1918–1920; 1922) and Arnold Toynbee (1889–1975), brain-father of the twelve volume *A Study of History* (1934–1961). It was also a period of Christian interest in the theology of history of an intensity unprecedented since patristic times.[71]

Progress and Religion (1929), intended as a summary synthesis of the entire work, announces the principal theme of Dawson's enterprise. A society's vitality is bound up with its religion. He wrote elsewhere:

> The great civilizations of the world do not produce the great religions as a kind of cultural by-product; in a very real sense the great religions are the foundations on which the great civilizations rest. A society which has lost its religion becomes sooner or later a society which has lost its culture.[72]

And whereas Spengler in his 'morphology' of civilisations treated each culture as a closed system, Dawson's chart was based on a principle of spiritual fecundity whereby parent cultures, in their deaths, give rise to offspring cultures which can continue their genes. But as with his Russian Orthodox contemporary Georges Vasileivich Florovsky (1893–1979),who also attempted a Christian theology of cultural history, Dawson's deeper presupposition here concerns human freedom, especially in its mode of creative victory over resistant materials, what

Florovsky termed *podvig*, 'ascetic achievement'.

> If man is not the slave and creature of time, but its master and creator, then history also becomes a creative process. It does not repeat itself meaninglessly; it grows into organic unity with the growth of human experience. The past does not die; it becomes incorporated in humanity. And hence progress is possible, since the life of society and of humanity itself possesses continuity and the capacity for spiritual growth no less than the life of the individual.[73]

As the tone and substance of these comments suggest, Dawson had not only an analysis to offer, as historian; he also had a prescription, as lay prophet. As he wrote in his (immediately post-Second World War) Gifford Lectures:

> We are faced with a spiritual conflict of the most acute kind, a sort of social schizophrenia which divides the soul of society between a non-moral will to power served by inhuman techniques and a religious faith and a moral idealism which have no power to influence human life. There must be a return to unity − a spiritual integration of culture − if mankind is to survive.[74]

Indeed, for all his criticism of Spengler (and also of Toynbee, whom he chastised for too sharp a distinction between primitive and civilised societies and too blunt a one between the higher religions and civilisations), Dawson defended the 'meta-historians' against the charge that prophecy and history were disreputably combined in their work.[75] Such creative vision, he held, typified great historians: witness Ranke (Leopold von Ranke 1795–1886) and de Tocqueville (Alexis Henri Charles Maurice Clerel, Comte de Tocqueville, 1805–1857). Dawson's own work is best thought of as a latter-day *City of God* (his favourite text among Christian sources), which tries to show the special history of Christian revelation confronting and transforming the general history of the world, while remaining conditioned by its possibilities and limitations. The same task was carried out simultaneously by the poet, essayist and visual artist David Jones (1895–1974), who recast elements of Dawson's work in mythopoetic form.[76]

2 | The Innsbrück School

The difficulty involved in turning so doctrinal a religion as Catholic Christianity into a proclamation about the meaning of history was encountered in very different guise by the Jesuit theologians of the inter-War 'Innsbrück School'. The prophetic tone audible in much of Dawson's writing connects his work to the missionary or 'kerygmatic' mode in which a portion of Germanophone theology began to present itself in his lifetime. Conscious of the unsettling effect on not only civil society but also Church of the passing of an entire European order with the First World War – a lost world not more peaceful or comfortable, except for a few, but with greater confidence in its values and standards than its disoriented successor,[77] Catholics in the most intellectually sophisticated segments of the defeated Central Powers where dislocation was at its worst – Germany, Austria – looked for a more vital theology, more freighted with immediate significance for human life, with even greater urgency than had their pre-War counterparts.

The implied comparison was with Scholasticism in its least attractive form: manual theology. With the exception of the Dominican study houses where the *Summa Theologiae* of Aquinas was the *texte de base*, most students read manuals — simplified schematic textbooks for philosophy and theology, where the principal points the student was expected to retain were isolated in advance as 'theses', self-contained propositions, for which concise argumentation and citation of relevant authorities were provided, and objections considered and countered. Whereas in the 'controversial theology' of the sixteenth and seventeenth centuries (between Catholics and Protestants and, if more rarely, Catholics and Orthodox) such theses were drawn directly from the sources of revelation, Scripture and Tradition, by the early years of the twentieth century they were more likely to be taken from that handy vade mecum, Denzinger's *Enchiridion*, considered a *résumé* of the doctrine produced by the magisterium of the Church. Writers of the Neo-Thomist school did not shun manuals, but expanded the very limited speculative content of their non-Thomistic rivals, *ad mentem sancti Thomas*: 'according to the mind of St Thomas'. The need to struggle, in the Enlightenment period and through various phases of nineteenth-century intellectual fashion, with deism, atheism, immanentism, had sharpened the wits of the Church's apologists: one merit of the manuals, to orderly minds, was their progressive exposition of the arguments for religion at large (*demonstratio religiosa*), with an accent on the possibility, appropriateness and necessity of supernatural divine revelation; the Gospel in general (*demonstratio christiana*), centring on the claims of Jesus of Nazareth to be an accredited divine legate; and Catholicism in particular (*demonstratio catholica*) with especial reference to the claims of the Catholic Church to be the Church Christ founded. From analysis of the latter it was then possible to show the authoritative structure to which appeal must be made in the dogmatic manuals — or dogmatic sections of more comprehensive handbooks. The style of thinking of the manuals was, clearly, objective and rational, if also polemical; the clergy whom it formed had, in all probability, a better conceptual grasp on the Catholic faith than their modern successors. The drawback was that so crystalline an intellectual structure, whose forms were as discrete as the prose of the manuals was sub-divided, could not easily be turned into a preaching and catechesis that moved souls. Though with the quasi-extinction of printed sermons, the homily became an oral form and the historian must largely rely, accordingly, on anecdote for such judgements, it seems likely that the standard of preaching fell between the later nineteenth century and the inter-War years.

It was into this situation that 'Innsbrück theology' moved. It aimed to be a truly evangelical theology which would identify the central core of the Gospel — God in Christ, with his good news of salvation — and relate all else to that. Among the Jesuits of the Canisianum, the theology faculty of Innsbrück University, a school of kerygmatic theology arose concerned to produce an articulation of the original proclamation in compelling language. Such men as Josef Andreas Jungmann (1889–1975), a liturgical historian, and Hugo Rahner (1900–1968), a patrologist, were scarcely 'Simple Simons': in their chosen specialisations, each was a scholar of international repute. But each produced a theology where luxuriance was cut back to reveal, if starkly, the great outlines of a tree. Jungmann's *Die Frohbotschaft und unser Glaubensverkündigung* (1936) drew on the Bible and the Liturgy to suggest what was really paramount in Christian faith, the one thing necessary that might get lost in too abundant a plethora of doctrines; such a 'theology of proclamation', *Verkündigungstheologie*, a catchphrase taken from the title of a major statement of its principles by Hugo Rahner, was expected to provide marching orders for catechetics, as Jungmann's *Katechetik. Aufgabe und Methode der religiösen Unterweisung* (1939) demonstrated. While such a concept of theological pedagogy was doctrinally sparing in comparison with the Catechisms in general release, with their hundreds of propositions on everything from the immortality of the soul to guardian angels, it was certainly no warmed-up humanism, but focused on the offer of salvation in a Christ-centred way, as unmistakably expressed in Jungmann's *Christus als Mittelpunkt religiöser Erziehung* (1939).

It was not likely, however, that Catholic thinkers would content themselves with the prospect of *kerygmatische Theologie* (to give it its alternative German name). In the first place, the plain diet which it prescribed would render the richness of *ressourcement* — the abundant documentation gathered together in the liturgical, ecclesiological, biblical and patristic revivals — unpalatable if not altogether indigestible. Yet were these gains to be reserved in practice to those with technical expertise of a specialised sort, and left unintegrated with common doctrine? Secondly, a slimline theology concentrating on essentials expressed well enough the idea of a 'hierarchy of truths'. But that not everything in Catholic doctrine is equally important did not entail that not everything was important: a truth of doctrine occupying, to all

appearances, quite a humble niche could prove to have crucial importance, not least (pace the Innsbrück Jesuits) for the practice of faith in
everyday existence. Using the example of the freedom of the will (a
philosophical truth connected with the deposit of faith and so capable
of authoritative teaching by the Church), Chesterton — in characteristic
vein as a layman theologising seriously in the comic mode — had
spoken of its potential to introduce 'a sparkling and crystal clearness'
into 'relations with the housemaid', prior to drawing, the wider lesson:

> The Christian puts the seed of dogma into a central darkness; but
> it branches forth in all directions with abounding natural
> health.[78]

And thirdly, it was argued that kerygmatic theology was born of
misplaced despair — the disbelief that dogmatic theology could renew
itself by re-establishing contact with the Church's Liturgy, her sense of
identity (communitarian, historic, missionary), and her Scriptures. The
principal question was not whether this should happen but how — in a
Scholastic mode, or some other? For without dogmatic reflection of an
ordered kind, Catholic thought could not get under way. Kerygmatic
theology itself, no matter how admirably Christocentric, would be
unable permanently to avoid comment on issues like the relation of religious experience to revelation, the relation of revelation to dogma, the
relation of dogma to its own history, which Modernism had raised but
failed acceptably to solve.

The Innsbrück School had little time for such ponderings before the
inhibitions on Church activity imposed by the National Socialists over-
took Austrian Catholicism with the Anschluss of 1938. It is in any case
unlikely that such small resistance as was offered, largely by the
peasantry, to that débâcle owed much to kerygmatic theology. The
evidence — the flashpoints of tension between the faithful and the
new order over the removal of crucifixes from public places, the celebra-
tion of church festivals and the like — points to a custom-sustained
traditional Catholicism (not necessarily unaware of the deeper issues
beneath) as the main obstacle to the cultural hegemony of Nazism.[79]

3 | Henri de Lubac and *nouvelle théologie*

In attempting to extract the pure essence of the Catholic Gospel from the toils of Clio, muse of history, the Innsbrück School resembled (though in little else) the high-and-dry Thomism of the years before and after the Second World War. Not Tyrolese but Lyonese (and Parisian) theology, however, stalked the waking nightmares of the best Thomistic minds. It was the wider strategy they saw implied in the patristic scholarship of de Lubac (at Lyons) and Daniélou (in Paris) that aroused the anxieties of the pure Thomists of the time, most fully represented as these were by the Dominicans of Saint-Maximin (Var) and Toulouse — though important outposts of their school included Rome, where the *Collegio Angelico*, if staffed by the Order of Preachers as a whole, was dominated theologically by a Toulouse friar, Réginald Garrigou-Lagrange (1877–1964), and Fribourg, whose major seminary was home to Charles Journet (1891–1975), a close collaborator of Maritain, made cardinal under Paul VI.

In the 1946 essay 'La Théologie et ses sources', the editor of the *Revue Thomiste*, Marie-Michel Labourdette (1908–1990), signalled in the pages of his own journal an attack on neo-patristic theology in the

Catholic Church. Naturally enough, his studied criticism of two projects launched a little before by the French Jesuits — *Sources Chrétiennes* itself and the series of historical-theological monographs *Théologie* — was not animated by hostility to the readier availability of the works of the Fathers, or the scholarly investigation of the history of Christian doctrine as such. Rather, Labourdette divined in both series a 'hidden agenda' of a kind unacceptable to a disciple of St Thomas. They were affected by a disapprobation of, and even contempt for, the Scholastic and especially the Thomist achievement, and — worse still — by a depreciation of intelligence itself in its search for abiding truth. The two series were tainted, he considered, by both a historical relativism which treats truth as truth for this or that historical period, and an experiential relativism where a subjectivism of inner experience could undermine (by appeal to the demands, or the limitations, of this or that 'spirituality') the objective value of the truths of faith. The slope on which the authors concerned had positioned themselves, the better (no doubt) to dialogue with Existentialists and historical materialists, was an impossibly slippery one that could only end in the evacuation of the idea of speculative truth, of time-transcending truth, and even, ultimately, of truth itself.[80] This would have been a generous quart to extract from a pint pot, had Labourdette not been aware of more pointed comments on the deficiencies of Neo-Scholasticism passed by not only Daniélou and de Lubac but also Balthasar, Pierre Teilhard de Chardin (1881–1955), and others. In an influential article on 'the present orientations of religious thought' in his journal, *Etudes*, Daniélou, for instance, while trumpeting the glories of the biblical, liturgical and patristic *ressourcements*, had spoken of the peculiar unfittedness of Scholastic thought — owing to its comparative lack of interest in the topics of history and subjecthood — for the engagement with contemporary thinkers which was also needed. Henceforth, Daniélou had concluded, some kind of phenomenological philosophy would better serve, in the light of the priority now given to the 'dramatic world of persons', for the description of 'religious realities in their concrete form'.[81] While Labourdette called for a pacific if far-reaching debate on the nature and task of Catholic theology in the light of these proposals, Garrigou-Lagrange, to whose mind they were even more antipathetic, considered the menace so serious as to require an intervention of the papal magisterium with a view to re-establishing the primacy of Christian Scholasticism as the classical expression of the philosophy and theological doctrine approved by the Church. That would take place in 1950 in Pius XII's letter *Humani Generis*, with its significant sub-title 'Concerning certain False Opinions which Threaten to Sap the Foundations of Catholic Teaching'.

That Labourdette's criticisms did not wholly miss the mark is shown by the career of Daniélou's *beau idéal* of a theologian, de Lubac — whose writings make plain, however, that more than pastoral accommodationism was at stake. In the 1929 lecture which began his teaching at Lyons, de Lubac had warned, in Blondelian accents, against dividing theology from life by treating dogma as:

> ... a thing in itself, like a revealed block without relation of any sort to natural man as a transcendent object whose manifestation (as indeed, a greater part of its content) is governed only by arbitrary divine decree.[82]

To shut one's eyes to concrete problems, or believe all issues resolved, is to cripple the missionary outreach of the Church. It should be noted however, that the reasons de Lubac adduced for these statements were not of a pragmatic order. First, the writing of a separated theology, a separated philosophy, and an apologetics based on 'natural faith' is untraditional (this was not how Augustine, Möhler, Newman, apologised), and moreover brings the Church's learning into disrepute. De Lubac's own theological apologetics, *Catholicisme. Les aspects sociaux du dogme* (1938), would, in its evocation of the 'social aspects of dogma', offer the Catholic faith as the answer to a very human problem, the unity and peace of mankind, achieved in God, certainly, and not in quasi-humanist abstraction from him. Second, God is author not only of supernature but of nature, and of nature, moreover, in view of grace. The human being is at no time simply a natural object, for he or she is, from the very start, *imago Dei*. The supernatural, however freely given — and here de Lubac had in mind man's elevation through the grace of Christ, to share in the inner life or the Holy Trinity — is never simply the adventitious. By this claim, de Lubac anticipated his later attempts to clean the Baroque tincture from the spectacles by which Augustine and Thomas were read in *Surnaturel. Etudes historiques* (1946) — the work most centrally contested in the substantive (as distinct from methodological) issues debated in the Church before (and after) *Humani generis*.[83]

To suppose that de Lubac wished to return to the Fathers so as to finish up with a less developed theology, which might by that very token be more acceptable to non-Catholic Christians who had either not shared (Orthodox) or repudiated (Protestants) the mediaeval inheritance of the Latin Church, was also — for the anxiety was entertained — far from the truth. De Lubac's expository (rather than remedial) work as a historical theologian was directed just as much to mediaeval as to patristic theology, especially in the history of biblical interpretation, the four-volume *Exegese mediévale* (1953–1964). More apposite is the judgement that he tended to prefer early mediaeval *Vorscholastik* to the full-blown Scholasticism of the high Middle Ages (something most clearly evidenced in his study of the relation between Church and Eucharist, *Corpus mysticum*, 1950, an important text for the 'eucharistic ecclesiology' apparent, in part, at Vatican II), and even the theology of the Christian Renaissance (little respected by the neo-mediaevalists of the 'Third Scholasticism, but fêted with aplomb in de Lubac's study of the Catholic humanist Giovanni Pico della Mirandola, 1463–1494).

To Labourdette, an exclusive delight in historical truth was an obstacle to any mind desirous of an integral intellectual development. It is not enough to be a historical theologian, to know how problems were posed in the past, for the Church needs answers to them now. Nor is there need to cobble together a new philosophy and theology for this purpose, since one already exists that can do the job. The Thomist synthesis was essentially true in its principles; though imperfect it was therefore eminently perfectible by contemporary and future labour. While with critical vigilance and constructive effort the nuggets of truth occurring in systems of thought otherwise false could be built into its edifice, no house could be raised simultaneously on Scotist and Hegelian, Existentialist and evolutionist foundations. In the thirteenth century there took place a providential encounter of the true religion with the true philosophy, and the faith of the Church Fathers, which hitherto had not found its proper conceptual instrument, now had this within its grasp. Though much in historic Aristoteleanism had to be re-thought by Christian theologians, the idea of attempting to go behind the 'Thomist miracle' to an understanding of the faith typical of an earlier epoch is inadmissible, a betrayal of theology's very essence.[84]

Garrigou-Lagrange, decanting the quintessence of a Thomist Catholicism in all the major areas of doctrine in *Le Synthèse thomiste* (1950), rejected, in evident agreement with Labourdette's criticisms, all mere 'Christian eclecticism', and deplored the attempt to minimise, in the spirit of Le Roy, or at least Blondel, the claims of an objective meta-physic, set to work in the service of dogma, in favour of those of practical relevance, defined in terms of the cultural programme of some immediate time and space.

4 | Teilhard de Chardin

Not the least respect in which Scholastic philosophers and theologians felt uneasy at de Lubac's work was his championship of the highly personal attempt at 'meta-history' — not from a theology-of-history starting-point, or drawn from a kerygmatic concept, but one that was, ostensibly at least, natural-scientific in character — by his older confrère Teilhard de Chardin.[85] A theological cosmology had been implicit in the Judaeo-Christian revelation ever since the sapiential books of the Hebrew Bible. Important to patristic and mediaeval divines it was almost inevitable that in the later nineteenth and twentieth centuries, when natural science became the paradigm of veridical knowing, and through technology affected human life more and more pervasively, an attempt should be made to restore cosmology to the proud place it once had occupied. The synthesis of evolutionary science and Catholicism fashioned by Pierre Teilhard de Chardin was flawed but fascinating. While Daniélou at first rejected it for its excessive optimism about how the world enters (or becomes) the Kingdom, he came to appreciate some at least of Teilhard's positions; and de Lubac defended the fundamental orthodoxy of his writing in two substantial studies, comparing him, in his union of science and mysticism, to Origen. The comparison was apt, for Origen also aroused both admiration and suspicion in Church tradition. The relation between this-worldly reality and the Kingdom of God, and so the relationship between the world and the Church, would be a singularly contraverted topic in the years immediately preceding the Second Vatican Council. Indeed, these questions define the greatest area of dispute between traditional and progressive Catholics in the era that Council initiated.

The notion of evolution as taken up theologically in Teilhard's work is larger than the zoologist's hypothesis to account for adaptation and change in species associated with the name of Charles Darwin. Teilhard's broader sweep (even leaving aside the specifically biblical and dogmatic contribution to his vision) derives from the thought of Le Roy, who in *Les Origines humaines et l'évolution de l'intelligence* (1928) had spoken of a diffused cosmic energy that is latently 'psychic' – tending to consciousness, concentrated in organisms of growing complexity, whose realm – the 'biosphere' – is, however, transcended when man appears. Thereafter evolution is continued in the 'nosphere' or realm of spirit – while always subject to God's transcendently creative action. Essentially, Teilhard introduced Christological and sacramental dimensions into Le Roy's cosmology. He thereby enabled it to enter into direct discussion with Catholic theology, but in doing so also exposed the inherent difficulties of its project.

If *L'Apparition de l'homme* (1956) sums up Teilhard's general phenomenology of the evolutionary process (and the difficulty of finding a term for someone who developed their own conceptual idiom on the remote basis of biology and palaeontology has left 'phenomenologist', *faute de mieux*, as Teilhard's philosophical niche),[86] then *Le Milieu divin* (1957) provides it with its theological context, for the word *'milieu'* – in the original French of Teilhard's writing – signifies not only an environment but a governing centre or expansively influential source. If the process of evolution is not to end in absurdity, by cosmic death, it must possess a centre of convergence of a divine, transcendent kind. The Church's Gospel must be, accordingly, profoundly concerned with human progress. However, the faithful performance of the duties of one's state in life which Teilhard, as a disciple in spiritual theology of the French Jesuit masters of the seventeenth century, took to be the normal form of self-insertion into that forward movement, will include a 'divinisation of our passivities', a self-abandonment to God's presence in the suffering and death that touch all life short of the 'Omega-point' of the glorious Parousia. (The ultimate-reality in eschatological perspective is rightly named, as the Seer of the Apocalypse names him, with the last letter of the Greek alphabet.)

In *Le Phénomène humain* (1954) and *L'Avenir de l'homme* (1959), Teilhard put together his cosmic phenomenology with his theological doctrine, extrapolating (as he thought) from the past how the future will be built through a process of *amorisation* whereby the free circulation of love-energy between persons will resolve the dreadful antimony of liberty and fraternity which the Revolution had with such little sagacity taken to be *idées-soeurs*. That future is itself, however, only thinkable if a divine personal Omega draws human persons, who as yet cannot love universally, to himself, by activating the love-energy present in the world.

The imprecision, metaphysically and dogmatically, of much of Teilhard's language rendered his attempts to link the Bergsonian *élan vital* to transforming grace less than fully persuasive to both philosophers and theologians. These critics wished to know how trends of increasing complexification (and 'interiorisation') in the realms of biology and culture could indicate their final convergence in God if, as both theistic rationality and biblical revelation suggest, it is by the free grace of God that the ultimate outcome of history, and the meaning of the cosmos, is decided.[87] Unfortunately the Catholic *pietas* of Teilhard towards the mystery of the Word incarnate, the Church, the Blessed Virgin and the Eucharist — essential, on his view, to our personal contribution to divine world-making — proved less easily communicable in the period (the 1960s) when his writings, long ecclesiastically inhibited, became generally available, than a secularising reading of his thought which confirmed the 'horizontalism' of the times.

5 | Karl Rahner

The tendency to elide the distinction between natural and supernatural under the influence of de Lubac's discovery that there is but one
history of grace embracing, if in differentiated ways, every person in the
world, can also be observed in the work of Hugo Rahner's younger (and
more famous) brother, Karl. For Rahner it was insufficient to inject
dosages of the repristinated liturgical, ecclesial, biblical, patristic and
kerygmatic sense into the existing body of Scholastic thought. A more
intimate transformation was required. In effect, what would remain
would be the deep springs of Christian Scholasticism in its Thomist
form: the theological epistemology that saw the knowing subject as
open to the divine mystery, the dynamic and mutually supportive relationship of nature and grace. Rahner's new conceptuality draws on the
philosophical enterprises of not only Kant and Hegel but also Martin
Heidegger (1889–1976) in order to transform traditional Scholasticism
into a theological anthropology that remains oriented, however, toward
the mystery of God. All human life was to be seen as permeated by the
offer of God's grace. Since the offer of grace was universal, Rahner
deemed it to be 'existential', a constituent feature of human existence.
But, since grace was thus present only as offer, Rahner qualified this

existential as 'supernatural' — not, in other words, given in and with humanity as such, but God's free gift to those who stand before his saving mystery. Rahner became thereby one of the founders of 'transcendental Thomism', a Thomism which accepts the post-Kantian stress on man's creative contribution to knowledge but (with Maréchal) finds latent in his drive toward knowledge an implicit self-direction toward God.

Unlike Maréchal, Rahner ranged widely over the entire landscape of Catholic doctrine. Though he left few major studies in dogmatics (as distinct from metaphysics, *Geist in Welt*, 1939, and the philosophy of religion, *Hörer des Wortes*, 1941), he published hundreds of thousands of words in other genres. When in 1948, with the Allied victory, the Jesuits were able to re-open their theology faculty at Innsbrück, Rahner, rudely uprooted from the Tyrolean capital where his superiors had sent him to teach, was able to return there. In the course of a three-year cycle he was needed to lecture on most of the great doctrinal themes. Thus the main period of his literary output began. We can divide it into four chief categories.

First, there were the essays that he gathered into the twenty-three volumes of his 'Theological Investigations' — thus the English title, with a genuflexion toward the *Philosophical Investigations* (1953) of the Cambridge philosopher Ludwig Wittgenstein (1893–1951). In the German original they were, more simply, *Schriften zur Theologie*. The implied comparison with Wittgenstein is not entirely whimsical when one bears in mind Augustine DiNoia's nutshell description of them:

> ... a series of brilliant, often successful, but relatively unsystematic experiments, intended to advance the state of discussion of particular Christian doctrines by pressing at the boundaries of prevailing neo-Scholastic formulations.[88]

Second, Rahner undertook a mighty task of lexicography when in 1955 he was made responsible for a new edition of the prestigious German Catholic encyclopaedia *Lexikon für Theologie und Kirche*.[89] The German bishops (a successor of whom, Walter Kasper, 1933–, would after Rahner's death commence a further revision) insisted that the *Lexikon* must, of its nature, present the *doctrina recepta et communis*, the generally accepted teaching of Catholic divines, though they did agree that Rahner's version (1957–1968) might seek to arouse interest in new issues. In 1961 Rahner got a freer hand when he began planning a second, and more Rahnerian, *Lexikon*. This was *Sacramentum Mundi* (1967–1969), described by Rahner as a '*summa* of theological knowledge in alphabetical order'. But most Rahnerian of all was the pocket version (well, by Teutonic standards), the 1961 *Kleine theologische Wörterbuch*. Co-authored with Rahner's future biographer and fellow Jesuit, Herbert Vorgrimler, this 'dictionary' was deliberately set within the perspectives of Rahner's personal thought.

The third genre to which Rahner set his hand (and the hands of others) was the *quaestio disputata*, a series of which began to appear from the publishing house Herder of Freiburg in 1958, sixteen from Rahner's pen, either alone or with a co-author. Re-opening questions often considered closed in Neo-Scholastic divinity, a number of these volumes influenced the fathers of the Second Vatican Council. Thus the *questio disputata* on revelation and tradition written jointly by Rahner and Joseph Ratzinger (1927–) had its effect on *Dei Verbum*, Vatican II's Dogmatic Constitution on Divine Revelation; and that on episcopacy and primacy (from the same hands) influenced *Lumen Gentium*, the Dogmatic Constitution on the Church;[90] while the ample treatment accorded to the deacon's office in *Diaconia in Christo* played a major part in securing the restoration of the permanent diaconate in the Latin Church.[91] The hundredth *Quaestio disputata*, the penultimate volume prior to Rahner's death and the last he co-authored (with the German Jesuit historian of theology Heinrich Fries) was the controversial proposal for Church reunion *Einigung der Kirchen: reale Möglichkeit* (1983).[92] Fourth, convinced that, owing to the mushrooming of theological specialisations, it was no longer possible for one person to write a Catholic dogmatics, Rahner organised a team of writers to produce *Mysterium Salutis* (1965–1976). The finest (multi-volume) study to emanate from the theologians of the generation of the Council, and far from exclusively (or even predominantly) Rahnerian in mould, it remains the best guide to the thought world in which the Council proceeded. It is a beautiful recreation of the common doctrine of the Church, the last till the production of a *Catechism of the Catholic Church* in the early 1990s. Rahner's pessimism about the way pullulating erudition and the philosophical pluralism of Catholic intellectual life in the later twentieth century had disabled any individual from writing a dogmatics did not extend, however, to fundamental theology, where, in a long tradition of German Catholic thinkers since the Enlightenment he produced — and this was his final major undertaking — his own account of the rational grounds for treating key claims of Christian doctrine as truth-inducing, in the shape of the *Grundkurs des Glaubens. Einführung in den Begriff des Christentums* (1976), in English translation *Foundations of Christian Faith*.

If during his lifetime Rahner's Mariology and Eucharistic theology were, even before Vatican II opened, treated with wariness by Church authority, by the time of his death a more wide-ranging debate about the salutariness of his (undoubtedly extensive) influence on modern Catholic theology was gestating. In part, Rahner stood trial for transcendental Thomism as a whole, with its particular view of the all-important relation joining humankind (too deterministically?) with the God of grace. Here the concept of 'anonymous Christianity', and its implications for missionary activity, classically understood, was key. But in part the anxieties arose from the deployment of the variegated Rahnerian inheritance by others, among whom were those more consistently radical than himself. From Rahner's basic option in linking the theology of creation so intimately to soteriology, via the concept of the supernatural existential affecting as it does every man who comes into this world, it followed that:

> ... the kingdom of God itself is coming to be in the history of the world (not only in that of the Church) wherever obedience to God occurs in grace as the acceptance of God's self-communication.[93]

The desire to revalorise the theological significance of the world could not, however, be satisfied at the expense of taking away the unique salvific role of the Church (and so of explicit faith in Christ as Saviour). The critics of Rahner's 'anonymous Christianity' notion were not always content with Rahner's formulation of the Church-world distinction as when, for instance, he called the Church

> ... the eschatological and efficacious manifestation (sign) in redemptive history that in the unity, activity, fraternity, etc of the *world* the kingdom of God is at hand.[94]

If the world simply needs the Church so as to become in the widest sense 'sacramental', then both the creational sacrality of the cosmos and the unique soteric reality of the Church seem devalued.

6 | Incarnation or eschatology?

These assertions (and the questions they provoked) formed part of a wider debate in Catholic theology on the eve of the Second Vatican Council's opening, especially in the French-speaking *milieux* largely responsible for *Gaudium et spes*, the Council's Pastoral Constitution on the Church in the Modern World. The French Catholic Renaissance, co-terminous, more or less, with the Third Republic, had been originally literary and social in character. Through their prose and poetry, Péguy and Claudel had invoked a new vision of Christian society. Turning to the Latin Middle Ages for inspiration they hoped for a re-birth of specifically Christian philosophy and social values, expressed in a Christian architecture and a Christian music (these were the years of the recovery of the Latin church's classical voice, Gregorian chant) — and even a renaissance of Christian chivalry, *le scoutisme*. In the sharp dispute over whether to permit non-believing (or Jewish) artists to produce work in radically contemporary styles for use in places of cult, the '*querelle de l'art sacré*' which agitated Catholic opinion from 1945 to 1955, their 'integral' successors argued for retaining the absolute integrity of the faith through detachment of the Church from the secular cultural milieu.[95] In Belgium, by contrast, the apologists of the *Jeunesse ouvrière chrétienne* or Young Christian Workers began from the opposite conviction: just because they were living in a largely dechristianised society they must re-implant the Church and its doctrine at an elementary level. It was no longer the historical method but history with a capital 'H' which exercised their house theologians, such as the Dominican Marie-Dominique Chenu (1895–1990). Here the watchwords were those of engagement, incarnation and presence in the world. These differing inspirations form the background of much Francophone theology just before the Council, as also after it, and from the two groups of partisans that correspond to them — 'integral Catholics' and 'theological humanists' (also referred to on occasion in the literature as 'integral humanists') — the considerable internal tensions of French Catholicism today largely derive.[96]

The integralists had it in their favour that a rich and complex religion aiming of its nature at the transformation of the whole of life cannot exist without creating a culture to sustain it. The theological humanists had on their side the fact that the secular world — in its very secularity — contains elements of truth and goodness, and with that secular world the history of the Church shows a constant give-and-take. Over against both of these tendencies, however, and less connected with the stratagems of cultural politics, stood a third party, whose watchword was 'eschatological theology'. Daniélou (at any rate until the later sessions of the Council) and his fellow patrologist Louis Bouyer (1913–1997), priest of Bérulle's *Oratoire de France*, set themselves resolutely against any confounding of the Kingdom of God with human achievement. There is a duty to transform *les réalités terrestres* insofar as that lies in our power, but to speak of such transformation as, in a phrase beloved by some theological humanists, the 'flower' which becomes the 'fruit' of the Kingdom, makes of that Kingdom no more than the result of human progress. Treating historical forms of human organisation, the arts and even the advances of technology as prefigurements of the Kingdom was at best a gross Neo-Pelagianism, and at worst smacked of a pagan apotheosis of created things. In the German-speaking Church, Guardini and Josef Pieper (1904–1997) concurred: the transposition of the temporal into the supra-temporal can only be achieved by God; history's meaning lies in his judgement, to be anticipated only in hope. Marxism and Existentialism as Promethean revolts against the Christian doctrine of history could hardly expect to be accommodated within it.

There were also intermediate positions, such as that of Yves Congar (1905–1995), for whom only the Church is meta-history rather than history, since in its life mysteries lying beyond time are actively present; still the Christian is called to 'christo-finalise' the world, for which both engagement (incarnationalism) and detachment (eschatology) are required, thus his ecclesiological studies *Esquisses du Mystère de l'Eglise*, whose second edition appeared in 1953, and *Jalons pour une théologie du laïcat* of the same year. A Christological (rather than ecclesiological) attempt to reconcile the parties was represented by Balthasar's *Theologie der Geschichte* (1959): since Christ is the only norm of history, Christians can elect to exemplify different aspects of that norm, by keeping eschatological distance from the world, or by choosing incarnationally some position in the world under Christ.

The three-cornered controversy between eschatological theologians, theological humanists and integralists foreshadows the debate over a theology of secularisation (ushered in by an over-zealous humanism) and theology of liberation (formally speaking, in its rejection of an autonomous natural sphere in civil society closer to integralism) in the years following the Second Vatican Council.

VII THE COUNCIL AND BEYOND

1 | The Second Vatican Council

At the Second Vatican Council, 'the Rhine' (which washes both France and Germany) 'flowed into the Tiber': for the Council's teaching can be seen as a precipitate of the intellectual activity of the finest German- and French-speaking theology of the inter-War period. If many of the distinctive emphases and insights of the Council derive from that source, they were also contextualised in documents offering overviews of the whole Christian economy in a way reminiscent of patristic theology at its best, and exhibiting at least at times the concern for careful conceptualisation typical of Christian Scholasticism – for, despite the impression left on some, it was by no means the Council fathers' intention to drop Scholastic thought from the Church's baggage-train.

While addressing itself to almost every major aspect of Church life, the Council had surprisingly little to say about the place of theologians in the Church. Its concept of theology, if clearest in *Optatam totius*, an account of priestly formation, must be pieced together from here and there in its documents. It emphasised (though the stress fell on many deaf ears) the importance of philosophy's role in Catholic thought – both 'that philosophical patrimony which is forever valid', an obvious reference to Thomism and related approaches as a *philosophia perennis*, and also 'modern philosophical studies', notably those influential in the student's own region. The Thomists were thus to be rewarded — but not at the expense of *nouvelle théologie*. For this was no mere matter of 'Know your enemies'. In recommending that

> ... the history of philosophy should be taught in such a manner that students may grasp the fundamental principles of the various systems, retaining those elements which are proved to be true while being able to detect and refute those which are false,[97]

the Council fathers steered a middle course between the Toulouse Thomists — not only incidental truths mentioned *en passant* but also elements from other 'fundamental principles' may be borrowed — and the 'new theologians', to whom the idea of an enhancement (however thoroughgoing) of the 'perennial philosophy' did not appeal. In continuity with the Leonine programme, students must be helped to see the connection between such philosophical argumentation and the mysteries of salvation as contemplated by theology 'in the higher light of faith'.

In its account of the sources of theology the Council gave priority to Scripture, and here too it could echo Leo XIII in the latter's description of the Bible as the 'soul of theology'. It proposed that students be trained in both literal and spiritual interpretation, receiving after a suitable introductory course (here no doubt the broad lines of a Catholic approach to Scripture in the great tradition would be sketched) an initiation into exegetical method — of a contemporary (evidently) historical-critical kind. They were to study the principal 'themes' of divine revelation — a reference, this, to the 'biblical theology' in which both Protestant and Catholic authors had hoped, despite the diversity of the biblical Canon (and even of particular books within it), to lay out in coherent fashion the content of this or that motif as found in Scripture as a whole. They were also to find personal nourishment in the spiritual exegesis of the sacred writings, thus showing that the predominant 'technique' of Fathers and mediaevals as well as the mystics and the Liturgy was not, in a fit of enthusiasm for the higher criticism, to find itself shelved.

After Scripture, the Council unhesitatingly placed next the Fathers of the Church. The theological student is to learn

...what the Fathers of the Church, both of the East and West, have contributed towards the faithful transmission and elucidation of each of the revealed truths...[98]

though in point of fact the presence of the Fathers in much progressive post-Conciliar theology was as little palpable as in the most maligned manualist Scholasticism — indeed, less so.

Furnished with this solid biblical and patristic basis for his investigation of the Church's faith, the student should then proceed to the history of dogma (note the salutary lesson learned from Modernism), finishing with a more speculative exploration of the mysteries of salvation, 'with St Thomas as teacher' (hardly a Modernist conclusion). That last requirement underlined the uniquely exemplary fashion in which Thomas is a *doctor fidei*, with particular reference to the comprehensiveness of his account of revelation and his sense of the inter-connection of all its parts.

The investigation of the sources of theology does not take place, however, in the Council's ideal construction of Catholic thought, without some reference to 'experience' — that elusive concept which, tarred and feathered in the turn-of-the-century doctrinal crisis, had gradually been rehabilitated when considered in its office as an 'aid to discernment' for the scanning of revelation — in the 1940s and 1950s. If a reference to experience in *Optatam totius* is somewhat guarded (students should 'learn to seek the solution of human problems in the light of revelation'), a more generous account is offered in *Gaudium et spes*:

> With the help of the Holy Spirit, it is the task of the whole people of God, particularly of its pastors and theologians, to listen to and distinguish the many voices of our times and to interpret them in the light of the divine Word, in order that the revealed truth may be more deeply penetrated, better understood, and more suitably presented.[99]

But the results of such interpretative activity remain within the general rubric which governs the Council's entire account of the theological enterprise:

> Theological subjects should be taught in the light of faith, under the guidance of the magisterium of the Church.[100]

The Council's own teaching was, of course, an exercise of that same magisterium: what did it add to the common doctrine of the entire period this study has covered? Since its *modus operandi* was renovation by recovery of the sources modified by adjustment to the changed conditions of the times,[101] it did not so much innovate as re-present — hence its frequent denomination as a 'pastoral' Council. *En route*, however, it re-shaped the doctrinal tradition in some not negligible respects. Thus in its fundamental theology, expressed in the Dogmatic Constitution *Dei Verbum*, it emphasised in holistic manner that revelation is a disclosure of the divine life and salvation through Christ to persons — while leaving, however, a salient place to articulate teaching (sometimes called the 'propositional view of revelation') in its scheme. It gave priority, accordingly, to the unity of Sacred Writ and Holy Tradition over against their differentiation. *Dei Verbum* spoke for the first time in any document of the magisterium of the factors impelling that homogeneous development in the understanding of doctrine to which the First Vatican Council had already drawn attention, singling out contemplation and believing study for special comment. It emphasised that the 'sacred deposit of the Word of God' (Scripture interpreted in Tradition) is entrusted to all the faithful *in solidum*, whilst insisting on the uniquely authoritative role of the construal of the transmitted revelation by pope and bishops. It commended investigation of the historical-critical method in its illumination of the literal sense of Scripture while warning against an exegesis that would undermine historicity — above all in the crucial area of the Gospels. It probably (but not certainly, the burden of the text is disputed) spoke of that consequence of biblical inspiration which theological tradition has termed 'inerrancy' as truth relevant to God's saving purpose summed up in Christ, rather than truth *simpliciter*.

The heart of the Council's teaching lay in its ecclesiology — even if, in a sociologically preoccupied age the fathers wisely did not let evocations of the churchly society stand alone, without reference to the Word of God. In *Lumen Gentium*, the Dogmatic Constitution on the Church, the Second *Vaticanum* completed the project of the First by promulgating a doctrine of the episcopate, but contextualised this within an account, at once mysteric and institutional, of the wider Church. Only after speaking of the origins of the Church in the Trinity (the Father calls believers together in the Church; the Son enjoys there the anticipation of his reign over the human race for man's salvation; the Holy Spirit indwells it and hallows it), does the Constitution describe the Church in and for itself. Touching on a large number of biblical figures for the Church, verbal icons which serve to indicate facets of its form, *Lumen Gentium*, following the example of Pius XIII's *Mystici Corporis Christi* gives pride of place to the language of the body of Christ as a way of expressing the Church's transcendentally mysterious yet concretely social being.

> The society equipped with hierarchical organs, the visible group, the earthly Church, is not to be viewed as a different entity from the mystical body of Christ, the spiritual fellowship, the Church endowed with heavenly blessings; they constitute one complex reality, made up of a human and a divine element. It is no trivial analogy which likens the Church to the mystery of the Word incarnate. The nature assumed by the divine Word serves him, to whom it is indissolubly united, as a living organ of salvation; in like fashion the social structure of the Church serves Christ's Spirit, who vivifies it, for the increase of the body.[102]

This was a lesson ill learned by those who after the Council, disappointed at the moderation of its reform, would rapidly become disenchanted with what they termed (in the light of this passage we must say in 'Nestorian' fashion) the 'institutional Church'.

The life of the Church is, then, sacramental — a matter of visible signs for invisible grace. Now sacramental signs make sense only communally, for without the specifying discourse of a community their 'language' cannot be read. And so before *Lumen Gentium* describes the sacramental ordering of the Church's life by its hierarchy, it must speak of the unique people of God (Christian, but with a vital Jewish pre-history) as a whole. Those who make up that people constitute a royal priesthood — something seen most clearly in their participation in the apogee of the sacramental 'system', the Mass. They compose a people of prophets not only by virtue of their obligation, one and all, to witness to the gospel, but owing also to the profusion of *charismata* or more personalised gifts, whether ordinary or out-of-the-ordinary, which help to build up the Church. Above all, and this was another signal theme likely to be obscured by a multitude of post-conciliar organisational concerns, the faithful universally are called to holiness.

While there is no suggestion that holiness admits of no grada-
tions or that a general call to holiness may not become the basis
of a more specific and even more urgent divine invitation, it is
clearly laid down that a horizon of infinite holiness is opened up
for everyone by his incorporation through baptism in the body of
Christ, who is the archetype of all creaturely holiness.[103]

Unlike the more imprudent post-Conciliar radicals, the Council treated
the people of God not as a crowd, but as a structured whole. And here its
adjudication of the respective roles of episcopate and papacy was of
great importance, both theological-doctrinal and practical, if not in all
respects entirely clear. By its teaching, couched in language verging on
that used for solemn definitions, that episcopal ordination confers the
fullness of the ministerial priesthood (and hence of the apostolic
ministry, of which that priesthood is the central office), the Council
restored to vigour in Latin theology the high patristic and Oriental
doctrine of the bishop's office; by presenting the bishops as not simply
a collection of individuals but a *collegium* ('college'), *ordo* ('order'),
coetus ('group'), *Lumen Gentium* re-created the notion of the global episcopate as the proper vis-à-vis of the universal pastorate of the pope. The
episcopal college, it stressed, does not, however, exercise supreme
authority without its papal head; whether the pope's office is to be
understood isomorphically, as the expression of his headship of the
college, remains a moot point among the Council's interpreters. What
was clear, at any rate, was that mutual *affectus* should circulate among
the members of the college, and between college and head; or to render
that point made by *intimiste* language in a vocabulary better suited to
the Church's public mission: impulses beneficial for her apostolic life
were to reach the pope (and, in practice, his curia) from the bishops,
and by the same token, impulses were not to be prevented from
reaching the bishops, and the rest of the Church, from its papal head
(and his curial instrument). This interflow did not always work
smoothly in the Church after the Council and, given the imperfect
state of human affairs even in the church, the removal of all such friction
is unlikely before the End. The eschatological thrust of the closing
sections of the Constitution, on monasticism and the Blessed Virgin
Mary as lodestar of the pilgrim Church, put such matters in their proper
perspective.

The third and last of the Dogmatic Constitutions (though the first to be voted), *Sacrosanctum Concilium* on the Sacred Liturgy, may be dealt with more briefly. Its preamble saw the Church's worship (with the Eucharistic Sacrifice at its heart) in exalted terms: the continuance of our redemption; the manifestation of the mystery of the Church; the fortifying of the faithful for preaching to others. In terms indebted to Casel:

> Recalling thus the mysteries of redemption, the Church opens to the faithful the riches of her Lord's powers and merits, so that these are in some way made present at all times, and the faithful are enabled to lay hold of them and become filled with saving grace.[104]

Recommending (in, for the most part, rather perilously general terms) the 'promotion and reform' of, in particular, the Roman rite, the council fathers drew on the best insights of the Liturgical Movement, while also incorporating into their text formulae favouring 'noble simplicity' and 'active participation' which somewhat played into the hands of iconoclasts and populists, opening the door in the post-Conciliar period to deformations of liturgical practice inspired by excessive didacticism, the instrumentalisation of worship for purposes of group solidarity, and a wholly inappropriate 'entertainment' ethos.

The Pastoral Constitution on the Church in the Modern World, *Gaudium et spes*, a kind of manifesto of the Church's policies towards the economically, socially, politically and culturally organised 'world' of the time, represented an innovation in genre with which not all the bishops, or their theologians, were well pleased. It constituted, however, a means of bringing together the otherwise scattered statements of the modern popes on issues of public policy, now placed within a theological framework owing much to the debate between incarnationalist and eschatological thinkers in the Church of France. While finding many hopeful symptoms of the tacit working of grace in civil society, *Gaudium et spes* (which after those opening words mentions in the very next breath 'griefs and anxieties') was not so bland as subsequent critics made out. A more substantial criticism may be that it encouraged a tendency by Church leaders to prefer windy statements of grand objectives beyond the attainment of a non-hegemonic religion, when the building up of local projects of an exemplary kind might have borne more fruit. The 'houses of hospitality' of the

American laywoman Dorothy Day (1897–1980) and the more authentically ecclesial of the 'base communities' of Latin America were, however, instances of the latter way.

The Council indeed had of set purpose weakened Catholicism's civil role in societies where Catholics made up the great majority of state citizens by certain concessions to the classically Liberal view of the relation between religion and the civil order. Here the influence of the American Jesuit philosopher John Courtney Murray (1904–1967) was paramount, though Murray himself considered his attack on the confessional State to be, rather, a Thomistic recovery of the dual finality of supernatural and natural, Church and civil polity, most clearly displayed in John of Paris (d 1306).[105] *Dignitatis humanae*, the Council's Decree on Religious Freedom, while maintaining in principle the duty of the juridical 'person' of the State to accept the claims of revelation, directed as these are to public life together as well as to the *foyer* of the heart, simultaneously renounced the traditional call of Church authority on the rulers of Catholic societies to inhibit the open propagation of moral and religious positions alien to the orthodox Gospel. The claim that the document represented nonetheless a case of homogeneous doctrinal development (specifically of the firm datum of the tradition that no one can be coerced into professing the Catholic religion) would subsequently be disputed, and produce the only significant act of schism to follow on the Council, with the departure from Catholic communion of the former archbishop of Dakar, Marcel Lefebvre, and five fellow bishops, of whom four were his own consecrees. The canonical situation of priests and layfolk in the Lefebvrist movement, much of which was fuelled by a perception of liturgical abuses, remained obscure.

'False' ecumenism was a further gravamen of traditionally minded Catholics against their more 'Progressive' brethren; the 'true' ecumenism which is its foil had nowhere been set out more clearly, however, than in the Council's own 'Decree'.

2 | Catholic ecumenism

The objection of the Papacy to the Ecumenical Movement as originally constituted was to its confessedly non-doctrinal character. Pragmatic, idealist (in the ethical sense of that word), theologically liberal, the 'Life and Work' phase of early ecumenism was unpropitious to Catholic participation. Its 'Faith and Order' counterpart — brought later to birth but soon shooting past its sibling in inter-church stature — took seriously the doctrinal and structural elements in ecclesial life, and so had better claims as a conversation partner. Anglican as distinct from sheerly Protestant in complexion, at a time when the Catholic move-ment in Anglicanism was still buoyant, if past the crest of its wave, Faith and Order yet aroused reservations among the Orthodox (who for reasons both theological and political participated nonetheless in its Conferences). As for the Catholics, Pope Pius XI spoke a firm *non possumus* in his encyclical letter *Mortalium animos* of 1927. The reason was the same in both cases: by speaking of the Church of Christ as, like Humpty Dumpty, needing putting together again, official ecumenism was still too little sensitive to the perils of indifferentism. Neither Ortho-doxy nor Catholicism could regard themselves as just possible variants of the Gospel: each saw itself as morally and mystically identical with the Body of Christ.

Pius XI's letter had not closed all doors, however, and under his successor, Pius XII, the Holy Office by its letter *Ecclesia sancta* of 1949 recognised that the movement derived its basic impulse from the inspiration of 'the Holy Spirit', and so should constitute a 'source of holy joy' for Catholics. They were to take its efforts seriously while simultaneously insisting on the need for return to the divinely established centre of unity for the Christian world, the Petrine see. In this perspective, the setting up of a 'Secretariat for Promoting Christian Unity' by Pope John XXIII in 1960, and its members' contribution to the Council's Decree on Ecumenism, was by no means a *volte-face*, a case of adoring what one had burned. An 'ecclesiology of return' (to Catholic unity, around Peter) was nuanced in the reigns of the conciliar popes by the admission that authentic 'elements of the Church' (and not simply uncovenanted graces) persisted even where bonds of visible fellowship were broken (or had never existed), and the consequent confession that Christ's Church 'subsists in', but is not exhaustively coterminous with, the Catholic body. The determination, expressed by the Conciliar decree *Unitatis redintegratio*, to affirm, by way of priority, what Christians hold in common, and to express that shared heritage by programmes of joint action and a degree of *communicatio in sacris* (common worship), struck nevertheless what were to all but a minority of Catholic thinkers (and believers) unaccustomed notes.

If in the decades immediately succeeding the Council's close, observers would note a degree of 'Protestantisation' of Western Catholic attitudes, this could hardly be laid, however, at the Decree's door. The text not only warned against an evil spirit of concessionary compromise that would sell doctrine short; it also placed *rapprochement* with the separated Eastern churches at the head of its agenda. Though in the period, with its more doctrinally responsible Protestantism, there was as yet no sense of a tug-of-war between those favouring ecumenism with the separated East and those who preferred to seek common ground with the Reform, still, of the three founding fathers of Catholic ecumenism only one, the abbé Paul Couturier (1881–1953), looked chiefly Westwards.[106] Of the other two, the Dominican Yves Congar had early set his face Eastwards, though with more than occasional glances at Canterbury and Wittenberg,[107] while the fact that Dom Lambert Beauduin (1873–1960) was the founder of a bi-ritual (Latin-Byzantine) 'monastery of union' whose energies were fully directed to the world of the Orthodox speaks for itself.[108]

The Conciliar decree had distinguished between 'churches' – bodies isomorphic with the local churches of the Catholic Church itself save for the feature of communion with the Roman see – and 'ecclesial communities', where other crucial elements of a Christian commonwealth were lacking – above all, continuance in the apostolic succession to which a plenary sacramental life and corporate instinct for the apostolic preaching are linked. The Catholic Church after the Council might recognise, therefore, a degree of limited communion with the latter groups on the basis of the baptismal priesthood of all believers (and that is far from nugatory), but with the Orthodox it could speak a language of imperfect eucharistic communion that enabled it to offer its own sacraments to Orthodox cut off by circumstances from their own and desiderate like privileges in return.

Not all dialogues with particular Christian confessions aimed in the short or even middle term at organic reunion.[109] In those that did, one of two methods was adopted. Either the dialogue partners sought to return beyond the historical moment of schism to the patristic and scriptural origins of disputed doctrines and practice (as in the conversations between Rome and Canterbury) or they proposed to build on common ground before exploring disputed territory (the procedure adopted with the Eastern Orthodox). With the smaller Oriental churches out of communion with Rome, where the disputed questions, formally at least, affected only Christology, a suggested formula of concord and a package of practical assistance for what were by and large beleaguered communities comprised the contents of the ecumenical box of delights. While the response of the Chalcedonian Orthodox (those living in peace and communion with the church of Constantinople) was, in general, cool, other non- or 'pre'-Chalcedonian churches, like the Syrian Orthodox in communion with the Jacobite patriarch of Antioch, were more forthcoming. Into all such questions there entered, however, issues of national, ethnic, and cultural belonging where those who represented Catholicism in the various 'bilateral' dialogues were relatively impotent to leave much mark. In the case of dialogue with those communities dating from the sixteenth-century Western Reformation that had retained (or regained) much of the patristic (and even mediaeval) development, notably Anglicanism, what set limits to advance was, rather, awareness of the internally heterogeneous character of their doctrinal identity and the consequent impossibility, in bodies lacking some dialogue to the Catholic magisterium, of making credal compacts stick.

If the likelihood of any major Christian body resuming bonds of ecclesial fellowship with Rome was small (the most hopeful of such openings, from the vantage point of the later 1990s, were with such relatively minor bodies as the Assyrian 'Church of the East' and the Polish National Church, a discontented annex of the Old Catholic Union of Utrecht, though at the time of writing negotiations are afoot for a restoration of local Catholic-Orthodox unity in the patriarchate of Antioch — with all the problems of 'mediate communion' that may raise), Catholic theology (and to a lesser extent philosophy) had been affected nonetheless by exposure to the theological worlds of Anglicanism, Lutheranism and Orthodoxy. The question for the future would be how well the antennae of intellectual discernment were operating, as they sought to distinguish what in these various inheritances was congruent with Catholic faith, and what sat, merely, in uneasy juxtaposition.

The principal benefit of ecumenical reflection was practical: the more generous atmosphere in which relations with separated Christians, with Jews,[110] and ultimately with the adherents of other religions (and none),[111] were carried on. Its subsidiary benefit lay in the realm of ideas, where notions derived from non-Catholic religious (and not simply philosophical) contexts could more readily be borrowed as instruments for the re-appropriation of the Church's own belief. Unfortunately, Catholic ecumenism when considered en bloc, prior to the differentiation of its 'true' and 'false' morphologies, also had the vices of its virtues. Softening the urgent tones in which the uniqueness of Catholic and, in the context of other religions, Christian claims had hitherto been announced, it blurred the contours of theological identity and thus helped precipitate the formation of those 'party' responses, whether Conservative or Progressive, which are so marked a feature of modern Catholicism. If Paul VI had predicted that the Second Vatican Council would be the most positive of all ecumenical councils thanks to 'the Church's spiritual and numerical confluence' and 'the complete and peaceful unity of its hierarchy',[112] observers with hindsight during the

162

pontificate of Pope John Paul II Wojtyła (b 1920) could comment ruefully that, while the Council might perhaps have augmented the unity of Christians, it had certainly diminished that of Catholics themselves.

3 | *Concilium* or *Communio?*

The Conciliar fathers of the Second *Vaticanum* had, then, underestimated the unsettling effect of disturbing the post-Tridentine religious culture in place in the Church at the beginning of the 1960s. Or to be more precise, they did not reckon with the heady cocktail which resulted when the policies they put in place (or were believed by not always disinterested critics to have authorised) mixed with the crisis of general culture in Western Europe and North America in that decade. The frames of reference within which the Council texts could be understood suddenly multiplied — and shifted. If any Catholic theologians, including *periti* from the Council sessions themselves, took it as axiomatic that the conciliar teaching of Vatican II could only legitimately be interpreted (like all other Councils) within the great tradition, others (who also numbered former *periti* among their ranks) sought to radicalise the Council's achievement by reference to the demands of a changed modernity in culture and society, to the needs, real or supposed, of a global future that transcended a 'Eurocentric' Church, of ecumenism (whether intra-Christian or the 'wider ecumenism' of inter-religious dialogue), and the hope, expressed in Marxian or other fashionable terms, for a large-scale emancipation of men and women from human bondage. The journal founded, in the first flush of conciliar optimism to continue, at the level of theology and related disciplines, the impetus of the Council (named, accordingly, *Concilium*) had become within a five-year period the effective preserve of the second group, those who proposed a hermeneutic key of a liberal-radical kind, and considered the conciliar texts to be only a beginning. Inhospitable, so it was felt, to representatives of the first group, the latter re-constituted themselves in the service of an alternative organ, *Communio*, whose name, with its implicit reference not only to the inner mystery of the Church but also to the Trinitarian persons themselves, suggested their main message: only by continuous contact with the dogmatic heart of revelation could Catholicism offer to humanity something qualitatively distinct, indeed unique, as opposed to a swiftly baptised version of secular panaceas. The question '*Concilium* or *Communio*?' is not altogether inapt, therefore, as a label for the post-Conciliar theological *mêlée*.

The Swiss-born Tübingen professor Hans Küng (b 1928) and the Dutch-based but Flemish-born Dominican Edward Schillebeeckx (b 1914) can stand for the first. Küng (who was deprived of his *missio canonica* or licence to teach in the Church's name in 1979 and strictly speaking, therefore, no longer counts as a recognised Catholic theologian) began writing in a philo-Barthian spirit and has (so far) ended in a somewhat bare monotheism intended to reconcile the three 'Abrahamic' faiths of Judaism, Christianity and Islam. He is the stormier petrel of the two. Schillebeeckx, whose early theology (now largely repudiated by its author) consisted of a Thomism warmed by personalist elements and rendered more modern in tone by phenomenological ones, did not move so far to the 'left', either absolutely or even proportionately, when, convinced in the late 1960s of a massive rupture in the human outlook, he determined to clothe in the mantle of the human sciences the body, stripped of its antique clothing, of Christian belief. The two men are joined, however, by similar options in Christology and ecclesiology, regarding the definitions of the patristic Councils about Christ as largely irrelevant to a contemporary, 'praxis-oriented' faith which looks to other aspects of the New Testament Scriptures than the high Christology of John for its presentation, and viewing the inherited structure of the Catholic Church — a hierarchically ordered, sacramentally hieratic institution — as alien both to primitive Church order and the democratic spirit of the times.

If such shared positions of Küng and Schillebeeckx are commonplaces of Liberal Protestantism, their more specific emphases are comparatively *sui generis*. If Küng's early writing (until 1970) transgressed the distinction between true and false ecumenism by down-playing distinctively catholic Christian tenets and re-constructing Reformation history in the interests of eirenicism,[113] and his middle period (1970–1983) showed a determination to interpret New Testament origins (vis-à-vis various aspects of Christian doctrine) through the lens of the historical-critical method,[114] his latest writing (from 1983 onwards) takes as its *Leitmotiv* the global convergence of religions through a 'critical conversation' between them.

Schillebeekcx's theological career divides into two sections only, separated by his experience of the fallout from the explosion of student radicalism in both North America and Western Europe in the years 1967–1968. Struck by the predominance in the United States (which he toured in 1967) of (Protestant) theologies of secularisation and the 'death of God', he was shattered by the cognate experience of alienation from the traditional language of faith of the 'New Left'-influenced segment of university students nearer home. Believing that the doctrinal, catechetical and homiletic tradition had undergone rupture, he conceived of a need to forge a new 'God-language', based on eschatological notions of God as the 'Future of man', and given cutting-edge, in a sociologically obsessed age, by the utopian critique of human social arrangements such a concept fostered. Immersing himself in the writings of the Frankfurt School of heavily revisionist Marxism, as later in the theory of ideal communication originated by the German philosopher Jürgen Habermas (1929–), Schillebeeckx befriended at once the so-called 'critical communities' of the Dutch church, hostile not only to papal but also to episcopal leadership as these generally were, and also a group of younger Dutch and Belgian 'theologians of contestation' in the Faculty of Münster — though it is important to note that what these gentlemen were contesting was not only 'institutional Catholicism' but also the theology of secularisation, now seen as a capitulation to bourgeois man. Schillebeeckx's watchword or phrase became 'mystical politics', where the Church will speak of God chiefly by a rhetoric, in gesture as in word, of resistance to the negativities of man's inhumanity to man.

Communio brought together those Council *periti* who were most disturbed by the disorientation of the post-Conciliar period (this was not the Church they had hoped to see) — thus de Lubac and Ratzinger, as well as figures who had not attended its sessions — either because they were insufficiently favoured by bishops, as with Balthasar, or simply too young, as with Walter Kasper. And the second of each of those pairs may stand proxy here for the rest. Ratzinger's career was unique in that alone of all the Catholic thinkers this book has considered he was given official responsibility for the state of the Church's intellectual culture — as Prefect of the Congregation for the Doctrine of the Faith (the former Holy Office of the Inquisition). In this onerous apostolate he drew on a wide-ranging historical-theological culture (he had written major works on Augustine's ecclesiology and Bonaventure's theology of history) and the experience of teaching all the major dogmatic tractates in a variety of German universities. Equipped with an acute philosophical sense and an eye for the directions in which political, cultural and even liturgical choices might lead (qualities not always possessed by simple historians of theology), he aimed to consolidate the common doctrine of the Church both by criticising the not always felicitous theological work of others and proposing happier conceptual mediations of his own. That twofold aim translated easily enough into the post-Conciliar redefinition of the Holy Office's task: not only to censure bad theology but also (through the instrumentality in particular of the Pontifical International Theological Commission of which the Prefect was simultaneously president) to encourage good.

If Ratzinger was Bavarian and not too many worlds removed in outlook from the nineteenth-century Munich school, Kasper was a Swabian, born near Tübingen and destined to spend his entire studious and professorial life in that university (bar a short spell at Munich) until his nomination as bishop of Stuttgart-Rottenburg (the diocese of which Tübingen is the jewel) in 1981. His intellectual nourishment came, then, from the Catholic Tübingen school, to which diet supplementation was added from the teaching of its mid-nineteenth-century Roman counterpart, thanks to the doctoral research which produced *Die Lehre von der Tradition in der Römischen Schule* of 1962. And if, in arguing for the consonance of those two schools, he identified their common theme as the primacy of Tradition as the perennially fruitful principle of authority for Catholic thought (the role of the magisterium being, simply, the making of partial yet abidingly valuable determinations of Tradition's content), he did the philosophical aspect of the Tübingen inheritance no less justice in his retrieval, in the service of faith, of Schelling's thought, and notably his concept of the Absolute as freedom: thus *Das Absolute in der Geschichte. Philosophie und Theologie der Geschichte in der Spätphilosophie Schellings* (1965). Conscious of the need for metaphysical authority in theological discourse (despite, or because of, the neglect of the same by theologians who looked to phenomenology, the philosophy of language, sociology or psychology as their preferred intellectual handmaiden), Kasper was able to make the Schellengian questions — How do created spirits as finite freedoms come forth from the infinite Freedom which is God? and, How, when they oppose themselves to God, is the resultant estrangement from him overcome? — *Leitmotiven* to guide the two dogmatic studies of his mature period, *Der Gott Jesu Christi* (1982) and *Jesus der Christus* (1974). Kasper's formula for the re-invigoration of theology was 'a renewal of both tradition and speculation', for over against reductionist theological programmes he considered a truly theological theology to be the 'only appropriate answer to modern atheism'[115] (hence speculation), while theological progress is only possible when we act on the truth that remembrance is the essence of the psyche (hence tradition).

4 | Liberation theology

Liberation theology in its European — as distinct from Latin American — roots derives from the severe critique mounted against the theology of secularisation by a school of theologians in Münster, in Westphalia, who gathered around the figure of Johann Baptist Metz (b 1928). That theology of *'les réalités terrestres'*, with its concern for the historical process, for the nature of economic society, and for the problem of work, which had preoccupied the theological humanists, of whom Marie-Dominique Chenu was the most distinguished representative in immediately pre-Conciliar France, had taken a metaphysically (but hardly socially) radical turn. The dominant sociological thinking of the early 1960s believed in a global process of secularisation — meaning not, as previously, the transfer of church institutions to state direction or church property to civil ownership, but the very effacement of the sacred itself. Among a number of Protestant theological radicals, both German and Anglo-Saxon, the advent of a 'religionless Christianity' in a 'secular city' was hailed with enthusiasm as a set of peculiarly propitious conditions for a Gospel which proclaimed the end of immature dependence on the deity and in its place, empowerment to act as free men and women, thanks to the spirit (capitalised or not) released by

Christ on the Cross. Such writings, in translation or otherwise, began to affect Catholics in a Church more disoriented by the Conciliar reform than the latter's makers had believed possible.[116] By 1970, however, a brand of political theology was emerging, notably in Münster but also in Louvain, for which such aspersion of secular liberalism with holy water was deemed no more than a new Constantinianism, a convenient marriage of the Gospel with the existing world, an abandonment of Christianity's innovatory quality and prophetic cutting edge.[117] 'Secularisation theology' thus found itself under attack from the Church's political Left (most sharply by Metz, these were the years of radicalisation of a hitherto staidly stable federal Germany) as also from the theological Right (of whom Daniélou, horrified by the collapse of doctrinal confidence in the Church of France, was in this respect the most prominent representative).

The 'political theology' or 'theology of revolution' produced in Münster derived from the reflection that transcendental Thomism (the intellectual background of the new school) had given precious little attention to human sociality. Its philosophical starting-point was the individual human spirit, not the social relations it enjoyed (or endured) through bodily communication with others. But devotees of the Judaeo-Christian Scriptures would hardly be content with that anodyne appreciativeness of the contemporary *polis* found among theologians of secularisation. In a sense the debate concerned two views of Hegel: did that master of modern political thought identify (correctly) as the true end of the social process a civil society capable of satisfying (and stimulating) multifarious human needs (in which case welfare capitalism did rather well), or did he suppose (quite properly) that the crucial issue is the final working out of the dialectic of 'lordship' and 'bondage', the probably (or even certainly) conflictual creation of a world without a whiff of servitude − in a word, a socialist society.

In Latin America, meanwhile, human needs far more palpable than those registered by the Protestant divines of the East Coast academies, and slavery of a sort far grosser than that identified by the post-Hegelian conscience of politicised theologians in the German faculties, were pressing bishops at the Medellín Congress of the Latin American episcopate in 1968 to adopt high-profile positions on such burning issues, for the abjectly poor, as reform of landholding. Liberation theology results from the meeting between social ferment in Latin America and the emergence of political theology in Western Europe, an encounter taking, often enough, the concrete form of doctoral research by Hispanic or Lusitanian American students in the Catholic faculties of Belgium and Germany. In the event both sides were changed: if Western theologians saw more clearly that secularisation was frequently de-Christianisation and so began to rediscover the pertinence to their theme of the great doctrinal tractates (the Incarnation, the Atonement, grace and salvation), the Latin Americans ran the risk of creating a rupture with not only the popular Catholicism of their continent but also the faith of the wider Church, re-defining redemption as they did in terms of the Godward significance of social, political and economic emancipation — rather than its own. The acceptance by such liberation theologians of a Marxist analysis of society and the historical process (though not of the human person or, of course, of God) did not commend them to Church authority: understandably so, from the view-point of Western scholars, to whom the social and historical elements in dialectical materialism appeared altogether bound up with the meta-physical and areligious.

To say in such a context that henceforth, in the Church, 'practice' must determine 'theory' was not to appeal, in large terms, to the totality of the Christian life, found in the Church's tradition, as the criterion of theological renewal. Rather was it to affirm something more specific. A pre-reflective commitment to those who are exploited (of whom the proletariat will be the most manifest example) was to serve as the originating and self-correcting foundation of all theological theory. It was to prevent this political imperative from becoming an ideological imperialism, however well intentioned, holding both theology and Church in thrall that the Roman see, not without prompting from within the Latin American hierarchies, proposed in a two-part response (negative critique first, 1984, then in 1986, positive) the re-casting of the legitimate evangelical 'option for the poor' into a form more consonant with the tradition at large. Some, like the Peruvian Gustavo Gutiérrez (b 1928), the standard-bearer in his enormously successful *Teologia de la Liberación* (1971) of the new school, listened hard; others, like the Brazilian Franciscan Leonard Boff (b 1938), who after the condemnation of his 'liberation ecclesiology', as found in *Igreja, carisma e poder* (1981) and *E a Igreja se fez povo* (1986), abandoned both priesthood and religious life, did not. In chastened form, liberation theology had won its place in the charmed circle of Catholic theologies — as a theology of the social implications of redemption, rather than an exhaustive account of the redemptive act. Whether the abandonment of Catholicism for evangelical sects by a proportion of the population of Central and South America should be ascribed to the insufficient influence of liberation theology or, on the contrary, to its excessive predominance (or to other factors altogether) remains for historians of the Americas a disputed point.

5 | Morals and man

After liberation theology, the greatest high-tension flash point in post-Conciliar Catholic thought concerned moral theology. In terms of sheer bulk, the most substantial contribution to the immediately pre-Conciliar literature on that subject had come from Jesuits — though the practical conclusions the moralists of the Society arrived at differed little from those urged by their *confrères* in the Dominican, Franciscan and Redemptorist schools. The intellectual roots of the post-Tridentine manuals in morals lay in the declining Middle Ages — and the burgeoning Renaissance. Conscious — as what reader of Scripture could not be? — of the role of divine commandment in biblical ethics, Jesuit moralists took up in moderated form the teaching of Duns Scotus and his successors that morality is founded 'voluntaristically' (from *voluntas*, 'will') on the precepts of God or of those authorised in ecclesial or civil society to speak in God's name. Such a view did inadequate justice *both* to that revelation of the human vocation which is human nature — with the virtues that make it flourish — *and* to the supernatural régime of grace — the infused virtues and other gifts of the Holy Spirit — under which Christians live. The Thomist revival was nowhere more salutary than in its emphatic reiteration of these points.

Unfortunately, the happy alliance of Thomistic and biblical ethics celebrated around the time of the Council was to give way in remarkably
short time to the emerging predominance of novel theological methodologies. It was characteristic of the German Redemptorist Bernard
Häring (1912–) and the American secular priest Charles Curran (1934–)
to retain the general framework of the 'natural law' theory of Thomism
while attempting to reconcile the latter with an appeal to 'contemporary Christian experience'. Criteria for what was authentically evangelical in the latter, and what derived, rather, from a culture presided
over by secular humanists, were not, however, readily forthcoming.
The rise to fortune of the new picture of moral decision-making was
assisted by the adoption of pragmatic standards of morality – largely
determined by the state of the civil law, as well as popular psychology
and notions of 'political correctness' – on the part of a considerable
section of the nominally churched population. Equally unfriendly to
the ethical absolutes for which many of the Christian martyrs had died
was the theory of the moral good dubbed 'proportionalism' from the
fact that it proposed the hegemony, in moral judgement, of a single
principle of 'proportionate reason'. The question, for Proportionalists,
is whether, in some human act, the *proportion* of positive values may
be said to win out over negative – something which can only be nicely
calculated in a way reminiscent of Consequentialism or even Utilitar-
ianism in non-Christian ethical systems. Here one might detect the
influence of Karl Rahner's 'Transcendental Thomist' fundamental
ethics, influenced as these were by the thought of Max Scheler (1874–
1928), transitory convert to Catholicism from early twentieth-century
German phenomenology. For Scheler, absolute moral *values* exist, and
can be known to exist *a priori*, but their decanting in the form of
concrete moral decisions is always a matter of creative flair for which
there can be no absolute *rules*.

The diffusion of these methodologies, in the context of a permissive and
pleasure-seeking (or at least pain-avoiding) culture, already signalled by
clerical and lay dissent from *Humanae Vitae*, Paul VI's 1968 encyclical
letter setting out once again the objections of Catholicism to contracep-
tive practice, caused the greatest difficulties for Church authority in the
realms not only of sexual ethics but of bioethics – the ethics of the origination, health care, parenthood, and dignified dying of the human
person at large.

By the 1990s, however, the revival of virtue ethics, most spectacularly by the Northern Irish lay philosopher Alasdair McIntyre (1929–) and the development of a sophisticated theory of the moral good as comprising irreducibly basic goods of any offence against which must necessarily be an evil (also the work of laymen, the American German Grisez, 1929–, and the Australian John Finnis, 1940–), enabled orthodox moralists in the Catholic tradition to recover much lost ground.

That process was aided by the emphasis on the narrative 'shaping' of the moral life in any distinctively Christian ethics which reached such thinking about human behaviour from 'narrative theology'.

6 | Narrative theology

Broadly defined, narrative theology is discourse about God in the setting of story. Though such disciplines as psychology, linguistics, social ethics and communications theory had some part in the emergence of narrative theology, its chief parent is literary criticism — the discipline best placed to understand what any genre of literature (such as 'narrative' surely is) might be. In narrative, while historical elements may be important or even foremost, we are not dealing with a chronicle of events based on empirical investigation (even if that investigation be, as in historiography, prompted by imaginative hypothesis). The historian in the last analysis must defer to facts; the narrator, in his plotting of a story, feels no such necessity. It is his vision which is primarily responsible for the coherence, meaning and direction of a narrative. The term 'narrative theology', coined, it seems, by a German Catholic professor of Romance languages, Harald Weinrich (1927–), was taken up by Metz, moving as the latter was from his 'political-theological' phase to one he termed 'memorative-narrative-theological'. For narrative theologians, great stories — including the sagas of faith of Old and New Testaments — have a unique power to move human beings at large, perhaps because they kindle a universal hope, or reverence suffering and honour struggle, or (on yet another view) reflect the three main aspects of our temporality, as they point to the past by way of memory, to the present through attention, and the future in anticipation.

The rise of narrative theology was owed to the convergence of three factors. First, there was the interest of religious phenomenologists in such themes as the interrelation of religion and the arts, the connexion between myth and truth, and the nature of symbol. Also pertinent, second, was the conviction of a number of biblical scholars not just that the Scriptures contain stories (so much leaps to the eye), but that even aspects of their writing which do not, at first sight, seem narrative in structure turn out, on further investigation, to be so. Thus one might argue that the Torah is more fundamentally narrative than law-code, since only within the story shape of the Pentateuch do the divine ordinances for Israel have their meaning — or that the parables of Jesus are essentially narrative in format. Last, shifts in cultural sensibility in the West played their part — a disenchantment with the cerebral, abstract, and prosaic, as also with the technocratic and scientistic (if not scientific), and an attraction to the concrete, intuitive and spontaneous.

Two more factors, a good deal more ambivalent in their implications, should also be noted. First, in a period of remarkably fast change both in society and mentality, the problem of historical relativism, shelved in the Modernist crisis, aired briefly in the *nouvelle théologie*, was released with a vengeance into Catholic theology. Can any truth be freed from the concrete circumstances in which it was born and to which it must presumably refer? Are not all truths inevitably (in this sense) contingent? Perhaps what people in the past have called 'true' is simply what they found of practical assistance in expressing their basic values and commitments. Or, if this is going too far, given that any one historical period is inevitably limited because conditioned, shall we not have to think of the 'truth' it came up with as 'insights', merely — contributions to some larger picture which will necessarily modify their position and importance when it is complete? And in any case, if we can only look out through the spectacles of our own time, will not all truths have to be filtered through a process of interpretation, from their original context to ours, and in this who can guarantee that they will really stay the same? If the Catholic tradition had largely evaded the perils of historical relativism, this was not merely because orders had been given from the Roman foc'sle to avoid rocks; it was also thanks to the tradition's own combination of supernaturalism with adherence to a rational and metaphysical *philosophia perennis*. But now, with relativism's invasion of the sanctuary, narrative theology could come forward and say: Fear not! Telling a story — which is what, *au fond*, revelation is — always suggests a narrator's limited perspective, and a story does not need universal truth claims to make its impact.

The second ambivalent factor, similar and related, was the emergence of Existentialism, favouring as the latter did personal self-engagement but looking with a jaundiced eye on attempts to set out the intrinsic being of things which it spurned as its own contrary, 'Essentialism'.

What, then, of the content of narrative theology? Narrative theologians often distinguish between the 'canonical story' — that of the Bible, studied with much help from literary scholars; 'life story' — the exploration of personal experience, carried out with numerous genuflections towards psychology and sociology; and 'community story' — which looks at communal lore and oral tradition. This trio can be correlated with three elements to be found in more classical theologies: Scripture, experience and tradition.

So far as Scripture is concerned, the best narrative theology is anxious to do justice both to the many individual stories of the Bible and to the overarching canonical story as a whole. Interpreters sometimes distinguish here between 'disclosive' elements in those stories, where something is revealed of a reality beyond myself, and 'transformative' ones, where the important thing is the power of the story to re-orient my life. In each case, reality meets us not in analytic discourse or mystical *ekstasis* but in the concrete mode of time, place, persons. But though most interpreters of the canonical story speak of the (capitalised) One we have to do with in the episodes of the 'history-like' biblical narrative, others, influenced by a secular and pluralist context, seem to find this further reality metaphysically elusive.

With regard to 'life story', the peculiar focus of narrative theology is directed to what is immediate and intimate, with a privileging of such values as spontaneity and self-expression over against the dominance of external structures and authoritarian traditions. Where a social element is invoked as a counterpoise to absorption in the individual in his or her difference, it is usually in terms of the 'right to tell one's story' : a weapon of the 'marginalised' in their struggle against cultural captors, or at the least by way of preserving identity in a uniform world. Under this general heading narrative theologians cite a variety of texts from the Christian past like the *Letter of Polycarp* and Augustine's *Confessions*, as well as biographies, but they also set out to create such materials *a novo* by encouraging people in small groups or parish settings to 'tell their own story', linking that story to the story of Christ.

'Community story', the story told by tradition, is conceived – in the case of a self-consciously Catholic narrative theology – as both encompassing and reflecting the canonical story of Scripture (in different respects), as well as englobing the many stories of personal and social experience. The attempt to construct a 'cosmic story' or 'world plot', drawing for assistance on the classical doctrine of the Church, is not supported, however, by all narrative theologians, for some would regard it as unfaithful to this style of theology's primary commitment to the partial and particular, the allusive and exploratory. Final resolutions, in narrative, are suggested, but no more. Faced with such an evident danger to the Christian religion as a totality others reply that, while in the case of such a world saga it is, admittedly, Church tradition which imposes a narrative ordering on Scripture, nonetheless the flow of this narrative order is already implicit in the biblical stories of the Canon thanks to the interrelation of those stories which the Canon itself creates. After all, even the Apostles' Creed or the Creed of Nicaea-Constantinople may be said still to possess a narrative frame. Thus, if we regard the Trinitarian content of the Creed as the most important doctrinal truth which that frame yields, we could well claim that the development of the doctrine of the 'economic' Trinity shows precisely awareness of the narrative structure of Scripture. And as to the companion doctrine of the 'immanent' or 'absolute' Trinity, that is simply a way of saying that at each turn of the tale it is the true God with whom we have to do.

The basic difficulty with narrative theology from a more traditional theological standpoint lies in negotiating the shift from an anthropocentric perspective where the Trinitarian Persons are part of a story I tell so as to make sense of my existence to a properly theocentric perspective where the actions of those Persons are precisely what constitute the story of the world and my story – granted, of course, that they are seen as envisaging creating and guiding in all liberty *free* spirits, men and women who also contribute to the story though only within the bounds set by providence and grace.

While in Anglo-Saxon countries narrative theology started life as a Protestant enterprise (of particular importance was the Yale scholar Hans Frei's Barth-influenced *The Eclipse of Biblical Narrative*, 1974, with its argument that, in that narrative, God's character is not simply described but enacted), it has enjoyed a Catholic reception of a widespread kind. Catholic theologians can hardly deny that the Gospels are stories, the central act of the Eucharist is a re-enacted narrative, the lives of the saints have a story-line — and thus much of Scripture, and a number of the monuments of Tradition, do consist of narratives. But if narrative theology concerns itself with stories seen as literary constructions aimed at disclosing a meaning and truth which goes beyond that of merely historical reporting, we can still ask whether the dictum 'The story is the meaning' captures all that the sources of revelation have wished to convey. Surely, for instance, the incarnational narrative of the Gospels does reveal something *doctrinal* about God and his nature, and man and his need for redemption, even though we can agree that is not the narrative's sole achievement.

The point has been put more sharply by asking whether narrative theologians are interested in meaning, only, or in truth as well. When Bernd Wacker in his *Narrative Theologie* describes how non-narrative forms of theology could emerge only in a society with a common horizon whereas in our own, faith must substitute for that horizon, and the saving message 're-find its radical forms and theology return to being experienced in saving recountals and arousing good narrators', he confirms the suspicions of such commentators as Edward Oakes of the Society of Jesus about, precisely, narrative theology's withdrawal from the task of communication with the unbelieving (or differently believing) world.[117a] 'Pure' narrativists, so it would seem, have abandoned

> ... the attempt to ground the meaning they find in narrative in anything other than the response of the individual person or community to the story itself.[118]

In rejecting apologetics (a telltale sign), such 'pure' narrativists sacrificed the assumption — dear to Catholic theology — that human culture must be in some way one, or else norms for the true, good and beautiful can nowhere be found, and rules for evidence and criteria of coherence for common conversations do not exist. 'Impure' narrativists, contrastingly, hope to find in the structure of narrative a clue to the ontological pattern of the world. They presuppose that narratives always make reality appear in one way or another, above all for that central feature of the real which is time.

Whether post-Conciliar theologians were giving enough weight to the complexity of theological method which changing contexts in culture entailed was the question which David Tracy (1939–), the younger of the two North American thinkers who set their minds to methodology, would put to his elder colleague and erstwhile model, Bernard Lonergan (1904–1984).

7 | Bernard Lonergan and David Tracy

The Canadian Jesuit Bernard Lonergan became, in the course of the 1970s and early 1980s, something of a cult figure in English-speaking Catholic theology. A veritable Lonergan industry led to the establishment of Lonergan centres in various parts of the world, including Rome; annual Lonergan workshops; a Lonergan bulletin, the 'Lonergan Studies Newsletter', and a Lonergan review, whose title is *Method: Journal of Lonergan Studies*. There are, so far as the present author is aware, no Rahner centres or regular Küng workshops or Congar bulletins, nor are there reviews of Schillebeeckxiana. A clue may lie in the fact that, alone of all these writers, Lonergan produced not only a concept of what theology should be but a total map of human knowing − human cognitional activity − into which to fit it. He proposed to realise the dream of reason, an exhaustive cartography of the world of the mind − something which, according to Rahner and in a less emphatic way Schillebeeckx, we must abandon all hope of, if we are to practise theology realistically in the pluralistic cultural and philosophical ambience of today.

When in 1953 Lonergan brought out the book that would make his name, *Insight*, sub-titled (with a forthright challenge to parity of esteem with Locke's 1690 *Essay concerning Human Understanding*) 'A Study of Human Understanding', it was natural to suppose that the budding speculative theologian who chose as his doctoral dissertation at the Gregorian (the old Collegium Romanum) the topic of human freedom and divine grace[119] had become a pure philosopher. That impression was mistaken, for the articles on cognitional theory published from 1946 to 1949 in the newly founded journal of the American Jesuits *Theological Studies* from which *Insight* took its rise themselves started life as an attempt to clarify a point in the theology of the Trinity. Without a better theological grasp of the eternal generation of the Word, whose created analogue – following Augustine and Aquinas – is human understanding, there could be no progress, Lonergan suggested, in clarifying what is distinctive of the eternal procession of the Spirit – that problem which had left the Greeks speechless, and Augustine ill at ease. As Lonergan's lifelong friend and epigone Father Frederick Crowe has written:

> Theologically, the articles are a study of the life of God in its internal dynamism and movement. But philosophically, they are a study of human life in its internal dynamism and movement on the level of spirit, that is, in the twofold procession of inner word and love, and so, to return to theology, in the image of God.[120]

The understanding which Lonergan would set out to describe so exhaustively in *Insight* as 'the dynamic structure immanent and recurrently operative in human cognitional activity'[121] is itself understood as the ground of the more familiar items in Scholastic epistemology – concepts, judgements, syllogisms – and the human echo of the coming to be, from out of the superabundance of the divine self-understanding, of the eternal person of the Word.

This connexion – easily missed by anyone who consults simply the final form of Lonergan's writings – between cognitional theory and Trinitarian theology explains the fact that Lonergan followed up the publication of *Insight* by three Latin treatises, aimed at the enlightenment of his Gregorian students, on, respectively, the ontological and psychological make-up of the Saviour, the triune God (a massive work in two volumes, partly translated into English as *The Way to Nicaea: The Dialectical Development of Trinitarian Theology* (1976) and, returning to Christology again, the Word incarnate. Lonergan's tendency to read the history of Christian doctrine as the corporate expression in the Church's life of the dynamic cognitive structure of the human mind itself testifies to the influence on his theology of a theory of human understanding which first saw life as an attempt to illuminate a dogmatic problem.

Though Lonergan's Christological and Trinitarian studies of the late 1950s and 1960s are already influenced by the thinking in *Insight*, they are also Lonergan's last offerings in a recognisable Scholastic mould. In the epilogue to *Insight*, he explains how

> After spending years reaching up to the mind of Aquinas, I came to a twofold conclusion. On the one hand, that reaching had changed me profoundly. On the other hand, that change was the essential benefit.[122]

Though a genuflexion is made, no doubt sincerely, in the direction of *Aeterni Patris*, these words, which close Lonergan's claim to intellectual continuity with Leo XIII, look ahead — and this is for the future their more important charge — to a new and, as Lonergan would envisage it, 'post-classical' version of what Catholic theology should be. That this transformed version of theology will owe more to *Insight*, now conceived as a separate philosophy of mind, than to Aquinas, Lonergan's influential, if also much criticised, *Method in Theology* of 1972 would show. Taking the truth of Catholicism for granted, Lonergan portrayed the basic 'functional specialities' of modern Catholic theology as following from the encounter between the Gospel of grace and a human intellect which scans the data of revelation in a four-step movement which can be summed up in four corresponding imperatives: be attentive to the facts; be intelligent (try to understand them); be reasonable (make rational judgements on them); and be responsible (use them properly in your life) — except that, in the case of revelation, we can only be responsible if we are first converted or, as Lonergan puts it, are in a state of unrestricted being in love with God.

If this be transcendental Thomism (a historic debt to Aquinas combined with an ambitious account of the a priori structure of knowing), it is a curious example, for it is a Thomism restricted to cognitional theory, albeit in theology's service. If for historic Thomism of many colours the subjective aspect of knowledge is always tributary to knowledge's objective content, Lonerganianism must be judged something of a paradox, in its silence about those realms where Thomists of another stamp made so marked a contribution earlier this century – in the philosophy of nature, ethics, politics, aesthetics and, indeed, metaphysics itself.

David Tracy addressed himself in his own prescriptive writing about theology to two gaps in the tissue of Lonerganianism. First, since Lonergan's centre of interest is conversion not criticism, he had asked not whether the truth-claims of Christian tradition are well grounded, but rather what is the importance, for a Christian mind, of intellectual, moral and religious conversion in the distinctive Lonerganian sense of those words? The foundation of Lonergan's theological practice is the graced subjectivity of the alert theologian – and is not this too narrow a point of entry upon the faith?

Second, like other critics, Tracy regarded *Method in Theology* as, despite its own protestations of 'post-classicism', excessively intellectualistic (a classic 'classicist' vice!) in the sense of neglectful of the underlying experience of value and meaning embedded in religious tradition in all the latter's concrete complexity (one need think only of the tremendous variety of texts, symbols, relations, attitudes, rituals, artefacts, that compose a Catholic culture and its faith-practice). It was, accordingly, to these two issues – the truth of Christianity, justified before 'the public and the 'academy', and the concreteness of tradition as a medium of meaning – that Tracy would turn.

Tracy calls his own project 'revisionist' theology, and this alerts us to its specific, and somewhat worrying, difference. Enthusiasm for the direction of his corrections of Lonergan may be muted when we read that theologians are to

> ... join other humanists in the demand for a more comprehensive understanding of rationality, in a discourse rationally and responsibly informed in its fuller theories of the good by the symbolic resources of art, philosophy and revelation...[123]

where, in a manner reminiscent of the semi-rationalism of Günther, revelation stands on a level playing-field with philosophy, as also (and here we can note a very desirable overcoming of the limits of rationalism by a broader sense of rationality which takes into account the aesthetic

dimension of human culture) with art. 'Praxis', which in Lonerganianism would have meant holiness of heart and in liberationism actually did mean socially emancipatory action, becomes in Tracy a matter
of articulating mutually critical 'correlations' between the meaning of
the 'Christian fact' and the meaning (supposing anybody can supply
one) of the contemporary situation. Sensitive to charges that he had
reduced the Church's theological life to an ongoing seminar with representatives of the secular humanities, Tracy would later attempt to integrate with his thought the 'mystical-political' (or as he preferred to say:
'mystical-prophetic') emphasis of his *Concilium* colleagues Schillebeeckx and Metz. Indeed, so many 'hermeneutical' — interpretation-
aiding — considerations and conditions are insisted on by Tracy that
the theologian finds its hard to get beyond methodological prelimin-
aries and reach his subject matter.

Tracy believed nonetheless that he had hit upon the perfect way to
present that subject matter eye-catchingly, namely as what he called a
set of 'classics'.

> This argument is dependent upon the assumption that 'classics'
> — understood as those texts, events, images, persons, rituals and
> symbols, which are assumed to disclose permanent possibilities
> of meaning and truth — actually exist... Since even their most
> sceptical critics grant that the Hebrew and Christian traditions
> do include classical texts, the hermeneutical theologian can
> argue that they perform a genuinely public function for both
> society and academy analogous to the philosopher's interpreta-
> tion of the classics of philosophy or the literary critic's interpreta-
> tion of the classics of literature... The notion of the religious
> classic as a cultural classic can assure the entry of all theological
> classics into the public realm of culture...[124]

— though not all topics lend themselves equally well to Tracy's
account. In pneumatology, for example, the Spirit is not tangible in the
way that are Christ and the Church (the two chief topics of Tracy's
dogmatics) in their self-expressions, though he is the divine medium in
which we touch these mysteries.

It would be cheap to write of Tracy's intriguing *via media* between
Catholic dogmatics and a universal philosophy of religion as issuing
from the need of a theologian in the divinity school of a secular univer-

sity to make himself acceptable to his fellows. The Church, he would persuade us, must allow itself to be challenged by the 'other', so as to be ready again to be addressed by its own classics and thus move forward to more adequate self-understanding. In a Church, however, which has opened all too fully to the secular the challenges may be more palpable than the addressing. It is owing to the quality of his response to that 'addressing', as well as to his ability to sum up much of the best in Catholic thought since, as before, the Enlightenment, that our last port of call will be Hans Urs von Balthasar.

8 | Balthasar

Before the Second Vatican Council, Balthasar was known, if at all, as a somewhat eclectic writer who had written learnedly but to no very consistent purpose on a variety of authors and themes, from the Greek Fathers to modern Catholic novelists, from German philosophy to the Holy Trinity. Critical both of Neo-Scholasticism and of the inadequation to mission of a sometimes ossified Church structure, he evidently belonged, with such figures as Henri de Lubac and Jean Daniélou, members of the Society of Jesus he himself had left, to that stable praised or stigmatised in the 1950s as *'nouvelle théologie'*. But in the last thirty years of his life (he died in 1988, shortly before receiving the cardinalatial insignia from the pope), this Swiss polyglot published the most amazing trilogy of works, each in multiple volumes of which only the prolegomena to a 'logic' was the product of his pre-maturity. His reputation underwent immediate revision: here was one of the greatest Catholic theologians of this, or any, century. At the same time, Baltha-sar's reaction to the runaway horse of the post-Conciliar 'renewal' — this was not the neo-patristically inspired reinvigoration of catholicity which the pre-Conciliar reformers had sought — led him to become the prime mover in the founding of the theological journal *Communio* whose aim (so we have noted) was to maintain the thrust of the best writing from before the Council — going back to the sources, within the unity of the faith — over against the liberal-radical accommodation to world culture, in a spirit of hospitality to pluralism, represented by *Communio*'s rival and predecessor, *Concilium*.

Balthasar furnishes an appropriate ending — provisional, as history moves continuously on, though it must be — precisely because of his attempt to unify what is valuable in the philosophical and theological tradition (not least of the period since the Enlightenment) in the service of the common faith of the Church. For Balthasar, it was characteristic of Catholics from the Baroque age in which the Enlightenment had its setting to the late nineteenth century with its habit of extending evolutionary ways of thinking to anything and everything that they treated the faith's expansion into a many-branched tree of doctrine as self-evidently a good thing. But in the twentieth century, theologians from Jungmann to Rahner have pressed a case for the contrary process, the contraction of the complexity of inherited Catholicism into an elemental simplicity — a project both stimulated and impeded by the ever-greater specialisation of theology's ancillary disciplines not least in the movements of *ressourcement*. Balthasar proposed to show how the diversity of theological disciplines, and indeed of theologies, could be turned into a symphony played by a well-schooled orchestra — and not left as the cacophony which could only be expected if a random collection of musically inclined people of varying tastes as well as gifts appeared unprepared for the performance.[125] Not only the doctrines of Catholicism but its various spiritualities and theologies, with their philosophical underpinnings, must be drawn back to the origin — defined by Balthasar as 'the divine, incarnate, crucified, love'[126] — not to deprive the Church of its 'wealth', but to manifest its abiding source. For a revelation transmitted as Tradition, to 'simplify' can only mean to 'integrate'. Both meanings are contained in a key-term of Balthasar's vocabulary, *Einfaltung*.

In part, that process was carried out in the writing of Balthasar's own chief work, the 'trilogy' — fifteen volumes consisting of a theological aesthetics — a study of the beauty or glory of God; a theological dramatics — a study of the saving action of God in the theatre of the world; and a theological logic — a study of the truth of God, which comes to light in those first two,[127] for in that trilogy Balthasar develops his case by way of a polyphonic conversation with a variety of voices in the tradition (so much so that whole tracts of the aesthetics, in particular, read like small monographs on figures from Irenaeus of Lyons [c 140 – c 202] to Charles Péguy [1873–1914]).

But in another sense Balthasar's desire to see the theological tradition of Catholicism better integrated (though not at the expense of its rich profusion) was manifested in the programmatic statements in which he offered a vision of theology's future as that orchestra of players producing a symphony for an undivided Church.

For Balthasar, the transcendent form set in the midst of history and changing its total direction − namely Christ's death and resurrection as reconciling man to God and summing up the entire cosmos as its new and eternal centre (shades here of Teilhard) − 'releases' the three chief types of theology the tradition has known.

First, there is theology as *doxological contemplation* of the fundamental form (*Gestalt*) of revelation − the God-man in his death and resurrection. This sort of theologising is not, for Balthasar, just one kind among others, in that its ethos − the glorifying of God's grace − needs to be present in other theological styles as well, if they are to be Christian. He emphasises that, while from Augustine to Anselm (1033/4–1109) and the new masters of the twelfth century, this is chiefly a contemplative theology of immersion in the saving events so as to fathom their divine dimensions, it is not one cut off from the practice of Christian existence. It is the whole person who must respond to the Father's self-gift in the Son. The paraenetic and the dogmatic are interwoven in such thinking, just as they were at the New Testament origins of the Church's faith, with Paul. The other-directedness of this theology, its openness in this way to the brother, links it to the second great type, which is kerygmatic.

For Balthasar *kerygmatic* theology is a missionary translation of sapiential theology and one that is ordered to preaching, catechising and teaching. It is, essentially, a *useful* theology, but not a merely utilitarian one, for it turns on the great presupposition that the particular acts of God in Jesus Christ (and their pre-history in Israel) possess a universal validity which is right for all peoples − and so is linked by Balthasar to the Ascension, the mystery of Christ's Lordship.

The demand for translation which lies in the command to be understandable to all nations is not free to make concessions ('teach them to observe everything'); the translation, then, must proceed ever anew out of the vision of the whole (the 'first' theology), and is to make use of the peoples' form of thought, in critical observation.[128]

And this brings Balthasar to the third main type: *dialectical* theology, meaning in effect an improved apologetics such as is needed by Christians in a world of unbelievers. This is an apologetics that improves by being transformed, for what Balthasar envisages is a greater crediting of the capacity to 'correspond' to the unknown God which the hearer already possesses — and so the unbeliever's becoming a genuine interlocutor who may perhaps have painful things to say about the Christian and the Church. Here Balthasar does justice to the message of Tracy.

> We do not wish to advocate an equal status for all religions or false religions, for the Christian has perceived that in Christ God has acted not only uniquely ('once for all') but also unsurpassably (*id quo nihil majus cogitari nequit*). Yet the Christian must remain aware, not only that 'there is something true' also in other points of view, but that the Christian truth is always greater than what he, in thinking, proclaiming, and indeed living, can capture, that he himself then, precisely because he knows this, remains under the judgement of the Word he proclaims, and that this judgement may also meet him through his brother.[129]

But as with the kerygmatic theologian, the dialectical theologian must enter into the river of contemplative theology in order to draw power for encounter, just as his kerygmatic counterpart must do if he is to find resources for proclamation. So the three forms are in a condition of constant circumincession.[130]

It is possible, however, to think of the unity and plurality of theologies not in terms (as here) of overall purpose but rather of the various theological departments or specialisations, as did Lonergan — and Balthasar has a word to say on that as well, notably on the interrelation of dogmatics and ethics or spirituality on the one hand, dogmatics and exegesis on the other. The spiritual, the ethical and the doctrinal are necessarily interactive because

> ... faith is a surrender by man to the fidelity of God in which he
> agrees with God from the very beginning (it is faith in God's
> word) and adapts himself by that agreement (as trusting obedi-
> ence of life).[131]

If the covenant with Israel was inseparably knowledge ('dogma') and
service ('ethics'), the same is true of the God-man who, in his fulfilment
of that covenant, both is God's Word and keeps it. So whatever the
offices or charisms of the Church's faithful, none can dispense with
that unity and become a specialist, simply, in 'knowledge of God' on
the one hand, or in 'acknowledging action' on the other. Only those
theologies that are permeated by spirituality have, accordingly, any
lasting efficacy in the Church's life. And as to the interrelation of
dogmatics and exegesis, the relative independence of the exegete in
his often highly technical discipline does not exempt him from
acquiring that 'ecclesial sense' to which his own object of study ultimately directs him. The goal to which the Scriptures are inclined is
Christ and the Church,[132] even if there is also value in exploring their
links and analogies with the general phenomenon of human religion:
the 'hearer of the Word' is not disconnected from the rest of humanity.

> This openness of theology to everything human should in no way
> tempt it to dissolve formlessly into the generally human; it retains
> its precisely definable focal point in God's historically salvific
> action, which has received such an infinite fullness in Christ, the
> 'heir of all things' (Hebrews 1, 2) that it cannot be surpassed by any
> human, world-historical evolution (which will never develop
> anything but the possibilities of man).[133]

Those words, which are both a brotherly warning to Catholic thinkers
tempted to tread the path of Protestant Liberalism and a summons to
mission to the world, form a serviceable bridge to the conclusion of
this study.

CONCLUSION: CATHOLI- CISM AND MODERNITY

Owing, above all, to the masterful combination of percipience and vigour which characterised the combination of Polish Pope and Bavarian Prefect of doctrine, Catholicism approached the close of the second millennium with its intellectual house relatively in order – at any rate at the level of theory. The writing of a 'universal' *Catechism*, drawing on sources biblical and patristic, liturgical and magisterial, Scholastic and hagiographic, enabled the Papacy, with collaboration from the worldwide episcopate, to essay an overview of the Catholic faith as a whole – in its credal, sacramental, moral and spiritual dimensions – to name those in the order of the four sub-books of the *Catechism* itself.[134] Especially striking was the presence in the work of so much material from the Christian East, for the Eastern Catholic churches, whose voice has been theologically silent for too long, had never not been, in one or another form, part and parcel of the (by no means wholly Western, therefore) Catholic Church.

Other interventions, concerned to demarcate the authentically Catholic from distortions, had renewed the Church's commitment to the existence of moral absolutes, to a genuinely theological (and not simply naturalistic) ethics where creation delivers the natural law in its fullness only in the light of Christ, and a doctrine of the virtues (both natural and supernatural): thus John Paul II's *Veritatis splendor* of 1993; clarified what was and what was not acceptable in feminism -- thus the encyclical *Mulieris dignitatem* of 1988; re-affirmed the goal of unity for all Christians, but also the terms on which, for Catholicism, such reconciled diversity could be genuine unity, and not papering over cracks – thus *Ut unum sint* of 1995; and brought to bear principles of Catholic social teaching on issues of the hour (and more than the hour, for the North-South divide, and the amorality of liberal democracy we shall have if not always with us then at any rate chronically so): thus *Sollicitudo rei socialis* of 1987 and *Centesimus annus* of 1991. Speculations which exceeded the limits of the possible in ecclesiology, Christology, eschatology and other domains were briskly pruned yet the basic statute by which the theologian holds his or her place in the Church set out in positive terms in the Congregation for the Doctrine of the Faith's *Instruction on the Ecclesial Vocation of the Theologian* (1990). The labyrinth of contemporary exegetical method was mapped, and its crooked ways made plain by a judicious re-ordering to the ecclesial sense of Scripture in the Pontifical Biblical Commission's masterly *The Interpretation of the Bible* (1994).

The validity of these measures lay in their consolidation of Catholic identity; of themselves, however, they could not guarantee the fruitful manifestation of that identity in the earth of the modern world. For modernity is not in all respects good soil. Human autonomy, legitimate within certain boundaries, easily becomes there a practical atheism which renders God literally in-significant – unable to signal his presence to man. Human desires swell to grossness in the pursuit of consumer satisfactions – which have precious little to do with the *makariotês*; blessedness, of the Beatitudes, and rather more with what Hegel called the 'bad infinite', the malediction that is craving without end. Such concupiscence, it might be thought, will eventually deprive the spirit of man of its proper creativity. Meanwhile rationality is paced by absurdity as means-to-ends are ever better understood but the ends themselves dissolve.

Yet modernity is not a monolith: the ideologies it propounded, the attitudes to the past it prescribed, were not only disparate but frequently at odds. Admittedly, there were some constants amid the variables. In

Europe and the United States upheavals in the ethical order of civil society and family in the closing decades of the nineteenth century ushered in a period marked by accelerating technical change, artistic experimentalism, and finally, as the *belle époque* turned to wormwood and gall in the First World War and its aftermath, a pervasive sense of historical crisis. The 'modern' age entertained both a grandiose vision of the possibilities of human transformation, and gnawing self-doubt — for progress of the kind desiderated inevitably includes, as Malcolm Bradbury has written, 'fragmentation and loss'.[135] If Teilhard's futurology represents an attempt to baptise the optimistic thrust of the modern, the movements of *ressourcement* were no less modern in seeing, against the grain of a civilisation in crisis, authenticity, order — and even, in the early aesthetics of Maritain and the Liturgical Movement in its practical aspect, a (really quite fashionable) return to craft.[136] In coming to take stock of this period, in identifying its qualities and bounds, people subsequently saw themselves as located after it: the term 'postmodern', with all its vagueness of connotation, would soon be born.

The corporate ethos of modern society, once the crises of Fascism and Bolshevism had passed, was Liberalism. Like the agnostic modern State it accompanied, Liberalism was bred of the desire to escape the power of revealed religion. If church and city, or universal Church and Empire, had endured constant friction, petty or great, the political science stemming from the Renaissance — from the divorce, at the hands of Niccolò Macchiavelli (1469–1521), of the statesman's prudence from the good — got round the problem by establishing a social peace, while ignoring the condition of men's souls. The individual who in the thought of Thomas Hobbes (1588–1679) makes his contract so as to enter the social realm pays the price of the artificiality attaching to him as a pre-social construct; he enjoys rights, but not the good itself.[137] The society of which such individuals is composed necessarily faces sooner or later a crisis of meaning. The organised banality of such régimes renders them singularly impermeable to revelation — if the more in need of it.

It also spurs some to reject the Liberal world, and in the name of a further radicalisation of human freedom (here Rousseau blazed the trail) gives rise to utopian hopes of a revolutionary rather than evolutionary kind, though this may take the form of an invasion of the body rather than the future. Artificial contraception, legalised abortion and euthanasia, the manipulation of sexuality, gender, and human genes display modern man's insistence at having sovereignty over himself, at all costs. By contrast to what the French political philosopher Pierre Manent in his *La Cité de l'homme* (1994) has called this 'de-substantialization' of man, the Church stands out as possessed of a substantive humanism, at once of reason and of faith, from Athens and Jerusalem. Though the modernity addressed in somewhat optimistic terms by the Second Vatican Council did not notably respond (except by its representatives' rejoicing that Rome too was now converted to tolerance, religious freedom and the practical paramountcy of material development), the postmodern world whose water-springs are few and far between may be riper for conversion. To deny the *logos*, to deconstruct all universal human norms, is indeed to need healing from madness.

Still, as Blondel wrote in a graphic phrase in *Catholicisme sociale et monophorisme* (1910), Christ ought not to make his entry into the temporal domain with mace-bearer and beadles at his head — a comment on Maurras' willingness, in the event of a Positivist monarchy coming to power, to give the Catholic Church privileged political status irrespective of the degree of effective incorporation within it of the population at large. Catholic thought — like the Gospel itself on which it is dependent — cannot regain high ground unless and until it converts souls, and therefore hearts and minds. Fortunately, the modernist myth of the inevitability of secularisation is crumbling in the face of the massive evidence for a continuing spiritual hunger, to which the interest in Oriental religions and the syncretism of 'New Age' bear eloquent, if not always admirable, witness. A sane philosophy — the search for which, as this book has indicated, absorbed much of the intellectual energy of Catholics since the Enlightenment — is if not a *sine qua non*, then at least greatly to be desired. A scepticism about man's cognitive powers, leading to relativism and resignation, must be cleared away and replaced by a new confidence in our faculties as truth-oriented, so that knowledge is the realisable result of the processes by which they operate. The imperilled Western sense of the history of its own spiritual civilisation, after the style of Dawson, also needs strengthening, for Catholic Christianity, as a historical religion, cannot survive the acceptance of Michel Foucault's (proto-) postmodernist position that the past is radically other, so much so that all 'consoling games of recognition' must be abandoned.

And if the erosion of rationality and of awareness of the historical continuum in which human life is set are negativities that the Church must contribute to overcoming, more positively her doctrine contains, as Professor Colin Gunton has noted from the angle of a Reformed theologian, features peculiarly helpful to modernity — for dogmatic faith in the Triune God of creation and salvation is illuminating for such dark puzzles as universality and particularity; identity and otherness; the interconnectedness of goodness, beauty and truth.[138]

Unfortunately, the weaknesses of some Catholic theology today — notably in the feebleness of its metaphysical authority — makes the task of communicating such insights harder, just as it reflects and reinforces the difficulty many individual Catholics have in grasping their faith as a unitary vision of the world, a total way of understanding things — as well as an invitation to activity or, in that current vogue word, *praxis*, adequate to the human enterprise today. The attempt to replace philosophy by sociology as theology's handmaid in liberation theology, the use of the concept of narrative found in current literary theory in narrative theology, and the appeal to the interpretation theory of hermeneutical philosophy in its theological counterpart, these intellectual moves, whatever their advantages in particular contexts, make discourse the less able to render the theological totality of Catholic Christianity, which needs to speak about being as well as meaning, and eternity as well as time. Liberation theology, narrative theology, and hermeneutical theology have their own particular tasks to perform, tasks related to the nature of the human being, as a political animal, as a creature that expresses the meaning of existence by the telling of stories, and as someone stretched between past and present, scanning by interpretation the texts and other artefacts that come down to it in tradition. What is vital, however, is that such theologies do not set themselves up as the universal theology calculated to meet all the Church's needs, albeit on a local or regional scale. They must find ways of making space for other kinds of theological discourse and, above all, for those which, in their cherishing of ontology, enable the expression of Catholic doctrine as a description of reality in its two poles, finite and infinite, and the relation between them. At the same time, such other kinds of theology — for which Thomism may stand as the paradigm — by presenting human intelligence as, above all, the capacity for intake of the real, highlight in an irreplaceable fashion the Church's fundamental intuition about truth: namely, that it is not first and foremost an action to be done (cf liberation theology) or a story to be told (cf narrative theology) or a text to be interpreted (hermeneutical theology), though it may indeed be all of these. Primordially, truth is an encounter with what is not humanity's work, the deed of God in creation and salvation.

And so the Catholicism of the twenty-first century will need not only to maintain its own coherence by setting forth the limits of possible pluralism (as the Catholicism of the twentieth century has done), but (like that of the nineteenth century) to determine more clearly the central tasks for which it needs reflective thought and scholarship at all. And it must do these things not least for the salvaging of the modern itself.

NOTES

1   R B Pippin, *Modernism as a Philoso-phical Problem. On the Dissatisfac-tions of European High Culture* (Oxford, 1991), p 20.

2   F-J Niemann, *Jesus als Glaubens-grund der Fundamental-theologie der Neuzeit. Zur Genealogie eines Traktats* (Innsbruck 1983) traces the origin of autonomous apolo-getic along these lines to the Renaissance; but the soil is pre-pared in the Fathers, with Justin and the early ecclesiastical writers we call (precisely) 'the Apologists'.

3   For a fascinating account, see O Chadwick, *The Popes and European Revolution* (Oxford 1981), pp 3–341.

4   M J Buckley, SJ, *At the Origins of Modern Atheism* (New Haven and London 1987), pp 66–67.

5   J Müller, 'Zu den théologie-geschichtlichen Grundlagen der Studienreform Rautenstrauchs', *Theologische Quartalschrift* 144 (1964), pp 62–97.

6   S Schama, *Citizens. A Chronicle of the French Revolution* (London 1989), p 858.

7   S Bann, *Romanticism and the Rise of History* (New York 1995); that, owing to the variety of historians' conception of history, the achieve-ments of their discipline have a certain ambiguity attached is the message of the same author's *The Clothing of Clio. A Study of the Representation of History in Nine-teenth Century Britain and France* (Cambridge 1984) and *The Inven-tions of History* (Manchester 1990).

8   G Steiner 'Aspects of Counter-Revo-lution', in G Best (ed), *The Perma-nent Revolution. The French Revolution and its Legacy*, 1789–1989 (London 1988), pp 135–136.

9   Cf C S Evans, *The Historical Christ and the Jesus of Faith. The Incarna-tional Narrative as History* (Oxford 1996), p 196.

10 A Finkielkraut, *The Undoing of Thought* (Et London 1988), p 21.

11 J Leflon, 'Crise et restauration des foyers de science religieuse dans l'Eglise au XIXe siècle', in A Mandouze — J Fouilheron (eds), *Migne et le Renouveau des études patristiques* (Paris 1985), p 55.

12 E Poulat, *Eglise contre bourgeoisie. Introduction au devenir du Catholicisme actuel* (Tournai 1977).

13 P Gerbet, *Considérations sur le dogme générateur de la Piété catholique (Paris 1829)*.

14 R W Franklin, *Nineteenth Century Churches. The History of a New Catholicism in Württemberg, England and France* (New York 1987), p 381.

15 R Aubert, *Le Problème de l'acte de foi* (Louvain 1950).

16 G Steiner, 'Aspects of Counter-Revolution', art cit, p 148.

17 W Ward, *W G Ward and the Catholic Revival* (London and New York 1893), p 84.

18 Ibid, p 140.

19 J P von Arx, SJ, 'Archbishop Manning and the *Kulturkampf*', *Recusant History*, 21 2 (1992), pp 254–266.

20 J Forstman, *A Romantic Triangle: Schleiermacher and Early German Romanticism* (Missoula, 1977).

21 See J Ranft, 'Lebendige Ueberlieferung Ihre Einheit und ihre Entwicklung', in H Tüchle (ed), *Die eine Kirche. Zum Gedenken J A Möhlers, 1838–1938* (Paderborn 1939).

22 See, for instance, in brief compass, and within the context of Tractarianism at large, A Nichols, OP, *The Panther and the Hind. A Theological History of Anglicanism* (Edinburgh 1993), pp 114–128.

23 C S Dessain (ed), *The Letters and Diaries of John Henry Newman*, XI (London 1961), p 110.

24 F Evain, 'Antonio Rosmini-Serbati (1797–1855) und der Rosminia-

nismus im 19. Jahrhundert', in E Coreth, SJ, et al, *Christliche Philosphie im katholischen Denken des 19. und 20. Jahrhunderts II* (Graz, Vienna, Cologne, 1987), pp 607–608.

25 G M Cornoldi, SJ, *Il rosminianismo, sintesi dell' ontologismo e del panteismo* (Rome 1881).

26 Cf N Wolterstorff, 'Tradition, Insight and Constraint', *Proceedings and Addresses of the American Philosophical Association* 66.3 (1993), pp 43–57; idem, *John Locke's Ethics of Belief: When Tradition Fractures* (Cambridge 1977).

27 *Le cinque piaghe della Chiesa* and *La costituzione secondo la sociale giustizia*, both published in the Year of Revolutions, 1848, had their censures lifted in 1854.

28 G Perrone, *Analisi della 'Symbolica' del Signore Professore Möhler e considerazioni sulla medesima intorno alle sue relazioni coll' insegnamento cattolico e protestante* (Rome 1837).

29 J J von Döllinger, 'Die Vergangenheit und Gegenwart der katholischen Theologie', in P Gams (ed), *Verhandlungen der Versammlung katholischer Gelehrter in München* (Regensburg 1863), pp 25–59.

30 K H Neufeld, 'La Scuola romana', in R Fisichella (ed), *Storia della teologia, 3. Da Vitus Pichler a Henri de Lubac* (Bologna 1996), pp 271–272.

31 For Passaglia's muted welcome to Leonine Thomism see his *Sulla dottrina di San Tommaso secondo l'encicylica Aeterni Patris* (Turin 1880).

33 H E Manning, 'Roma aeterna. A Discourse before the Accademia of the Quiriti, in Rome, on the 2615th Anniversary of this City, 21 April 1863', idem, *Miscellanies* (London 1909), pp 16, 22.

33 For the background here, see J T Burtchaell, *Catholic Theories of Biblical Inspiration since 1810: A Review and Critique* (Cambridge 1969).

34 G A McCool, SJ, *From Unity to Pluralism. The Internal Evolution of Thomism* (New York 1989; 1992), p 12.

35 G K Chesterton, *Orthodoxy* (London 1900; 1963), p 36.

36 *Ethica ordine geometrico demonstrata* (Amsterdam 1677).

37 Cited in H Bouillard, *Blondel and Christianity* (Et Washington and Cleveland 1969), p 21.

38 M Blondel, 'Lettre sur les Exigences de la pensée contemporaine en matière d'apologétique et sur la Méthode de la philosophie dans l'étude du problème religieux', originally published in *Annales de Philosophie Chrétienne* for 1896.

39 *Histoire et dogme. Les lacunes philosphiques de l'exégèse moderne* (1904).

40 G E Michalson, Jr, *Lessing's 'Ugly Ditch': A Study of Theology and History* (University Park, Penn, 1985).

41 For the contradictions of such a view, see W J Abraham, *Divine Revelation and the Limits of Historical Criticism* (Oxford 1982).

42 A F Loisy, 'Chronique biblique', *Revue d'histoire et de littérature religieuse* 11 (1906), p 570; words written in the course of a review of A Houtin, *La Question biblique au XXe siècle* (Paris 1906), a *Loisyiste* account of the controversy sparked off among Catholics by *L'Evangile et l'Eglise* and *Autour d'un petit livre*.

43 R Aubert, 'Modernism', *Sacramentum Mundi* IV (Et London 1969), p 101.

44 N Sagovsky, *Between Two Worlds. George Tyrrell's relationship to the*

Thought of Matthew Arnold (Cambridge 1983).

45 F von Hügel, *Selected Letters, 1896–1924* (London 1927), pp 3–4.

46 A de Villeneuve-Bargemont, *Traité d'économie politique Chrétienne* (1834).

47 *Histoire parlementaire de la Révolution française* (1933–1838), co-authored with M Roux-Lavorgne.

48 P Misner, *Social Catholicism in Europe From the Onset of Industrialization to the First World War* (New York and London 1991), pp 139–140, paraphrasing Ketteler's text.

49 G A McCool, SJ, *From Unity to Pluralism. The Internal Evolution of Thomism*, op cit, pp 53–54.

50 See, for example, E Weber, *The Hollow Years. France in the 1930s* (London 1945).

51 G Greene, 'François Mauriac', in *The Lost Childhood and Other Essays* (London 1951), pp 70, 71.

52 R M Griffiths, *The Reactionary Revolution. The Catholic Revival in French Literature, 1870–1914* (New York 1965).

53 R H Harvanek, SJ, 'Philosophical Pluralism and Catholic Orthodoxy', *Thought* 25 96 (1950), pp 21–52; idem, 'The Unity of Metaphysics', ibid, 28 110 (1953), pp 375–411.

54 R W Franklin, *Nineteenth Century Churches. The History of a New Catholicism in Württemberg, England and France* (New York and London 1987).

55 Pius's work for the recovery of the Liturgy's full integrity certainly helps justify the claim that he was the greatest reforming pope since Trent: G Romanato, *Pio X. La vita di Papa Sarto* (Milan 1992), p 247.

56 *Das christliche Kultmysterium* (Regensburg 1969), p 79; cf *The Mystery of Christian Worship, and Other Writings* (Et Westminster, Md, 1960), p 54.

57 Cf C von Korvin-Krasinski, OSB, *Mikrokosmos und Makrokosmos in religionsgeschichtlicher Sicht* (Düsseldorf 1960).

58 Well set out in Y Congar, *Christ, our Lady and the Church* (Et London 1957).

59 R Guardini, *The Church and the Catholic* (Et London 1935), p 11.

60 Reviewing A von Harnack, *Dogmengeschichte* (Tübingen 1922), in *Theologische Quartalschrift* 104 (1923), pp 102–103, cited in R A Krieg, CSC, *Karl Adam. Catholicism in German Culture* (Notre Dame, Ind, 1992), p 11.

61 K Adam, *Christ and the Western Mind* (Et New York 1930), p 34.

62 Idem, *The Spirit of Catholicism* (Et London 1929; 1952), p 41, with an internal citation of Augustine's *Sermon* 96, 8.

63 S Jaki, OSB, *Les Tendances nouvelles de l'ecclésiologie* (Rome 1957); p 79. Here Jaki was responding to the severe criticisms of the post-Great War writers in D Koster, *Ekklesiologie im Werden* (Paderborn 1940).

64 K Adam, *The Spirit of Catholicism*, op cit, p 174.

65 Cited in B Montagnes, *Le Père Lagrange, 1855–1938. L'Exégèse catholique et la crise moderniste* (Paris 1995), p 33.

66 Ibid, p 60.

67 Cited ibid, p 198.

68 A Hamman, 'Patrologia-patristica' in A Di Berardino, *Dizionario patristico e di antichità cristiane* (Casale Monferrato 1983), II, col 2717.

69 J C Weber (ed), *In Quest of the Absolute. The Life and Work of Jules Monchanin* (Et Kalamazoo and London 1977).

70 Cited in C Scott, *A Historian and his World. A Life of Christopher Dawson, 1889–1970* (London 1984), p 49.

71 J M Connolly, *Human History and the Word of God. The Christian Meaning of History in Contemporary Thought* (New York and London 1965).

72 C Dawson, *The Dynamics of World History* (New York 1957), p 128.

73 Idem, *Enquiries into Religion and Culture* (New York 1933) p 252.

74 Idem, *Religion and Culture* (London 1948), p 217.

75 The 'Problem of Meta-History', in idem, *Dynamics of World History* (London and New York 1957). For a spirited modern defence, see C T McIntire and M Perry, 'Toynbee's Achievement', in idem (ed), *Toynbee Reappraisals* (Toronto 1389), pp 3–31.

76 T Dilworth, *The Shape of Meaning in the Poetry of David Jones* (Toronto 1988).

77 B Tuchman, *The Proud Tower. A Portrait of the World before the War, 1890–1914* (New York 1962; 1966).

78 G K Chesterton, *Orthodoxy*, op cit, p 28.

79 E Hanisch, *Der lange Schatten des Staates Oesterreichische Gesellschaftsgeschichte im 20. Jahrhundert, 1890–1990* (Vienna 1995).

80 M M Labourdette, OP, 'La Théologie et ses sources', *Revue Thomiste* XLVI 2 (1946), pp 353–371.

81 J Daniélou, 'Les Orientations présentes de la pensée religieuse', *Etudes* 249 (1946), pp 5–21.

82 Cited in A Russo, *Henri de Lubac. Teologia e dogma nella storia. L'influsso di Blondel* (Rome 1990), p 66.

83 For some, de Lubac might have rectified the misreading of the main Dominican commentator of the Second Scholasticism, Cajetan (Thomas de Vio, 1469–1534), but his Blondelianism led him into distortions of his own: thus J-H Nicolas, OP, 'Les rapports entre la nature et

le surnaturel dans les débats contemporains', *Revue Thomiste* XCV 3 (1995), pp 399–415.

84   S-T Bonino, OP, 'Le Thomisme du P Labourdette', in *Un maître en théologie. Le Père Marie-Michel Labourdette*, OP (Toulouse 1992 = *Revue Thomiste* XCII 1).

85   H de Lubac, SJ, *La Pensée religieuse du Père Teilhard de Chardin* (Paris 1962); idem, *La Prière du Père Teilhard de Chardin* (Paris 1964).

86   F Russo, SJ, 'La Méthode du Père Teilhard de Chardin', in idem, et al, *Essais sur Teilhard de Chardin* (Paris 1962 = *Recherches et débats* 40), pp, 13–23.

87   For these and other *quaestiones disputatae* raised by Teilhard's corpus, see O Rabut, OP, *Dialogue avec Teilhard de Chardin* (Paris 1961).

88   J A DiNoia, OP, 'Karl Rahner', in D E Ford (ed), *The Modern Theologians. An Introduction to Christian Theology in the Twentieth Century*, I (Oxford 1989), p 186. Collected separately were essays relevant to pastoral care, published in three volumes in 1959 as *Sendung und Gnade*; these were written with one eye on the approaching General Council of the Church.

89   Rahner's edition, in ten volumes plus indices, appeared at Freiburg between 1957 and 1967.

90   *Episcopacy and Primacy* (Et London, Edinburgh and New York 1962).

91   *Diaconia in Christo Ueber die Erneuerung des Diakonats* (Freiburg 1962).

92   On which see A Nichols, OP, 'Einigung der Kirchen: an Ecumenical Controversy', *One in Christ* XXI 2 (1985), pp 139–166.

93   K Rahner, 'Church and World', in idem et al (ed), *Sacramentum Mundi*, op cit, p 348.

94   Ibid, italics original.

95   W S Rubin, *Modern Sacred Art and the Church of Assy* (New York and London 1961), p 16.

96   There is a broad overview in R Virgoulay, *Les courants de pensée du Catholicisme française. L'épreuve de la modernité* (Paris 1984).

97   *Optatam totius*, 15.

98   Ibid, p 16.

99   *Gaudium et spes*, 44.

100 *Optatam totius*, 16.

101 For this interpretation of the phrase *accommodata renovatio* see B C Butler, *The Theology of Vatican II* (London 1967), p 20.

102 *Lumen Gentium*, 8.

103 B C Butler, *The Theology of Vatican II*, op cit, p 80.

104 *Sacrosanctum Concilium*, 102.

105 See D E Pelotte, SSS, *John Courtney Murray: Theologian in Conflict* (New York 1975). Certainly Murray's doctrine of faith, inspired as it was by that of Scheeben, gave no support to *theological* liberalism within the Church (thus D T Hughson, SJ, *Matthias Scheeben on Faith. The Doctoral Dissertation of John Courtney Murray* (Lewiston and Queenston 1987): the two issues, fundamentally distinct, would often be conflated in post-Conciliar controversy.

106 G Curtis, *Paul Couturier and Unity in Christ* (London, 1964).

107 A Nichols, OP, *Yves Congar* (London 1989), pp 96–140.

108 S A Quitslund, *Beaduin: a Prophet Vindicated* (London 1973).

100 The most complete collection of 'agreed statements' is the ongoing *Enchiridion Oecumenicum* (Bologna 1986–).

110 Thanks to the efforts of the first *praeses* of the Secretariat for Christian Unity, the Jesuit Cardinal Augustin Bea (1881–1968), relations with the Jews, the descendants of

the Church's spiritual ancestors, were confided to him and his successors; A Bea, *The Church and the Jewish People* (Et London 1966); A Gilbert, *The Vatican Council and the Jews* (Cleveland 1968); H Croner (ed), *More Stepping Stones to Jewish-Christian Relations, Christian Documents 1975–1985* (New York 1985).

111 The Council used the model of the (immediately pre-Conciliar) Secretariat to institute others for the non-Christian religions and non-believers.

112 Cited in T F Stransky, CSP, 'The Foundation of the Secretariat for Promoting Christian Unity', in A Stacpoole (ed), *Vatican II by Those who were There* (London 1986), p 81.

113 See G H Duggan, SM, *Hans Küng and Reunion* (Cork 1964).

114 C M LaCugna, *The Theological Methodology of Hans Küng* (New York 1982).

115 W Kasper, *The God of Jesus Christ* (Et London 1984), p 15.

116 For an example of such 'death of God' theology in (nominally) Catholic guise, see for instance J Cardonnel et al, *Dieu est mort en Jésus Christ* (Bordeaux 1967).

117 M Xhaufflaire, *Feuerbach et la Théologie de la sécularisation* (Paris 1970).

117ᵃE T Oakes, SJ, 'Apologetics and the Pathos of Narrative Theology', *Journal of Religion* 72.1 (1992), pp 37–58.

118 B Wacker, *Teologia narrativa* (Brescia 1981), p 27. German original 1977. The same refusal of 'an ontological narrative which underwrites or legitimates the Church's story and contradicts nihilism' can be seen in G Loughlin, *Telling God's Story Bible, Church and Narrative Theology* (Cambridge 1996), p 79. Loughlin is quite right, however,

that no ontology can do full justice to the divine narrative.

119 Published as: *Grace and Freedom Operative Grace in the Thought of St Thomas Aquinas* (London 1971).

120 F E Crowe, SJ, *Lonergan* (London 1992), p 49.

121 *Insight, A Study of Human Understanding* (New York 1970), p xxii.

122 Ibid, p 696.

123 D Tracy, *The Analogical Imagination Christian Theology and the Culture of Pluralism* (New York 1981), p 31.

124 Ibid, p 68.

125 H U von Balthasar, *Die Wahrheit ist symphonisch Aspekte des christlichen Pluralismus* (Einsiedeln 1972; Et *Truth is Symphonic Aspects of Christian Pluralism*, San Francisco 1987).

126 Idem, *Einfaltungen Auf Wegen christlicher Einigung* (Einsiedeln 1988; Et of first edition *Convergences: to the Sources of Christian Mystery*, San Francisco 1984).

127 *Herrlichkeit Eine theologische Aesthetik* (Einsiedeln 1961–1969); *Theodramatik* (Einsiedeln 1973–1983); *Theologik* (Einsiedeln 1985–1987).

128 Idem, *Convergences*, op cit, pp 63–64.

129 Ibid, p 67.

130 Idem, *Theo-drama. A Theological Dramatic Theory I. Prolegomena* (Et San Francisco 1988), pp 126–128.

131 Idem, *Convergences*, op cit, p 69.

132 Historical critical scholars and, if to a lesser extent, their competitors in such new forms of academic exegesis as the sociological, structuralist, post-structuralist and narrative schools make a desirable contribution to the Church's understanding of its own founding literature, in whose connexion nothing is too trivial to be worthy of notice. However, such scholars

are not necessarily better placed than members of another community than the academic — the Church itself — when it comes to ascertaining the meaning and truth of the texts: a point made from a non-Catholic perspective by J D Levenson, *The Hebrew Bible, the Old Testament and Historical Criticism: Jews and Christians in Biblical Studies* (Louisville, Ky, 1993).

133 H U Balthasar, *Convergences*, op cit, p 71.

134 *The Catechism of the Catholic Church* (Et London 1994); for a commentary thereon, the reader might consult A Nichols, OP, *The Splendour of Doctrine. The 'Cate-* chism of the Catholic Church' on Christian Believing* (Edinburgh 1996); and idem, *The Service of Glory. The 'Catechism of the Catholic Church on Worship, Ethics, Spirituality* (Edinburgh 1997).

135 M Bradbury, 'From Here to Modernity', *Prospect*, December 1995, p 35. Also in *International Affairs*.

136 R Golan, *Modernity and Nostalgia Art and Politics in France between the Wars* (New Haven 1995).

137 P Manent, *An Intellectual History of Liberalism* (Et Princeton 1994).

138 C E Gunton, *The One, the Three and the Many: God, Creation and the Culture of Modernity* (Cambridge 1993).

BIBLIOGRAPHY

GENERAL

R Aubert, *La Théologie catholique au milieu du XXe siècle* (Paris 1953);
idem, in S Neill (ed), *Twentieth Century Christianity* (London 1962).

V B Brezik, OSB, *One Hundred Years of Thomism* (Houston, Tx, 1981).

O Chadwick, *From Bossuet to Newman. The Idea of Doctrinal Development* (Cambridge 1957);
idem, *The Popes and European Revolution* (Oxford 1981);
idem, *The Secularization of the European Mind in the Nineteenth Century* (Cambridge 1977).

J Collins, *God in Modern Philosophy* (Chicago 1959);
idem, *A History of Modern European Philosophy* (Milwaukee 1954).

Y Congar, *A History of Theology* (New York 1968).

J M Connolly, *Human History and the Word of God. The Christian Meaning of History in Contemporary Thought* (New York and London 1965);
idem, *The Voices of France* (New York 1961).

E Coreth, SJ, et al (eds), *Christliche Philosophie im katholischen Denken des 19. und 20. Jahrhunderts* (Graz, 1987–1990, 3 vols).

P de Letter, 'Theology, History of', in *New Catholic Encyclopaedia*, 14 (Washington 1967), pp 49–58.

R W Franklin, *Nineteenth Century Churches. The History of a New Catholicism in Württemberg, England and France* (New York 1987).

H Fries — G Schwaiger (eds), *Katholische Theologen Deutschlands im 19. Jahrhundert* (Munich 1975, 3 vols).

R V Gucht — H Vorgrimler (eds), *Bilan de la théologie au XXe siècle* (Tournai–Paris 1970).

E E Y Hales, *The Catholic Church in the Modern World. A Survey from the*

French Revolution to the Present (London 1958).

E Hocedez, SJ, *Histoire de la théologie au XIXe siècle* (Brussels–Paris, 1947–1952, 3 vols).

H J John, *The Thomist Spectrum* (New York 1966).

A Kolping, *Katholische Theologie gestern und heute* (Bremen 1964).

G A McCool, SJ, *From Unity to Pluralism. The Internal Evolution of Thomism* (New York 1989); idem, *Nineteenth Century Scholasticism. The Search for a Unitary Method* (New York 1989).

A E McGrath (ed), *The Blackwell Encyclopaedia of Modern Christian Thought* (Oxford 1993; 1995).

B Mondin, *I grandi teologi del secolo ventesimo* (Turin 1969).

A Rauscher (ed), *Religiös-kulturelle Bewegungen im deutschen Katholizismus seit* 1800 (Paderborn 1986).

N Ravitch, *The Catholic Church and the French Nation 1589–1909* (London and New York 1990).

L Reinisch (ed), *Theologians of our Time* (Notre Dame, Ind, 1964).

S Schürer, *Katholische Kirche und Kultur im 18. Jahrhundert* (Paderborn 1941).

M Schoof, OP, *Breakthrough Beginnings of the New Catholic Theology* (Dublin 1970).

H J Schultz (ed), *Tendenzen der Theologie im zwanzigsten Jahrhundert* (Stuttgart 1966).

M F Sciacca (ed), *Les grands courants de la Pensée mondiale contemporaine* (Paris 1961).

N Smart (ed), *Nineteenth Century Religious Thought in the West* (Cambridge 1985, 3 vols).

G Thils, *Orientations de la théologie* (Louvain 1958).

K Werner, *Geschichte der apologetischen und polemischen Literatur der christlichen Theologie* (Schaffhausen 1861–1867, 5 vols); idem, *Geschichte der katholischen Theologie* (Munich 1867).

I.1 INTELLECTUAL ANTECEDENTS

M Buckley, *At the Origins of Modern Atheism* (New Haven and London 1987).

R M Burns, *The Great Debate on Miracles. From Joseph Glanvill to David Hume* (Lewisburg, NJ, 1981).

J Delumeau, *Catholicism between Luther and Voltaire. A New View of the Counter-Reformation* (Et London 1977).

A Koyré, *From the Closed World to the Infinite Universe* (New York 1958).

I O Wade, *The Intellectual Origins of the French Enlightenment* (Princeton, NJ, 1971).

I.2 CATHOLICS AND UNBELIEVERS

C Becker, *The Heavenly City of the Eighteenth Century Philosophers* (New Haven 1932).

G Craig, *The Church in the Age of Reason* (Oxford 1960).

P Gay, *The Enlightenment: an Interpretation* (New York 1966–1969, 2 vols).

P Hazard, *European Thought in the Eighteenth Century. From Montesquieu to Lessing* (Et London 1954).

R P Palmer, *Catholics and Unbelievers in Eighteenth Century France* (Princeton, NJ, 1939).

I.3 RESPONSE TO THE PHILOSPHES

E Dublanche, 'Bergier, Nicolas-Sylvestre', *Dictionnaire de Théologie catholique* 2.1 (Paris 1932), cols 742–745.

A Prandi, *Cristianesimo offeso e difeso: Deismo e apologia cristiana nel secondo Settecento* (Bologna 1975).

G Ruggieri, 'L'apologetica cattolica in epoca moderna', in idem (ed), *Encyclopedia di Teologia fondamentale I: Storia Progetto, Autori, Categorie* (Genoa 1987), pp 278–348.

I.4 THE HISTORY MEN

A Andreoli, *Nel mondo di Luigi Antonio Muratori* (Bologna 1972).

J Bergkamp, *Dom Jean Mabillon* (Washington 1928).

S Bertelli, *Erudizione e storia in Antonio Ludovico Muratori* (Naples 1960).

E Cochrane, 'Muratori: The Vocation of an Historian', *Catholic Historical Review* 51 (1965), pp 153–170.

T Facchini, *Il papato principio di unità e Pietro Ballerini di Verona. Dal concetto di unità ecclesiastica al concetto di monarchia infallibile* (Padua 1950).

H Quentin, *Jean Dominique Mansi et les grandes collections conciliaires* (Paris 1900).

E Raimondi, *I lumi dell'erudizione Saggi sul Settecento italiano* (Milan 1909).

D Scioscioli, FA, *Zaccarria erudito del XVIII secolo* (Brescia 1925).

I.5 CATHOLIC ENLIGHTENMENT, CATHOLIC IDENTITY

E Bene & I Kovacs (eds), *Les Lumières en Hongrie, en Europe centrale et en Europe occidentale* (Budapest 1975).

C A Bolton, *Church Reform in Eighteenth Century Italy: the Synod of Pistoia, 1786* (The Hague 1969).

W J Callahan & D Higgs (eds), *Church and Society in Catholic Europe of the Eighteenth Century* (Cambridge 1979).

O Chadwick, 'The Catholic Reformers', in idem, *The Popes and European Revolution* (Oxford 1981), pp 392–445.

E Hegel, *Die katholische Kirche Deutschlands unter dem Einfluss der Aufklärung des 18. Jahrhunderts* (Münster 1975).

S Merkle, *Die katholische Beurteilungen des Aufklärungs-zeitalten* (Berlin 1909);

idem, *Die kirchliche Aufklärung im katholischen Deutschland* (Bonn 1910).

L-J Rogier, 'L'Aufklärung catholique', in L-J Rogier, G de Bertier de Sauvigny, J Hajjar, *Siècle des Lumières, Révolutions, Restaurations* (Paris 1966 = *Nouvelle Histoire de l'Eglise*, 4).

M Rosa, *Cattolicesimo e lumi nel Settecento italiano* (Rome 1981).

L Swidler, *Aufklärung Catholicism, 1780–1850* (Missoula 1970).

E Winter, *Der Josephinismus. Die Geschichte des österreichischen Reformkatholizismus, 1740–1748* (Berlin 1962).

II.1 THE REVOLUTIONARY IMPACT

G Best (ed), *The Permanent Revolution. The French Revolution and its Legacy 1789–1989* (London 1988).

O Chadwick, *The Popes and European Revolution* (Oxford 1981), pp 446, 534.

F Furet, *Penser la Révolution* (Paris 1978).

J McManners, *The French Revolution and the Church* (New York 1969).

B Plongeron, *Conscience religieuse et Révolution. Regards sur l'historiographie religieuse de la Révolution française* (Paris 1969).

J L Talmon, *The Origins of Totalitarian Democracy* (London 1961).

A R Vidler, *The Church in an Age of Revolution* (Harmondsworth 1961).

J de Viguerie, *Christianisme et révolution* (Paris 1986).

II.2 ROMANTIC THEOLOGY

E Callot, *Les trois moments de la philosophie théologique de l'Histoire: Vico, Herder, Hegel* (Paris 1974).

A Dwight Culler, *The Victorian Mirror of History* (New Haven and London 1985).

J R Geiselmann, *Geist des Christentums und des Katholizismus. Ausgewählte Schriften katholischer Theologie im Zeitalter des deutschen Idealismus und der Romantik* (Mainz 1940).

T F O'Meara, 'The Origins of the Liturgical Movement and German Romanticism', *Worship* 59 (1985), pp 326–342;
idem, *Romantic Idealism and Roman Catholicism* (Notre Dame, Ind, 1982).

H G Schenk, *The Mind of the European Romantics* (London 1966).

T Strom, *Theologie im Schatten politischer Romantik* (Munich 1970).

R Switzer, *Chateaubriand* (New York 1971).

II.3 TRADITIONALISM

J-R Derré, *Lamennais, ses amis, et le mouvement des idées à l'époque romantique* (Paris 1962).

J Henry, *Le traditionalisme et l'ontologisme à l'Université de Louvain, 1835–1865* (Louvain 1922).

N Hötzel, *Die Uroffenbarung im französischen Traditionalismus* (Munich 1962).

L Marino, *La filosofia della Restaurazione* (Turin 1978).

G Merli, *De Bonald. Contributo alla formazione del pensiero cattolico della Restaurazione* (Turin 1972).

P Poupard, *L'Abbé Louis Bautain* (Tournai 1961).

P N Stearns, *Priest and Revolutionary. The Dilemma of French Catholicism* (New York 1967).

II.4 THEOLOGICAL COUNTER-REVOLUTIONISM

E M Cioran (ed), *J de Maistre. Du Pape et autres textes* (Paris 1957).

C Galli (ed), *I controrivoluzionari* (Bologna 1981).

J Godechot, *La Contre-révolution* (Paris 1961).

II.5 NEO-ULTRAMONTANISM

R Aubert, *L'Ecclésiologie au XIXe siècle* (Paris 1960).

M L Brown, *Louis Veuillot: French Ultramontane Catholic Journalist and Layman, 1813–1883* (Durham, NC, 1977).

K Buchheim, *Ultramontanismus und Demokratie: Der Weg der deutschen Katholiken im 19. Jahrhundert* (Munich 1963).

J D Holmes, *More Roman than Rome. English Catholicism in the Nineteenth Century* (London 1978).

P Spencer, *The Politics of Belief in Nineteenth Century France* (London 1954).

W Ward, *W G Ward and the Catholic Revival* (London and New York 1893).

III.1 SEMI-RATIONALISM

G Fritz, 'Semi-rationalistes', *Dictionnaire de Théologie Catholique* XIV 2 (Paris 1941), cols 1850–1854.

T Schäfer, *Die Erkenntnis-theoretische Kontroverse Kleutgen-Günther* (Paderborn 1961).

H Schwedt, *Das römische Urteil über Georg Hermes, 1775–1831. Ein*

Beitrag zur Geschichte der Inquisition im 19. Jahrhundert (Rome 1980).

P Wenzel, *Der Freundeskreis um Anton Günther und die Gründung Beurons* (Essen 1965); idem, *Das wissenschaftliche Anliegen des Güntherianismus* (Essen 1961).

III.2 THE CATHOLIC TÜBINGEN SCHOOL

H Brunner, *Der organologische Kirchenbegriff in seiner Bedeutung für das ekklesiologische Denken des 19. Jahrhunderts* (Frankfurt 1979).

J S Drey, *Brief Introduction to the Study of Theology: With Reference to the Scientific Standpoint and the Catholic System* (Notre Dame, Ind, 1994).

A Dru, *The Church in the Nineteenth Century: Germany, 1800–1918* (London 1963).

W L Fehr, *The Birth of the Catholic Tübingen School* (Chico, Calif, 1981).

J H Geiselmann, *Die katholische Tübingen Schule: ihre theologische Eigenart* (Freiburg 1964).

E Klinger, 'Tübingen School', *Sacramentum Mundi*, VI (London 1970).

R H Nienaltowski, *Johann Adam Möhler's Theory of Doctrinal Development* (Washington 1959); idem, 'Möhler, J A', *New Catholic Encyclopaedia* 9 (Washington, 1967), pp 1004–1005.

H Savon, *Johann Adam Möhler, the Father of Modern Theology* (Et Glen Rock, NJ, 1966).

L Scheffczyk (ed), *Theologie in Aufbruch und Widerstreit* (Bremen 1965).

B Welte, 'Zum Strukturwandel der katholischen Theologie im 19. Jahrhundert', in idem, *Auf der Spur des Ewigen* (Freiburg 1965).

B E Winze, *Narrating History, Developing Doctrine: Friedrich Schleiermacher and Johann Sebastian Drey* (Atlanta, Ga, 1993).

III.3 NEWMAN

G Biemer, *Newman on Tradition* (London and New York 1967).

J Coulson & A M Allchin (eds), *The Rediscovery of Newman. An Oxford Symposium* (London, 1967).

S Gilley, *Newman and his Age* (London, 1990).

I Ker, *The Achievement of John Henry Newman* (London 1990); idem, *John Henry Newman: a Biography* (Oxford 1988). idem (ed), *John Henry Newman. An Essay in Aid of a Grammar of Assent* (Oxford 1985); idem (ed), *John Henry Newman, The Idea of a University* (Oxford 1967).

M J Svaglić (ed), *John Henry Newman. Apologia pro Vita mea* (Oxford 1967).

J H Walgrave, *Newman the Theologian* (Et London 1966).

H D Weidner (ed), *John Henry Newman, The Via Media of the Anglican Church* (Oxford 1990).

III.4 ROSMINI

F Conigliero, *Immanenza e trascendenza del sopranaturale in Rosmini* (Palermo 1973).

G Cristaldi, *Antonio Rosmini e il pensare cristiano* (Milan 1977).

F Evain, *Introduction à l'ontologie personnaliste d'Antonio Rosmini* (Paris 1973).

C Leetham, *Rosmini Priest, Philosopher and Patriot* (London 1957; New York 1982^2).

K H Menke, *Vernunft und Offenbarung nach Antonio Rosmini. Der apologetische Plan einer christlichen Enzyklopädie* (Innsbrück–Vienna–Munich 1980).

A Rosmini, *Antropologia soprannatu-rale* (Rome 1983 = *Opere di Antonio Rosmini*, 39–40).
idem, *Anthropology as an Aid to Moral Science* (Et Durham 1991);
idem, *Dell' educazione; Sull' unità dell' educazione* (Rome 1994 = *Opere di Antonio Rosmini*, 3);
idem, *The Five Wounds of Holy Church* (Et London 1883);
idem, *Maxims of Perfection* (Et London 1889);
idem, *The Origin of Thought* (Et Durham 1989);
idem, *Il razionalismo teologico* (Rome 1992 = *Opere di Antonio Rosmini*, 43);
idem, *A Short Sketch of Modern Philosophies, and of his own System* (Et London 1882).

III.5 THE ROMAN SCHOOL

C Boyer, 'Passaglia, Charles', *Diction-naire de Théologie Catholique* XI 2 (Paris 1932), cols 2207–2210.
A Brent, 'Newman and Perrone: Un-reconcilable Theses on Develop-ment', *Downside Review* 102 (1984), pp 276–289;
idem, 'The Hermesian Dimension to the Newman-Perrone Dialogue', *Ephemerides Theologicae Lova-nienses* 61 (1985), pp 73–99.
M Hofmann, *Theologie, Dogma und Dogmenentwicklung im theolo-gischen Werk Denis Pétau's* (Frank-furt am Main–Munich 1976).
W Kasper, *Die Lehre von der Tradition in der römischen Schule* (Freiburg 1962).
K H Neufeld, 'Zur "Römischen Schule" im deutschen Sprachraum', in H Hammans (ed), *Geist und Kirche* (Paderborn 1990), pp 323–340.
idem, 'La Scuola romana', in R Fisi-chella (ed), *Storia della teologia 3. Da Vitus Pichler a Henri de Lubac* (Bologna 1996, pp 267–283).

C Passaglia – C Schrader (eds), *Dionysii Petavii Aurelianensis e Societate Jesu de Theologicis Dogmatibus* (Rome 1857).
P Walter, *Johann Baptist Franzelin, 1816–1886 Jesuit, Theologe, Kardinal* (Bozen 1987);
idem, *Die Frage der Glaubensbe-gründung aus innerer Erfahrung auf dem I Vatikanum. Die Stellung-nahme des Konzils vor dem Hinter-grund der zeitgenössischen römischen Theologie* (Mainz 1980).

III.6 PIUS IX AND HIS COUNCIL

R Aubert, *Le pontificat de Pie IX, 1846–1878* (Paris 1952);
idem, *Vatican I* (Paris 1964).
U Betti, *La costituzione dommatica 'Pastor aeternus'* (Rome 1961).
C Butler, *The Vatican Council, 1869–70, based on Bishop Ullathorne's Letters* (London 1930, 2 vols).
F J Cwiekowski, *The English Bishops and the First Vatican Council* (Louvain 1971).
G Martina, *Pio IX, 1846–1850* (Rome 1974);
Pio IX, 1851–1866 (Rome 1986).
J R Page, *What Will Dr Newman Do? John Henry Newman and Papal Infal-libility, 1865–1875* (Collegeville, Minn, 1994).
J R Palanque, *Catholiques libéraux et gallicans en France face au Concile du Vatican* (Aix-en-Provence 1962).
C Patelos, *Vatican I et les évêques uniates. Une étape éclairante de la politique romaine à l'égard des orientaux, 1867–1870* (Louvain 1981).
H J Pottmeyer, *Der Glaube vor dem Anspruch der Wissenschaft* (Frei-burg 1968).
F van der Horst, *Das Schema über die Kirche auf dem I. Vatikanischen Konzil* (Paderborn 1963).

III.7 SCHEEBEN

Auctores varii, *Matthias Joseph Scheeben. Un teologo tomista* (Rome 1988).

K Feckes, et al, *M J Scheeben, der Erneuerer katholischer Glaubenswissenschaft* (Mainz 1935).

E Paul, *Denkweg und Denkform der Theologie von Matthias Joseph Scheeben* (Munich 1970).

M J Scheeben, *The Mysteries of Christianity* (Et St Louis, Mo, 1946); idem, *Nature and Grace* (Et St Louis, Mo, 1954).

III.8 LEONINE NEO-THOMISM

R Aubert, *Aspects divers du néothomisme sous le pontificat de Léon XIII* (Rome 1961).

E Coreth, SJ, et al, *Christliche Philosophie im katholischen Denken des 19. und 20. Jahrhunderts*, II (Graz, Vienna, Cologne, 1987), pp 72–332.

P Dezza, SJ, *I neotomisti italiani del XIX secolo* (Milan 1942, 2 vols).

G A McCool, SJ, *Nineteenth Century Scholasticism: The Search for a Unitary Method* (New York 1989); idem, *From Unity to Pluralism. The Internal Evolution of Thomism* (New York 1989; 1992), pp 5–38.

IV.1 BLONDEL

M Blondel, *Action: Essay on a Critique of Life and Science of Practice* (Et Notre Dame, Ind, 1984); idem, *The Letter on Apologetics, and History and Dogma* (Et London 1964).

H Bouillard, *Blondel and Christianity* (Washington 1969).

H Duméry, *Raison et religion dans la Philosophie de 'L'Action'* (Paris 1963).

J P Golinas, *La restauration du Thomisme sous Léon XIII et les philosophies nouvelles: Etudes de la pensée de M Blondel et du Père Laberthonnière* (Washington 1959).

O König, *Dogma als Praxis und Theorie Studien zum Begriff des Dogmas in der Religionsphilosphie Maurice Blondels vor und während der modernistischen Krise, 1888–1901* (Graz 1983).

J Lacroix, *Maurice Blondel. An Introduction to the Man and his Philosophy* (Et New York 1968).

J J McNeill, SJ, *The Blondelian Synthesis. A Study in the Influence of German Philosophical Sources on the Formation of Blondel's Method and Thought* (Leiden 1966).

B Reardon, 'Maurice Blondel and the Philosophy of Action', in idem, *Liberalism and Tradition* (Cambridge 1975).

R Saint-Jean, *L'Apologétique philosophique. Blondel 1893–1912* (Paris 1966).

C Theobald, *Maurice Blondel und das Problem der Modernität. Beitrag zu einer epistemologischen Standortsbestimmung der zeitgenössischen Fundamentaltheologie* (Frankfurt 1988).

IV.2 MODERNISM

R S Appleby, *Church and Age Unite! The Modernist Impulse in American Catholicism* (Notre Dame, Ind, 1992).

R Aubert, 'Modernism', *Sacramentum Mundi* IV (Et London 1969), pp 99–104.

L F Barman, *Baron von Hügel and the Modernist Crisis in England* (Cambridge 1972).

J Böhm, *Dogma und Geschichte. Systematische Ueberlegungen zum Problem der Dogmenentwickung in der Auseinandersetzung zwischen*

Alfred Loisy und der Lehramt der katholischen Kirche (Bad Honegg 1987).

G Daly, *Transcendence and Immanence. A Study in Catholic Modernism and Integralism* (Oxford 1980).

D Donovan, 'Church and Theology in the Modernist Crisis', *Proceedings of the Catholic Theological Society of America* 40 (1985), pp 145–159.

B Dumry, 'Le Modernisme', in *Les grands courants de la Pensée mondiale contemporaine. Les Tendances principales* (Paris 1961).

M.-J Lagrange, OP, *M Loisy and le Modernisme. A propos des 'Mémoires'* (Paris 1972).

T Loome, *Liberal Catholicism. Reform Catholicism. Modernism. A Contribution to a New Orientation in Modernist Research* (Mainz 1979).

E Poulet, *Alfred Loisy. Sa vie, son oeuvre. Par Albert Houtin et Félix Sartriaux* (Paris 1960);
idem, *Histoire, dogme et critique dans la Crise moderniste* (Paris, Tournai 1962).
idem, *Intégrisme et catholicisme intégrale: un réseau secret international antimoderniste, la 'Sapinière'*, 1909–1921 (Tournai 1969).

M Ranchetti, *The Catholic Modernists. A Study of the Religious Reform Movement, 1864–1907* (Et London 1969)

B M G Reardon, 'Science and Religious Modernism. The New Apologetic in France, 1890–1913', *Journal of Religion* 56 (1977), pp 48–63.

J Riviére, 'Modernisme', *Dictionnaire de Théologie Catholique* X.2 (Paris 1935), cols 2009–2047;
idem, *Le modernisme dans l'Eglise* (Paris 1929).

N Sagovsky, *'On God's Side'. A Life of George Tyrrell* (Oxford 1990).

P Scoppola, *Crisi modernista e rinnovamento cattolico in Italia* (Bologna 1961).

A Vidler, *The Modernist Movement in the Roman Church* (Cambridge 1934);
idem, *A Variety of Catholic Modernists* (Cambridge 1970).

IV.3 THE SOCIAL CATHOLICS

O Arnal, *Ambivalent Alliance. The Catholic Church and the Action Française, 1899–1939* (Pittsburgh 1985).

E C Bock, *Wilhelm von Ketteler, Bishop of Mainz. His Life, Times and Ideas* (Lanham, Md 1977).

J-Y Calvez & J Perrin (eds), *The Church and Social Justice. The Social Teaching of the Popes from Leo XIII to Pius XII, 1878–1958* (Et Chicago 1961).

J Carron, *Le Sillon et la démocratie Chrétienne, 1894–1910* (Paris 1967).

A Curillier, *P-J-B Buchez et les origines du Socialisme chrétien* (Paris 1948).

D Dorr, *Option for the Poor. A Hundred Years of Vatican Social Teaching* (New York 1983).

W Gurian, *Die politischen und sozialen Ideen des französichen Katholizismus, 1789–1914* (Münchengladbach 1929).

E Hamisch, *Konservatives und revolutionäres Denken: Deutsche Sozialkatholiken und Sozialisten im 19. Jahrhundert* (Vienna 1975).

T S Hamerow, *Restoration, Revolution, Reaction. Economics and Politics in Germany, 1815–1871* (Princeton, NJ, 1988).

P Levillain, *Albert de Mun: Catholicisme Française et catholicisme romain du Syllabus au Ralliement* (Rome 1983).

K-E Lönne, *Politisches Katholizismus im 19. und 20. Jahrhundert* (Frankfurt 1986).

H Maier, *Revolution and Church: The Early History of Christian Demo-*

cracy, 1789–1901 (Notre Dame, Ind, 1969).

P Misner, *Social Catholicism in Europe. From the Onset of Industrialization to the First World War* (New York and London 1991).

J N Moody (ed), *Church and Society. Catholic Social and Political Thought and Movements, 1789–1950* (New York 1953).

H-S Reiss (ed), *The Political Thought of the German Romantics, 1793–1815* (New York 1955).

M Sutton, *Nationalism, Positivism, and Catholicism. The Politics of Charles Maurras and French Catholicism, 1890–1914* (Cambridge 1982).

A R Vidler, *A Century of Social Catholicism, 1820–1920* (London 1964; 1969).

L P Wallace, *Leo XIII and the rise of Socialism* (Durham, NC, 1966).

IV.4 ROUSSELOT AND MARÉCHAL

J Donceel, SJ, *A Maréchal Reader* (New York 1970).

E Kunsz, *Glaube, Gnade, Geschichte. Die Glaubenstheologie des Pierre Rousselot, SJ* (Frankfurt 1969).

J Maréchal, *Le point de départ de la Métaphysique: Leçons sur le développement historique et théorique du problème de la connaissance* (Paris 1944, 1949, 5 vols).

J McDermott, SJ, *Love and Understanding. The Relation between the Will and the Intellect in Pierre Rousselot's Christological Vision* (Rome 1982).

P Rousselot, SJ, *The Intellectualism of Saint Thomas* (New York 1935),

IV.5 MARITAIN AND GILSON

J Croteau, OMI, *Les Fondements thomistes du personalisme de Maritain* (Ottawa 1955).

E Gilson, *The Christian Philosophy of St Thomas Aquinas* (Et New York 1956); idem, *Elements of Christian Philosophy* (Garden City, NY, 1959); idem, *A History of Christian Philosophy in the Middle Ages* (New York 1955); idem, *The Spirit of Medieval Philosophy* (Et New York 1940); idem, *The Unity of Philosophical Experience* (New York 1937).

J W Hanke, *Maritain's Ontology of the Work of Art* (The Hague 1973).

J Maritain, *Art and Scholasticism* (Et New York 1962); idem, *Creative Intuition in Art and Poetry* (New York 1955); idem, *The Degrees of Knowledge* (Et New York 1959); idem, *Existence and the Existent* (Et New York 1948); idem, *Integral Humanism: Temporal and Spiritual Problems of a New Christendom* (Et Notre Dame, Ind, 1973); idem, *Moral Philosophy: an Historical and Critical Survey of the Great Systems* (New York 1964); idem, *A Preface to Metaphysics: Seven Lectures on Being*; idem, *Science and Wisdom* (Et New York 1940); idem, *The Person and the Common Good* (Et Notre Dame, Ind, 1973).

A H Maurer, CSB, 'The Legacy of Etienne Gilson', in V H Brezik, CSB (ed), *One Hundred Years of Thomism* (Houston Tx, 1981), pp 28–44.

A C Pegis (eds), *A Gilson Reader* (Garden City, NY, 1957).

J A Quinn, OSA, *The Thomism of Etienne Gilson* (Villanova, Pa, 1971).

L K Shook, CSB, *Etienne Gilson* (Toronto 1984).

V.1 CASEL AND THE LITURGICAL RENEWAL

J-D Benoit, *Liturgical Renewal* (London 1958).

B T Bogler, *Liturgischer Erneuerung in aller Welt* (Maria Laach 1950).

L Bouyer, *The Liturgy Revived* (Et Notre Dame, Ind, 1964).

P Duployé, *Les origines du Centre de pastorale liturgique* (Paris 1968).

R W Franklin, 'The Nineteenth Century Liturgical Movement', *Worship* 53 (1979), pp 12–39.

A Gozier, *Dom Casel* (Paris 1968).

R Guardini, *The Spirit of the Liturgy* (Et London 1930).

A Haquin, *Dom Lambert Beauduin et le renouveau liturgique* (Gembloux 1970).

C Johnson, *Prosper Guéranger, 1805–1875. A Liturgical Theologian* (Rome 1984).

E B Koenker, *The Liturgical Renaissance in the Roman Catholic Church* (St Louis, Mo, 1954).

F Kolbe, *Die Liturgische Bewegung* (Aschaffenburg 1964).

B Neunheuser, 'Odo Casel in Retrospect and Prospect', *Worship* 50.6 (1976), pp 489–504.

O Rousseau OSB, *Histoire du mouvement liturgique. Esquisse historique depuis le début du XIXe siècle jusqu'au pontificat de Pie X* (Paris 1945).

A Schilson, *Theologie als Sakramententheologie: die Mysterienlehre Odo Casels* (Mainz 1982).

W Trapp, *Vorgeschichte und Ursprung der liturgischen Bewegung* (Regensburg 1940).

R Tuzik (ed), *Leaders of the Liturgical Movement* (Chicago 1990).

V.2 ADAM AND THE ECCLESIOLOGICAL REVIVAL

K Adam, *The Spirit of Catholicism* (Et New York 1929).

R Aubert, 'Karl Adam', in H J Schultz (ed), *Tendenzen der Theologie im 20. Jahrhundert* (Stuttgart 1966), pp 156–162.

J Bluett, 'The Mystical Body of Christ, 1890–1940', *Theological Studies* 3 (1942), pp 261–289.

H Fries, *Die katholische Religionsphilosophie der Gegenwart* (Heidelberg 1949).

S Jaki, OSB, *Les Tendances nouvelles de l'ecclésiologie* (Rome 1957).

B Kreidler, *Eine Theologie des Lebens* (Mainz 1988).

R A Krieg, CSC, *Karl Adam. Catholicism in German Culture* (Notre Dame, Ind, 1992).

J Levie, 'Le Père Emile Mersch', in E Mersch, *Théologie du Corps mystique* (Brussels 1944), I, pp vii–xxxiii.

E Przywara, 'Le mouvement théologique et religieux en Allemagne', *Nouvelle Revue Théologique* 56 (1929), pp 565–575.

W Spael, *Das katholische Deutschland im 20. Jahrhundert* (Würzburg 1964).

F Viering, *Christus und die Kirche in römisch-katholischen Licht. Ekklesiologische Probleme zwischen dem ersten und zweiten Vatikanischen Konzil* (Göttingen 1962).

V.5 LAGRANGE AND THE BIBLICAL REVIVAL

A Bea, *The Word of God and Mankind* (Et Chicago 1967).

Biblical Interpretation in Crisis: the Ratzinger Conference on the Bible and the Church (Grand Rapids, Mich, 1989).

R E Brown, SS, *The Critical Meaning of the Bible* (London 1982), pp 1–81; idem, with T A Collins, OP, 'Church Pronouncements', *The New Jerome Biblical Commentary* (London 1989; 1991), pp 1166–1174.

C Charlier, *The Christian Approach to the Bible* (Et Westminster, Md, 1958).

G Ghiberti, 'Lettera e interpretazione della Bibbia dal Vaticano I al Vaticano II', in R Fabro (ed), *La Bibbia nell' epoca moderna e contemporanea* (Bologna 1992), pp 187–245.

O Kuss, 'Exegese als theologische Aufgabe', *Biblische Zeitschrift 5* (1961), pp 161–183.

M-J Lagrange, *Père Lagrange: Personal Reflections and Memoirs* (Et New York 1985).

J L McKenzie, 'Problems in Hermeneutics in Roman Catholic Exegesis', *Journal of Biblical Literature 77* (1958), pp 18–38.

B Montagnes, *Le Père Lagrange, 1855–1938 L'Exégèse catholique et la crise moderniste* (Paris 1995).

A Nichols, OP, 'François Dreyfus on Scripture Read in Tradition', in idem, *Scribe of the Kingdom. Essays on Theology and Culture* (London 1994), I, pp 32–77.

R Schnackenburg, 'Der Weg der katholischen Exegese', *Biblische Zeitschrift 2* (1958), pp 151–176.

C Theobald, 'L'Exégèse catholique au moment de la Crise moderniste' in C Savart — J N Aletti, *Le monde contemporain et la Bible* (Paris 1985, = *Bible de tous les temps*, 8, pp 387–439.

G Wood, 'Hermeneutics', *New Catholic Encyclopaedia 2* (Washington 1967), pp 507–512.

V.6 DANIÉLOU AND THE PATRISTIC REVIVAL

B Altaner, 'Stand der patrologischen Wissenschaft', *Miscellanea Mercati I* (Rome 1946), pp 483–520.

A Benoit, *L'actualité des Pères de l'Eglise* (Neuchâtel, Paris 1961).

'Bibliographie patristique du Cardinal Jean Daniélou', in J Fontaine & C Kanengiesser (eds), *Epektasis Mélanges patristiques offerts au Cardinal Jean Daniélou* (Paris 1972), pp 673–689.

J Daniélou, *The Bible and the Liturgy* (Et Notre Dame, Ind, 1956); idem, *Le Catéchèse aux premiers siècles* (Paris 1968); idem, *The Development of Christian Doctrine Before the Council of Nicaea. I: The Theology of Jewish Christianity* (Et London 1964); *II: Gospel Message and Hellenistic Culture* (Et London 1973); *III: The Theology of Latin Christianity* (Et London 1977); idem, *From Shadows to Reality. Studies in the Biblical Typology of the Fathers* (Et London 1960).

D Gorce, *Petite Introduction à l'étude des Pères* (Bruges 1946).

A Hamman, *Jacques-Paul Migne. Le retour aux Pères de l'Eglise* (Paris 1975).

P Lebeau, SJ, *Jean Daniélou* (Paris 1966).

VI.1 CHRISTOPHER DAWSON

C Dawson, *The Age of the Gods. A Study in the Origins of Culture in Prehistoric Europe and the Ancient East* (London 1928); idem, *Beyond Politics* (London 1959); idem, *Dynamics of World History* (London and New York 1957); idem, *Enquiries into Religion and Culture* (London 1933); idem, *The Gods of Revolution, Intro-*

duction by Arnold Toynbee (London 1972);
idem, *The Historic Reality of Christian Culture* (London and New York 1960);
idem, *The Making of Europe. An Introduction to the History of European Unity* (London 1952);
idem, *Mediaeval Essays. A Study of Christian Culture* (London 1954);
idem, *Progress and Religion. An Historical Enquiry into the Causes and Development of the Idea of Progress and its Relationship to Religion* (London 1929);
idem, *Religion and Culture* (London 1948);
idem, *Religion and the Rise of Western Culture* (London 1950).
C Scott, *A Historian and his World. A Life of Christopher Dawson, 1889–1970* (London 1984).

VI.2 THE INNSBRÜCK SCHOOL

B Fischer & H B Meyer (eds), *J A Jungmann. Ein Leben für Liturgie und Kerygma* (Innsbrück 1975).
J Hofinger, SJ, *The Art of Teaching Christian Doctrine: the Good News and its Proclamation* (Et London 1962);
idem, 'J A Jungmann', *Living Light* 13 (1976), pp 350–359.
J A Jungmann, SJ, *Christus als Mittelpunkt religiöser Erziehung* (Freiburg 1939);
idem, *Die Frohbotschaft und unser Glaubensverkündigung* (Regensburg 1936; synopsis translation as *The Good News and its Proclamation* (New York 1961);
idem, *Katechetik Aufgäbe und Methode der religiösen Unterweisung* (Freiburg 1939; 1955; Et *Handing on the Faith A Manual of Catechetics*, Freiburg and London 1959).
E Kappler, *Die Verkündigungstheologie* (Freiburg 1949).

H Rahner, SJ, *Eine Theologie der Verkündigung* (Freiburg 1939; Et *A Theology of Proclamation*, New York 1968).
M Schmaus, 'Ein Wort zur Verkündigungstheologie', *Theologie und Glaube* (1941), pp 312–322.
H Vorgrimler, *Den Vätern und dem Vater. Der Theologe und Historiker Hugo Rahner* (Freiburg 1963).

VI.3 HENRI DE LUBAC AND *NOUVELLE THÉOLOGIE*

S-T Bonino, OP, 'Le Thomisme du P. Labourdette', in *Un maitre en théologie. Le Père Marie-Michel Labourdette, O.P. (Toulouse 1992 = Revue Thomiste XCII. 1).*
N Ciola, *Paradosso e mistero in Henri de Lubac* (Rome 1980).
H de Lubac, SJ, *At the Service of the Church. Henri de Lubac Reflects on the Circumstances that Occasioned his Writings* (Et San Francisco 1989);
idem, *A Brief Catchesis on Nature and Grace* (Et San Francisco 1984);
idem, *Catholicism* (Et London 1950);
idem, *The Discovery of God* (Et London 1960).
T Deman, 'Tentatives françaises pour un renouvellement de la théologie', *Revue de l'Université d'Ottawa* (1950), pp 129–167.
A Dondeyne, *Contemporary European Thought and Catholic Faith* (Et Pittsburgh 1958).
N Eterović, *Cristianesimo e religioni secondo Henri de Lubac* (Rome 1981).
M Figura, *Der Anruf der Gnade. Ueber die Beziehung des Menschen zu Gott nach Henri de Lubac* (Einsiedeln 1979).
E Fouilloux, 'Dialogue théologique, 1946–1948', in S-T Bonino (ed), *Saint Thomas au XXe siècle. Actes du*

Colloque Centenaire de la 'Revue Thomiste', Toulouse, 25–28 mars 1993 (Paris 1994).

R Garrigou-Lagrange, La Synthèse thomiste (Paris 1950).

A J Lindsay, De Lubac's Images of the Church: A Study of Christianity in Dialogue (Washington 1974).

A Russo, Henri de Lubac. Theologia e dogma nella storia. L'influsso di Blondel (Rome 1990).

M Sales, Idée de Dieu et sens de l'homme. Essai sur la structure anthropo-théologique de la Révélation chrétienne dans la pensée du Père Henri de Lubac (Paris 1970).

H U von Balthasar, 'The Achievement of Henri de Lubac', Thought 51.200 (1976), pp 7–49;
idem, The Theology of Henri de Lubac (Et San Francisco 1991);
idem, with G Chantraine, Le cardinal Henri de Lubac. L'homme et son oeuvre (Paris 1983).

G Weigel, SJ, 'The Historical Background of the Encyclical Humani Generis', Theological Studies 12.2 (1951), pp 208–230.

VI.4 TEILHARD DE CHARDIN

C Cuénot, Teilhard de Chardin (London and Baltimore 1965).

H de Lubac, The Religion of Teilhard de Chardin (Et London and New York, 1967);
idem, The Faith of Teilhard de Chardin (London and New York, 1965).

C F Mooney, SJ, Teilhard de Chardin and the Mystery of Christ (London and New York 1966).

O Rabut, OP, Dialogue with Teilhard de Chardin (Et London 1961).

P Teilhard de Chardin, The Divine Milieu (Et New York and London 1960);
idem, Hymn of the Universe (London and New York 1965);
idem, The Making of a Mind (Et London and New York 1965);
idem, Man's Place in Nature (Et London and New York 1966);
idem, The Phenomenon of Man (Et London, 1959).

N M Wildiers, An Introduction to Teilhard de Chardin (Et London and New York 1968).

VI.5 KARL RAHNER

A Carr, The Theological Method of Karl Rahner (Missoula 1977).

J A DiNoia, OP, 'Karl Rahner', in D F Ford (ed), The Modern Theologians. An Introduction to Christian Theology in the Twentieth Century, I (Oxford 1989), pp 187–204.

G A McCool, A Rahner Reader (New York 1975).

L J O'Donovan, 'A Journey into Time: the Legacy of Karl Rahner's Last Years', Theological Studies 46 (1985), pp 621–646;
idem (ed), A World of Grace. An Introduction to the Themes and Foundations of Karl Rahner's Theology (New York 1980).

K Rahner, Foundations of Christian Faith (Et New York and London 1978);
idem, Hearers of the Word (Et New York 1969);
idem, Spirit in the World (Et New York 1968);
idem, Theological Investigations (Et New York and London 1961–1992, 23 volumes). This will eventually need amplification in the light of the forthcoming Karl-Rahner-Gesamtausgabe (Solothurn–Freiburg 1995–).

G Vass, Understanding Karl Rahner. I. A Theologian in Search of a Philosophy (Westminster, Md, and London 1985); II. Mystery of Man and the Foundations of a Theological System (Westminster, Md, and London 1985).

H Vorgrimler, *Understanding Karl Rahner. An Introduction to his Life and Thought* (Et New York 1986).

VI.6 INCARNATION OR ESCHATOLOGY?

H U von Balthasar, *A Theology of History* (Et London and New York 1963).

L Bouyer, 'Christianisme et eschatologie', *La Vie intellectuelle* XVI (1948), pp 6–32.

Y Congar, *The Mystery of the Church* (Et London and Baltimore 1960); idem, *Lay People in the Church* (Et London 1957; 1965; Westminster, Md, and London 1984).

J M Connolly, 'The Catholic Theologies of History', in idem, *Human History and the Word of God* (New York and London 1965), pp 155–200.

J Daniélou, *The Lord of History. Reflections on the Inner Meaning of History* (Et Chicago 1958).

A Dondeyne, *Faith and the World* (Et Pittsburgh and Dublin 1964); idem, 'A Catholic-Humanist Dialogue', in F Kurtz and idem, (ed), *Humanists and Roman Catholics in a Common World* (London 1972).

F G Fessard, SJ, *De l'Actualité historique* (Paris 1959–1960).

R Guardini, *The End of the Modern World* (Et New York 1956); idem, *Freedom, Grace, and Destiny* (Et New York 1961).

J Leclerq, *Christ and the Modern Conscience* (Et London 1962); idem, *Christians in the World* (Et London 1961).

H Lübbe, *Säkulisierung. Geschichte eines ideenpolitischen Begriffs* (Freiburg 1965).

J Mourroux, *Le Mystère du temps: approche théologique* (Paris 1962).

J Pieper, *The End of Time* (Et London 1954).

B Pruche, OP, *Histoire de l'homme: Mystère de Dieu* (Bruges 1961).

G Thils, *Théologie des réalités terrestres* (Paris 1948–1949).

B Welte, *Heilsverständnis* (Frankfurt 1965).

VII.1 THE SECOND VATICAN COUNCIL

G Barauna (ed), *L'Eglise de Vatican II* (Paris 1966).

B C Butler, *The Theology of Vatican II* (London 1967).

P Hebblethwaite, *John XXIII. Pope of the Council* (London 1984); idem, *Paul VI. The First Modern Pope* (London 1993).

B Kloppenburg, *The Ecclesiology of Vatican II* (Et Chicago 1974).

J C Murray, *The Problem of Religious Freedom* (Westminster, Md, 1965).

K H Neufeld, 'In the Service of the Council: Bishops and Theologians at the Second Vatican Council', in R Latourelle (ed), *Vatican II*; *Assessments and Perspectives I* (New York 1988), pp 74–105.

I de la Potterie, 'La vérité de la Sainte Ecriture et l'histoire du salut d'après la Constitution dogmatique *Dei Verbum*', *Nouvelle Revue Théologique* 88.1 (1966), pp 149–169.

W A Purdy, *The Church on the Move* (London 1965).

A Stacpoole (ed), *Vatican II Revisited by Those who were There* (London and Minneapolis 1986).

H Vorgrimler (ed), *Commentary on the Documents of Vatican II* (Et London 1967–1969).

VII.2 CATHOLIC ECUMENISM

A Bea, *The Unity of Christians*, ed B Leeming, SJ (St Louis, Miss, and London 1963).

Y M-J Congar, OP, *Dialogue between Christians* (Et London 1966); idem, *Diversity and Communion* (Et London 1984); idem, *Divided Christendom* (Et London 1939).

H A Fey (ed), *The Ecumenical Advance. A History of the Ecumenical Movement, 1948–1968* (London 1970).

H Meyer & L Vischer (eds), *Growth in Agreement. Reports and Agreed Statements of Ecumenical Conversations on a World Level* (Ramsey, NJ, 1984).

R Rouse & S C Neill, *A History of the Ecumenical Movement, 1517–1948* (London 1967)

T F Stransky, CSP, and J B Sheerin, CSP (eds), *Doing the truth in Charity, Ecumenical Documents, 1964–1980* (New York 1982).

VII.3 *CONCILIUM* OR *COMMUNIO*?

J Bowden, *Edward Schillebeeckx. Portrait of a Theologian* (London 1983).

N Greinacher — H Haag, *Der Fall Küng. Eine Dokumentation* (Munich 1980).

H Häring & K J Kuschel, *Hans Küng. His Work and his Way* (London 1979).

W Kasper, *The God of Jesus Christ* (Et London 1964); idem, *Introduction to Christian Faith* (Et New York 1980); idem, *Jesus the Christ* (Et London 1976); idem, *The Methods of Dogmatic Theology* (Et Shannon 1969); idem, *Theology and Church* (Et London 1989).

P Kennedy, OP, *Edward Schillebeeckx* (London 1993).

H Küng, *Christianity. Its Essence and History* (Et London 1995); idem, *The Church* (Et London 1967); idem, *Does God Exist? An Answer for Today?* (Et London 1980); idem, *Global Responsibility. In Search of a New World Ethic* (Et London and New York 1991); idem, *Infallible? An Enquiry* (Et London and New York 1976); idem, *On Being a Christian* (Et London and New York 1976); idem, *Theology for the Third Millenium* (Et New York 1988).

C M LaCugna, *The Theological Methodology of Hans Küng* (Chico, Calif, 1982).

A Nichols, OP, *The Theology of Joseph Ratzinger. An Introductory Study* (Edinburgh 1988); idem, 'Walter Kasper and his Theological Programme', in idem, *Scribe of the Kingdom. Essays on Theology and Culture* (London 1995), 11, pp 44–53.

W L Portier, 'Schillebeeckx as Critical Theorist: The Impact of Neo-Marxist Social Thought on his Recent Theology', *The Thomist* 48.3 (1984), pp 341–367.

J Ratzinger, *Church, Ecumenism, Politics* (Et Slough 1988); idem, *The Feast of Faith* (Et San Francisco 1986); idem, *Principles of Catholic Theology* (Et San Francisco 1987); idem, *Theological Highlights of Vatican II* (Et New York 1966); idem (with V Messori), *The Ratzinger Report: An Exclusive Interview on the State of the Catholic Church* (Et San Francisco 1985).

E Schillebeeckx, *Christ: the Christian Experience in the Modern World* (Et London 1900); idem, *Church: the Human Story of God* (Et London 1990); idem, *The Church with a Human Face. A new and Expanded Theology of Ministry* (Et London 1985); idem, *God the Future of Man* (London 1969); idem, *Jesus. An Experiment in Christology* (Et London 1979); idem, *Ministry: a Case for Change*

(Et London 1981);
idem, *The Understanding of Faith: Interpretation and Criticism* (Et London 1974).

M Schoof (ed), *The Schillebeeckx Case: Official Exchange of Letters and Documents in the Investigation of Fr. Edward Schillebeeckx by the Sacred Congregation for the Doctrine of the Faith, 1976–1980* (Et New York and Ramsey, NJ, 1984).

VII.4 LIBERATION THEOLOGY

L Boff, *Church: Charism and Power. Liberation Theology and the Institutional Church* (Et New York 1985).

M-D Chenu, *L'Evangile dans le temps* (Paris 1966).

C Duquoc, *Ambiguité des théologies de la sécularisation. Essai critique* (Gembloux 1972).

M H Ellis & O Madura (eds), *The Future of Liberation Theology. Essays in Honour of Gustavo Gutiérrez* (Maryknoll, NY, 1989).

R Gibellini, *Frontiers of Theology in Latin America* (Et Maryknoll, NY, 1979).

G Gutiérrez, *A Theology of Liberation* (Et Maryknoll, NJ, and London 1973).

A Hennelly, *Theology for a Liberating Church. The New Praxis of Freedom* (Washington 1989).

B Kloppenburg, OFM, *Temptations for the Theology of Liberation* (Et Chicago 1974).

B Mahan – L Dale Robinson, *The Challenge of Liberation Theology. A First World Response* (Maryknoll, NY, 1981).

J B Metz, *The Church in the World* (Et London 1968).

A Nichols, OP 'The Rise and Fall of Liberation Theology', in idem, *Scribe of the Kingdom. Essays on Theology and Culture* (London 1995), II, pp 101–123.

J L Segundo, *The Liberation of Theology* (Et Maryknoll, NY, 1977).

VII.5 MORALS AND MAN

B Ashley, OP, *Theologies of the Body: Humanist and Christian* (Braintree, Mass, 1985);
idem, 'The Loss of Theological Unity. Pluralism, Thomism and Catholic Morality', in M J Weaver and R Scott Appleby (eds), *Being Right. Conservative Catholics in America* (Bloomington, Ind, 1995), pp 63–87.

C E Curran, *Contemporary Problems in Moral Theology* (Notre Dame, Ind, 1970).

J Finnis, *Moral Absolutes. Tradition, Revision and Truth* (Washington 1991).

G Gilleman, SJ, *The Primacy of Charity in Moral Theology* (Et London 1959).

C Grisez, *The Way of the Lord Jesus* (Chicago 1983–).

B Häring, CSsR, *The Law of Christ* (Et Westminster, Md, and Cork, 1963–1966);
idem, *Free and Faithful in Christ* (Et Middlegreen, Slough, 1978–1979).

R A McCormick, SJ, *How Brave a New World? Dilemmas in Bioethics* (London 1981);

A MacIntyre, *After Virtue* (London 1981).
idem, *Whose Justice? Whose Rationality?* (London 1988).

S Pinckaers, OP, *Les Sources de la morale chrétienne. Sa méthode, son contenu, son histoire* (Fribourg 1985).

M Scheler, *Formalism in Ethics and Non-Formal Ethics of Value: A New Attempt toward the Foundation of an Ethical Personalism* (Et Evaneston, Ill, 1973).

VII.6 NARRATIVE THEOLOGY

J S Dunne, *Time and Myth* (Garden City, NY, 1973).

W Kasper, 'Systematisch-theologische Anstze, II. Narrative Theologie', *Theologische Quartalschrift* 156 (1976), pp 55–61.

R Krieg, 'Narrative as a Linguistic Rule', *International Journal for the Philosophy of Religion* 8 (1977), pp 190–205;
idem, *Story-shaped Christology* (New York 1988).

G Loughlin, *Telling God's Story. Bible, Church and Narrative Theology* (Cambridge 1996).

J B Metz, *Faith in History and Society* (Et New York 1980).

J Shea, *Stories of God. An Unauthorized Biography* (Chicago 1978).

VII.7 BERNARD LONERGAN AND DAVID TRACY

P Corcoran, SM (ed), *Looking at Lonergan's 'Method'* (Dublin 1975).

B Lonergan, *Grace and Freedom. Operative Grace in the Thought of St Thomas Aquinas* (London 1971);
idem, *Insight: An Essay on Human Understanding* (London 1957);
idem, *Method in Theology* (London 1972);
idem, *The Way to Nicaea. The Dialectical Development of Trinitarian Theology* (London 1976).

J Nash, 'Tracy's Revisionist Project: Some Fundamental Issues', *American Benedictine Review* XXXIV (1983).

J L Rike, 'Radical Pluralism and Truth in the Thought of David Tracy', in W G Jeanrond and J L Rike (eds), *Radical Pluralism and Truth. David Tracy and the Hermeneutics of Religion* (New York 1991), pp ix–xxiii.

W M Shea, 'The Stance and Task of the Foundational Theologian: Critical or Dogmatic?' *Heythrop Journal* XVII.3 (1974), pp 273–292.

D Tracy, *The Achievement of Bernard Lonergan* (New York 1970);
idem, *The Analogical Imagination. Christian Theology and the Culture of Pluralism* (New York 1981);
idem, *A Blessed Rage for Order. The New Pluralism in Theology* (New York 1975);
idem, 'On Naming the Present', *Reflections on God, Hermeneutics and Church* (Maryknoll, NY, and London 1994);
idem, 'The Necessity and Insufficiency of Fundamental Theology', in R Latourelle and G O'Collins (eds), *Problems and Perspectives of Fundamental Theology* (Et New York 1982);
idem, *Plurality and Ambiguity. Hermeneutics, Religion, Hope* (London 1987);
idem, 'The Task of Fundamental Theology', *Journal of Religion* 54 (1974), pp 13–54.

VII.8 BALTHASAR

H U von Balthasar, *Convergences. To the Source of Christian Mystery* (Et San Francisco 1983);
idem, *The Glory of the Lord. A Theological Aesthetics* (Et Edinburgh and San Francisco 1982–89);
idem, *Love Alone: the Way of Revelation* (Et London 1968);
idem, 'The Place of Theology', in idem, *Word and Redemption* (Et New York 1965), pp 7–22;
idem, *Theodrama. Theological Dramatic Theory* (Et San Francisco 1988–);
idem, *Theologik* (Einsiedeln 1985–1987).

B McGregor, OP, & T Norris (eds), *The Beauty of Christ. An Introduction to the Theology of Hans Urs von Balthasar* (Edinburgh 1994).

E T Oakes, *Pattern of Redemption. The Theology of Han Urs von Balthasar* (New York 1994).

J O'Donnell, SJ, *Hans Urs von Balthasar* (London 1992).

M Ouellet, 'The Message of Balthasar's Theology to Modern Theology', *Communio* XXIII (1996), pp 270–299.

J Saward, *The Mysteries of March. Hans Urs von Balthasar on the Incarnation and Easter* (London 1990).

D L Schindler (ed), *Hans Urs von Balthasar. His Life and Work* (San Francisco 1991).

CONCLUSION: CATHOLICISM AND MODERNITY

The Catechism of the Catholic Church (Et London 1993).

L Kolakowski, *Modernity on Endless Trial* (Chicago and London 1990).

J M McDermott, SJ (ed), *The Thought of Pope John Paul II — A Collection of Essays and Studies* (Rome 1993).

J Saward, *Christ is the Answer. The Christ-Teaching of Pope John Paul II* (Edinburgh 1995).

C Taylor, *Sources of the Self. The Making of the Modern Identity* (Cambridge 1989).

H G Williams, *The Mind of John Paul II. Origins of his Thought and Action* (New York 1981).